CUSTOM WOODWORKING

Classic Cabinetry

CUSTOM WOODWORKING

Classic Cabinetry

By the editors of *Woodsmith* magazine

CONTENTS

CUSTOM WOODWORKING

Classic Cabinetry

Tabletop Case

DISPLAY CABINETS — 6

STORAGE PROJECTS — 48

HEIRLOOM PIECES 84

Scandinavian Cabinet

Cherry Wardrobe

DISPLAY CABINETS

When it comes to display cabinets, the case itself can say as much about a woodworker's skill as it does about the items being displayed. This is particularly true of classic pieces, like the four cabinet styles presented in this section.

Starting small, the hanging wall case is ideal for displaying small objects, and it can be customized for a variety of collectibles. Next is a tabletop display case with a beveled glass top and a pull-out drawer. This small but elegant case gives you the option of making half-blind dovetails and lets you try detail carving.

The contemporary cabinet is perfect for displaying larger items with its open, understated appearance. And finally, the curio cabinet combines glass panels and adjustable shelves with dentil molding to create a distinctive look, whether you build the full-size standing version or the small hanging keepsake cabinet.

Hanging Wall Case

Whether you're showing spools or other small collectibles, this wall case will display them proudly. And building it gives you a chance to practice some classic woodworking techniques.

Many people collect small items such as thimbles, commemorative coins, and small car replicas. I don't have any of those things, but I have all sorts of wooden spools. So I decided to build a display cabinet for them. This case won't hold larger collectibles, but it also won't take up much space, so you can find a home for it in just about any room of the house.

TECHNIQUES. The small size of the project also gives you an opportunity to practice a few time-tested woodworking techniques on a smaller scale.

Those techniques include simple rabbet/dado construction on the basic box, and mortise and tenon joinery for the door frame. A detailed description of how to cut a mortise and tenon can be found on pages 13-17.

MATERIALS. The case in the photograph at right is made from $^3/_4$" red oak, but cherry or any other hardwood will do as well. You could also use pine, without the decorative inlay, and with either a natural or painted finish. The oak case shown here was finished with two coats of an antique oil finish.

Unless you're an expert in making inlaid marquetry, the best way to tackle the veneer inlay is to buy it ready-made from a specialty supplier (see Sources, page 126). The $2^1/_4$"-diameter inlay pictured at right is made from painted wood veneers that are fitted and glued to a paper backing (see Shop Tip on page 12). Remember, because pre-made inlay sizes vary, be sure to have your inlay in hand before laying out the scrollwork top.

OPTIONS. There are several simple ways to customize this case design, depending on your needs. If you won't be displaying spools, you could leave the pegs off the shelves, or change the number or positions of the shelves.

You could also replace the inlay with a small clock, a circular picture frame, a piece of decorative glass, or anything else that will fit the design.

EXPLODED VIEW

OVERALL DIMENSIONS:
11W x 3D x 19¼H

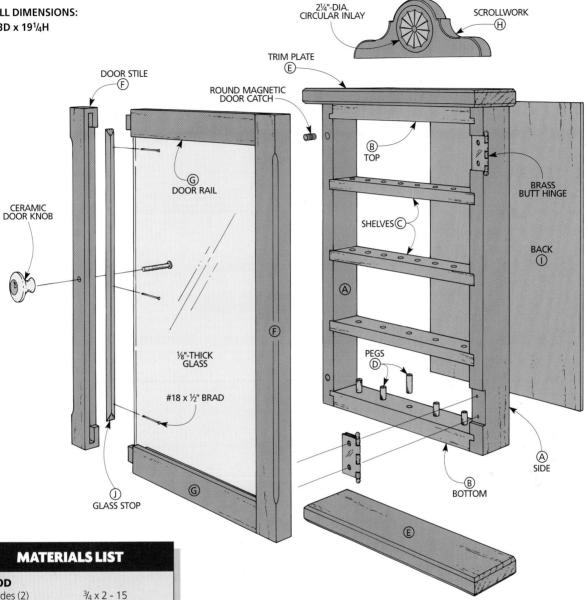

2¼"-DIA.
CIRCULAR INLAY

SCROLLWORK
(H)

TRIM PLATE
(E)

DOOR STILE
(F)

ROUND MAGNETIC
DOOR CATCH

(B)
TOP

BRASS
BUTT HINGE

SHELVES (C)

CERAMIC
DOOR KNOB

DOOR RAIL
(G)

BACK
(I)

(A)

⅛"-THICK
GLASS

PEGS
(D)

(F)

#18 x ½" BRAD

(A)
SIDE

(B)
BOTTOM

(G)

(E)

GLASS STOP
(J)

MATERIALS LIST

WOOD

A	Sides (2)	¾ x 2 - 15
B	Top/Bottom (2)	¾ x 1¾ - 9½
C	Shelves (3)	½ x 1¾ - 9½
D	Pegs (26)	¼ dowel x 1
E	Trim Plates (2)	¾ x 3⅛ - 11¼
F	Door Stiles (2)	¾ x 1⅛ - 15
G	Door Rails (2)	¾ x 1⅛ - 9⅞
H	Scrollwork (1)	¾ x 3 - 8⅜
I	Back (1)	¼ ply - 10 x 15
J	Glass Stops	¼ x ¼ - 48 rough

HARDWARE SUPPLIES

(32) No. 18 x ½" brads
(2) 1¼" x 1½" brass butt hinges w/ screws
(2) ⁹⁄₁₆" round magnetic door catches
(1) 1"-dia. ceramic door knob w/ screw
(1) ⅛"-thick glass, 8¾" x 13⅛"
(1) 2¼"-dia. circular inlay

CUTTING DIAGRAM

¾ x 7¼ - 36 (1.8 Bd. Ft.)

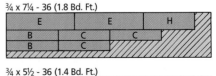

¾ x 5½ - 36 (1.4 Bd. Ft.)

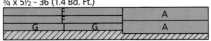

NOTE: CUT BACK (I) FROM 12" x 24" SHEET OF ¼" PLYWOOD. CUT PEGS (D) FROM 36" LENGTH OF ¼" DOWEL. ¼" GLASS STOPS (J) CAN BE CUT FROM LEFTOVER ¾" STOCK.

The case uses straightforward box construction: the top and bottom are joined to the sides with rabbet/dado joints, and all three shelves are dadoed into the sides. This requires a total of five dadoes on each side piece *(Fig. 1)*.

I knew these dadoes had to line up perfectly on both sides. So rather than trying to cut identical dadoes on two individual pieces, I cut only one set of dadoes — in one double-wide piece. Then after the dadoes were cut, I ripped this piece to get the matching sides.

To eliminate five individual setups for cutting these dadoes, I decided to make things easy by spacing the three shelf dadoes equidistant from both ends. This way, the setup for the top shelf could also be used for the bottom shelf by flipping the piece end for end.

To start this process, I cut the double-wide piece 15" long by $4\frac{1}{2}$" wide. (This is a little wider than needed to allow for trim cuts if any chipout occurs as the dadoes are cut.)

DADOES FOR SHELVES. I cut the dadoes for the shelves first. The dadoes for the top and bottom shelves are cut $3\frac{3}{4}$" from each end of the double-wide piece. And the dado for the center shelf is centered on the length — $7\frac{1}{4}$" from either end. All three of these dadoes are $\frac{1}{2}$" wide by $\frac{1}{4}$" deep *(Fig. 1)*.

DADOES FOR CORNER JOINTS. Next, I cut the dadoes for the rabbet/dado joint (used to attach the top, bottom and two sides of the cabinet). These $\frac{1}{4}$"-wide dadoes are positioned so the bottom edge of the dado is equal to the thickness of the top/bottom pieces *(Fig. 3)*.

RIP TO SIZE. After all the dadoes were cut, I ripped the double-wide piece into the two 2"-wide side pieces (A). Then I cut a $\frac{1}{2}$"-wide, $\frac{1}{4}$"-deep rabbet on the back edge of each side piece for the $\frac{1}{4}$" plywood back *(Fig. 4)*.

TOP/BOTTOM. This same basic procedure can be used to cut the top and bottom (B). First, I cut a double-wide piece to a length of $9\frac{1}{2}$". (This length allows for 9" between the sides, plus $\frac{1}{2}$" for the two $\frac{1}{4}$"-long tongues.)

Next, I cut rabbets on the ends of the double-wide piece to leave a tongue that fits the dado in the side pieces. This is the rabbet half of the rabbet/dado joint.

Note: It's called a rabbet/dado joint, but the only purpose of the rabbet is to leave a tongue to fit the dado *(Fig. 3)*.

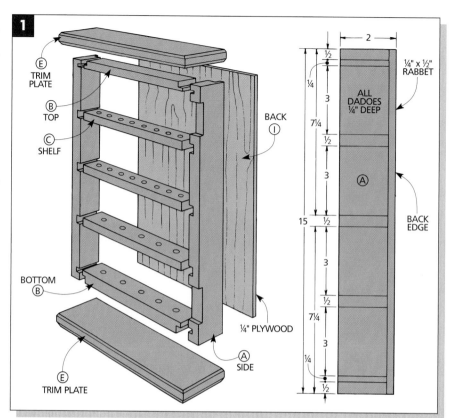

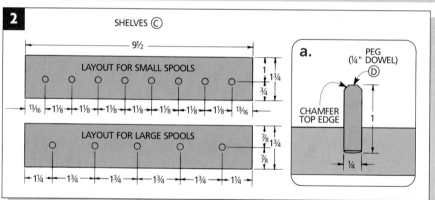

Finally, I ripped the double-wide piece to get the top and bottom (B). These pieces are ripped $\frac{1}{4}$" narrower than the cabinet sides to allow room for the $\frac{1}{4}$" plywood back.

NOTCHES FOR HINGES. To mount the door, notches have to be cut for the hinges. But rather than waiting until after the cabinet was already assembled, I decided I would go ahead and cut the notches while the sides were still easily accessible.

To simplify things, I cut these notches to a depth equal to the full thickness of the knuckle of the hinge *(Fig. 3)*. Then the hinge flap on the door frame could be surface-mounted, so no mortise is needed on the door frame (refer to *Fig. 8* on page 12).

SHELVES. I made the shelves (C) thinner so they wouldn't look too bulky and detract from any small collectibles.

Before resawing or planing the shelves to final thickness, cut the shelves to length. To determine this length, dry-assemble the top, bottom and two sides to form the basic shell of the cabinet. Then measure the distance between the bottoms of the dadoes, and cut the stock to this length.

Next, rip these three pieces to a width of $1\frac{3}{4}$". (This is $\frac{1}{4}$" less than the width of the sides to allow for the back.)

Finally, the three shelves can be resawn (ripped on edge) or planed to fit the $\frac{1}{2}$" dadoes in the cabinet sides. If you're resawing, set the cut to slightly over $\frac{1}{2}$", because you need a little extra thickness so the saw marks can be removed. (I used a cabinet scraper to remove the marks, but they could also be sanded off.)

HOLES FOR DOWELS. If the cabinet is used for spools, a series of $3/8$"-deep holes need to be drilled in the shelves for the pegs. I used a spacing of $1^1/8$" for the small spools on the top two shelves, and $1^3/4$" spacing for the large spools on the bottom shelf and cabinet bottom *(Fig. 2)*.

PEGS. Then the pegs (D) for the spools are cut 1" long. I chamfered their top edges by mounting them in the drill press (set at a slow speed) and using a file to knock off the edges.

ASSEMBLY. Next, the $1/4$" plywood back (I) is cut to fit between the rabbets in the cabinet sides. Its length is equal to the full height of the cabinet.

Finally, the cabinet (top, bottom, sides, and shelves) can be glued together, with the plywood back tacked in place to help keep everything square.

TRIM PLATES

At this point the cabinet is just a plain box. So to spice things up I added decorative trim plates (E) to the top and bottom. The length of these plates is a total of $3/4$" longer than the width of the cabinet. This allows a $3/8$" overhang on each outside edge *(Fig. 5a)*.

The width of these plates is equal to the cabinet's depth (2") plus the thickness of the door frame ($3/4$") plus $3/8$" for the overhang on the front. This totals $3^1/8$". But since the door frame isn't built yet, I cut them to rough width ($3^1/4$") for now, and trimmed them later.

CHAMFER EDGES. Finally, I cut $1/8$"-wide chamfers on the front edges and both ends of the plates. The edges on the back are left square *(Fig. 5)*.

DOOR FRAME

The door of the case is constructed with simple mortise and tenon joinery. (See pages 13 to 17 for detailed instructions on cutting this joint.)

STILES. The first step is to cut the stiles and rails $1^1/8$" wide. Then the stiles (F) can be cut to length to equal the full height of the cabinet.

This dimension is actually a little too long — the door would fit too tightly between the trim plates. But since the plates aren't mounted yet, I cut the stiles to full height first, and trimmed

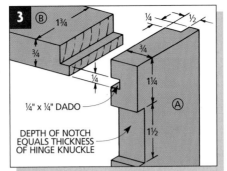

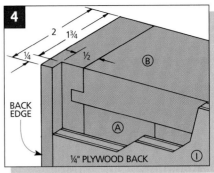

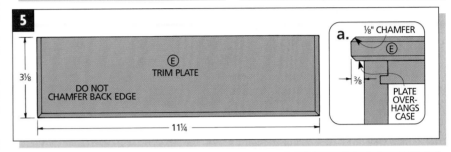

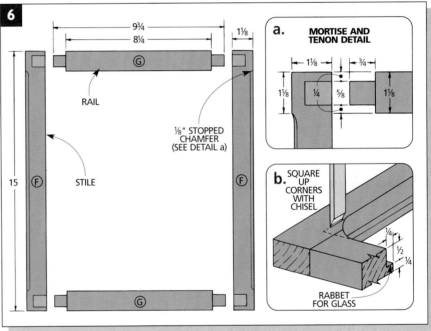

the door to size after it was assembled.

RAILS. The rails (G) are cut to length so the final width of the door frame is equal to the outside width of the cabinet *(Fig. 6)*. (The shoulder-to-shoulder length of the rail equals the outside width of the cabinet minus the combined width of the stiles. Then add $1^1/2$" for the two $3/4$"-long tenons.)

After the frame pieces are cut to size, I cut $1/4$"-wide mortises in the stiles, and cut the tenons to fit the mortises. Then you can glue the door together, making sure it's square and flat.

TRIM DECORATIVE PLATES. Once the door was assembled, I backtracked and

found the final width for the trim plates (E). These plates are trimmed and glued to the cabinet so they're centered on the width and flush with the back.

Finally, I trimmed the height of the door frame to allow clearance between the plates. (Trim a hair off both the top and the bottom of the door frame so the widths of the rails remain equal.)

RABBET FOR GLASS. To hold the glass that goes in the door frame, I routed a $1/4$"-wide by $1/2$"-deep rabbet on the back of the frame *(Fig. 6b)*.

CHAMFER. After sanding the door frame, I routed stopped chamfers on the outside edges of the stiles *(Fig. 6a)*.

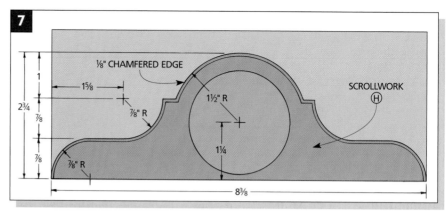

Once you have completed the basic cabinet with the door and trim plates, you could leave it the way it is for a formal, classic style.

But if you're interested in adding a little something extra to the case, you might want to try the scrollwork top and inlay. (I chose a ready-made starburst inlay, but you could use a different design. For sources of inlays, see page 126.) Although it's not necessary, it turned out to be a lot of fun.

MARK AND CUT. The first step is to mark the outline of the scrollwork on a piece of stock $2\frac{3}{4}$" wide by $8\frac{3}{8}$" long. (All of the necessary dimensions are shown in *Fig. 7*.) When the outline is marked, be sure to include the center point of the circle for the starburst.

Then cut the outline on a band saw (or jig saw), and smooth the edges with a drum sander (on a drill press) and a file.

CHAMFER EDGES. To soften the edges of the scrollwork, I routed a $\frac{1}{8}$"-wide chamfer along its front edge *(Fig. 7)*. The easiest way to do this is on a router table, with a chamfer bit equipped with a pilot guide.

Note: The pilot prevents the bit from completely chamfering the inside corners of the profile. So I wound up using a sharp chisel to touch up the areas missed by the router bit.

MOUNT INLAY. After the scrollwork is cut and chamfered, a circular recess

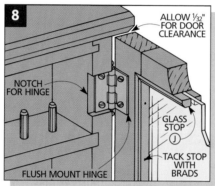

is cut for the starburst inlay. Since this particular inlay is a circle, the recess is relatively easy to cut with a circle cutter on a drill press. (Details for cutting the recess and mounting the inlay are described in the Shop Tip box below.)

MOUNT TO CABINET. After the inlay is mounted, the scrollwork is simply glued to the top of the cabinet, centered on the width and flush with the back.

DETAILS

At this point, the case is nearly complete. All that remains are the finishing details.

FINISH. First, to make things easier, I finished all the parts of the cabinet before adding the glass and hardware.

GLASS STOPS. Next, cut the stops (J) that will hold the glass in the door frame *(Fig. 8)*. These are simply tacked in place with brads.

HARDWARE. Then I installed the hinges. I used brass butt hinges on this cabinet, mounting them in the mortises on the edge of the cabinet side.

I centered two round magnetic catches on the cabinet side and door, and installed a ceramic knob.

HANGING. To hang the case, just drill two screw holes through the back, 1" down from the top and 2" in from each side. This way, the screws won't be visible when the door is closed. ■

SHOP TIP . . . . *Routing a Circular Inlay*

A marquetry inlay is a nice way to add a touch of class to any project. The problem is getting it mounted. For the hanging wall case, I used a "starburst" inlay, which has a circular shape that is easier to work with.

My inlay came mounted in a rectangular piece of veneer. So the first thing I did was remove the inlay itself by cutting around it (through the paper backing) with a razor knife. This backing is actually veneer tape that holds all the pieces of the pattern together.

When the inlay is removed, measure its diameter and cut a

recess to fit (see drawing). Because this particular inlay is close to a true circle, I used a circle cutter to score the outside edge of the recess.

Then I removed a majority of the waste in the recess with a router and a $\frac{1}{2}$" straight bit. Set the depth of cut to about three-fourths the thickness of the inlay and rout to within about $\frac{1}{8}$" of the score line. To remove the remaining waste, I used a sharp $\frac{1}{4}$" chisel.

To mount the inlay, apply a coat of contact cement in the recess and also to the "back" of the inlay.

Note: The side with the brown paper is actually the front, or top side.

Press the inlay into the recess (with the paper side up). Place a softwood

block over the inlay and tap it in place with a hammer. Then place a board on top of the inlay to clamp it down evenly. Finally, sand the inlay flush with the surface of the board.

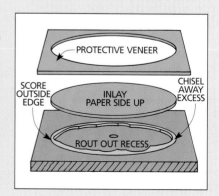

Although there are many variations of mortise and tenon joints, in this section I'm showing only the basic joint — but I'm including all the tricks I've learned to achieve good results.

The procedure I follow is not intended to cut one joint just to show off. The point is to cut four joints to form a good, sturdy frame — one that's square and has no twist to it.

Building a mortise and tenon frame involves several techniques, yet the entire process depends on four basic rules:

1) Use straight lumber.

2) Plan all cuts so you're working with "standard" settings. Once you set up for a cut, don't change it. Cut all pieces with exactly the same setting.

3) Make trial cuts each step of the way.

4) Be patient, and don't rush to get things done.

The full description of this procedure may seem overly detailed, suggesting that there's a tremendous amount of time and work involved. But once you're in the shop and start cutting the joint, things move along at a pretty good pace — fast enough to get the job done, but carefully enough to get it done right.

THE INITIAL PROCEDURE

When I set out to build a frame, I first decide the final size I want the frame to be. There are two choices: you can build the frame so the *outside* dimensions are a certain size, or build it so the *inside* dimensions are a certain size. As an example, I built a sample frame with outside dimensions of 12" high by 11" wide. (The hanging wall case frame is a little different size. See *Fig. 6* on page 11.)

STILES AND RAILS. To build a frame this size, the stiles (vertical pieces) will be 12" long, which is the final outside height of the frame. The length of the rails (horizontal pieces) is determined by this simple equation: rail length = (final outside width of frame) minus (2 times the width of the stile) plus (2 times the length of the tenon). To use this equation

I had to fill in the two variables: the width of the stile, and the length of the tenon. I chose a width of 1½" for the stiles.

Things get a little complicated when figuring the length of the tenon. In general, the tenon should be at least ¼" less than the width of the stile. That is, you want to leave ¼" between the bottom of the mortise and the outside edge of the stile. If the stiles are 1½"

RAIL ↓T

SHOULDER TO SHOULDER

TOTAL LENGTH OF STILE =
TOTAL HEIGHT OF FRAME (12")

TOTAL LENGTH OF RAIL =
OUTSIDE WIDTH OF FRAME (11")
MINUS 2 TIMES WIDTH OF STILE (3")
PLUS 2 TIMES LENGTH OF TENON (2")

RAIL ↑B

wide, this means a tenon length of 1¼".

However, another limiting factor for the tenon is the depth of the mortise. The mortise bits I like to use drill comfortably to a depth of 1". So I reduced the length of the tenon for the sample frame to 1" (which is also an even measurement that's easy to work with so there's less chance of an error.)

Back to the equation. The final outside dimension of the frame is 11". Subtract 3" (2 times the width of the stile). Add 2" (2 times the length of the tenon). Thus, the rail length equals 10".

CHOOSING THE WOOD. When choosing the wood to build a frame, it's important to choose good straight lumber — no warp, no twist, no cup. No matter how well the joints are cut, if the wood is warped, or especially if it's twisted, the frame will show it.

I also try to choose a piece that's oversized so there will be some scrap left over for trial cuts. When the scrap comes from the same board as the rails and stiles, you know the setting on the

trial cuts will apply to the "real" pieces. (For the sample frame I chose a piece of hardwood 3½" wide by 36" long.)

CUT TO LENGTH. First I cut rough length sections for the stiles and rails ½" longer than needed. Then the section for the stiles is cut to final length. (The rails are cut to final length later.)

When cutting to final length, I use a double-cut procedure, trimming one end of each board square and then trimming the other end to final length.

RIP TO WIDTH. Next I set up the saw to rip the stiles and rails to final width (1½"). Again, all pieces are double-cut. First rip them about ⅛" wider than needed, and then trim them to final width. This double cutting allows you to rip both edges of each piece so you know you're working with two clean edges.

CHECK FOR WARPING. Although I try to use good straight lumber at the outset, internal stress in the board can cause a piece to go "crazy" as it's ripped.

The worst thing to contend with is a piece that's twisted. To check for twist, lay each workpiece on a flat surface (I use the top of the table saw), and try to rock it by applying pressure to opposite corners. If a piece is twisted, set it aside and cut a replacement that is truly flat and straight.

LAY OUT GRAIN PATTERN. Now both the stiles and rails have been cut to "standard" width and the stiles have been cut to final length. (The rails are cut to final length when the tenons are cut.)

The next step is to lay out the pieces in their respective positions to form the frame. Then shuffle the pieces until they have their best faces forward and are arranged with a nice grain pattern.

MARK EACH PIECE. When all the pieces are arranged, I mark each piece so there's no confusion later. I just draw an arrow on the face side that points toward the inside edge of the frame.

I also mark each piece so I know which is right (R), left (L), top (T), and bottom (B). Then I'm ready to cut the mortises and tenons.

The difficulty in cutting a mortise and tenon joint is that it requires two separate operations. Yet the end result must be one perfectly matched joint. This problem is magnified when building a frame simply because there are four joints to contend with.

The key to making four good joints for a frame is to make each mortise and each tenon with standard settings — so they're all cut the same and don't have to be "customized."

So which do you cut first, the mortise or the tenon? I think it's best to cut the mortise first, because one of its dimensions (width) is limited to the size of the bit used to drill it out. The tenon, on the other hand, is exposed and relatively easy to get to if its dimensions need to be altered.

LAYING OUT

The first step in cutting a mortise is to lay out the dimensions (width, length, and depth) on the edge of the stile. I make these layout marks on only one stile. Then this stile is used to set up a special fence arrangement on the drill press to cut all the mortises with standard settings.

DETERMINE WIDTH. The width of a mortise is limited to the diameter of the bit you're using. In general, the mortise should be one-third the thickness of the stock you work with. For $3/4$"-thick hardwood, I cut a $1/4$"-wide mortise.

MARK LENGTH. For the length of the mortise, again there are limitations. The mortise should stop far enough from the end of the stile so it doesn't split out the end. Usually $1/4$" from the end is enough to eliminate problems.

The other end of the mortise is limited to the width of the rail. (Since the tenon can't be any wider than the width of the rail, the mortise is also limited to this size.) Keeping this in mind, I mark a boundary line on the stile equal to the width of the rail *(Step 1)*.

Now the other end of the mortise can be marked. You'll find this is where some consistency will pay off. Since the first mark was made $1/4$" from the end of the stile, the second line should be marked $1/4$" from the boundary line *(Step 2)*. (This will simplify cutting the tenons later.)

MARK DEPTH. Finally, the depth of the mortise is marked on the end of the stile *(Step 3)*. For the sample frame, I marked the depth at 1".

FENCE FOR DRILL PRESS

The jig I use to drill the mortises is a $3/4$" plywood base with a movable fence. To build this jig, cut the base about 12" wide by 48" long. Then cut two grooves on the bottom of the base, and glue in two stiffeners (see drawing below).

Next, rip three pieces of plywood to a rough width of $2^1/2$" for the fence. (Two of these pieces are 30" long, and the bottom piece is 36" long.) These three pieces are glued and clamped together. When the glue is dry, rip a clean edge on each face so the fence ends up $2^1/4$" wide. Also, cut a chamfer on the bottom edge of the fence as a sawdust relief.

To attach the fence to the base, drill a

series of $1/4$" holes at each end of the fence to form 2"-long slots, and another series of $1/4$" holes at each end of the base to form 8"-long slots.

Note: This combination of slots allows you to position the fence at an angle without causing it to bind.

Clean out these slots with a jig saw and file. And finally, use carriage bolts to fasten the fence to the base.

To prolong the life of the base, I cut a 3" x 3" square hole with a jig saw and cleaned up the edge with a router. Then I glued a backing piece to the bottom, and cut a replaceable square to fit the hole.

SETTING UP THE FENCE

All of the layout marks you made are used to set up the fence, stops and featherboard used to hold the stile in place as the mortise is drilled. An overview of this setup is shown in *Step 4*.

Note: The bottom corners of the stops should be chamfered to allow a sawdust relief. Also, the featherboard is raised up with a small block so it exerts pressure on the top edge of the stile. This is where all the action is, so you want the most support here.

CENTER STILE ON BIT. To set up the fence, the first step is to position the fence so the stile is centered on the bit. This is the critical step. It's possible to make alterations later, but things will go a whole lot smoother if the mortise is exactly centered on the stile.

To get the proper setting, I use a piece of scrap to make trial cuts. Place the scrap against the fence and adjust the fence so the bit is approximately centered on the thickness of the scrap.

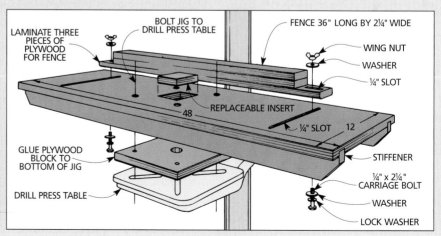

LAMINATE THREE PIECES OF PLYWOOD FOR FENCE

BOLT JIG TO DRILL PRESS TABLE

FENCE 36" LONG BY 2¼" WIDE

WING NUT

WASHER

¼" SLOT

REPLACEABLE INSERT

48

¼" SLOT   12

GLUE PLYWOOD BLOCK TO BOTTOM OF JIG

STIFFENER

¼" x 2¼" CARRIAGE BOLT

DRILL PRESS TABLE

WASHER

LOCK WASHER

There are a couple different kinds of bits you can use to drill out mortises. I've used both a traditional Forstner bit and a router bit called a spiral end mill.

The procedure is to drill a shallow test hole in the scrap piece — deep enough so the bit forms a complete circle. Then flip the scrap piece around so the other face is against the fence. Lower the bit to see if it drills in exactly the same hole *(Step 5)*. (This may take quite a few trial cuts, but the effort spent now will pay off later.)

DRILL END HOLES. Now you're ready to drill out the mortise. I start by drilling the two end holes to define the final length of the mortise *(Step 6)*. This is done with the face side (marked with an arrow) of the stile against the fence.

Note: When the depth of cut is set on the drill press, it's best to lower the bit just slightly deeper than 1" to be sure the bit actually cuts to full depth.

CLEAN OUT. After the end holes are drilled, the rest of the waste is removed. When I use the mortise bit, I drill a series of barely overlapping holes between the end holes *(Step 7)*.

After this first series of holes is drilled, there will be small V-shaped shoulders along the cheeks of the mortise. I center the bit over each "V"

shoulder and drill straight down on them. The bit may tend to argue a little when removing the V-shoulders, so I make repeated, shallow cuts until the V's are drilled to full depth.

MORTISE OTHER END. Up to this point all of these steps were for drilling one mortise on one end of the stile. This stile was positioned with its face side against the fence.

To cut the other end, the stile has to be turned around. But this puts the face side out. And if the bit is not exactly centered on the thickness of the stile, the mortises at each end will be off-center in different directions.

Just to maintain consistency, I cut only one end of all the stiles first (with the face side against the fence). Then I

reposition the stop blocks so I can keep the face side of the stile against the fence when cutting the mortises at the other end.

CHOP SQUARE. You should now have perfect slot mortises on all the stiles. From here you have two choices:

1) Leave the ends of the mortise rounded, and then round over the tenon to match.

2) Square up the corners of the mortise with a sharp chisel to accept the square corners of the tenon.

To square up the mortise, chop down on the end of the mortise with a sharp chisel *(Step 8)*. Make light taps and pry out the waste until you reach the bottom of the mortise. Then clean up the corners by paring down on the cheeks.

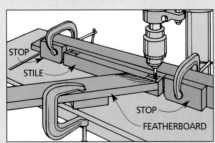

1 *Since the mortise's length is limited to the rail's width, first hold the rail at the end of the stile and mark a boundary line.*

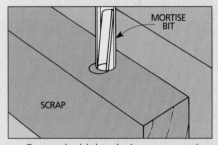

2 *To mark the final length, mark one line at least ¼" from the end of the stile and the other ¼" from the boundary line.*

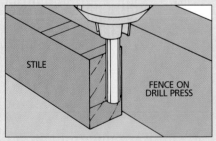

3 *Mark the depth of cut on the end of the stile. Lower the bit a little past this mark to be sure the bit cuts to full depth.*

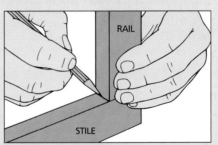

4 *Set the stop blocks to the maximum length of the mortise. Then fasten the featherboard using a block to raise it up.*

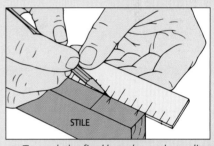

5 *Center the bit by placing scrap against the fence and making a shallow hole. Then flip it to see if the holes match up.*

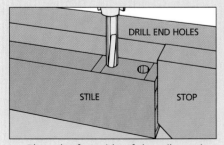

6 *Place the face side of the stile against the fence. Start the mortise by drilling the two end holes to define the length.*

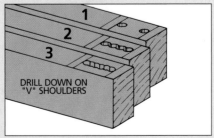

7 *Drill overlapping holes to clean out the waste. Then drill down on the V-shoulders, and make a final routing pass.*

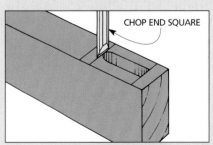

8 *To get square corners, start by chopping straight down at the ends. Then pare down on the mortise cheeks.*

When making a mortise and tenon joint there's a tendency to concentrate on the fit of one tenon in one mortise. But in a frame, the rails have two tenons (one at each end). This introduces another critical measurement: the distance between the shoulders of the two tenons.

This distance must be *exactly* the same on both rails, or the frame will be out of square. The method I use to cut the tenon is intended to get the tenon to fit the mortise, as well as produce the correct shoulder-to-shoulder distance.

LENGTH OF RAIL. First, the rails have to be cut to final length. (The rails were only cut to rough length earlier.) The final length of the rails is determined by the shoulder-to-shoulder distance, plus the length of both tenons.

Remember, the sample frame should have an outside width of 11". If the stiles are 1½" wide, their combined width is 3". Thus, the shoulder-to-shoulder distance of the rails must be 8". The other variable (the length of the tenon) is equal to the depth of the mortise (1").

Adding these variables together (8" for the shoulder-to-shoulder distance, plus 2" for the two tenons) equals the final length of the rail (10"). Trim the rails to this final length.

DEPTH OF CUT. Once you have this measurement, the technique I use to cut a tenon is to lay the rail flat on the table saw and make multiple passes over the blade to clean off the face of the tenon.

First, set the height of the saw blade to cut the tenon to the proper thickness. To do this, I use the mortise as a gauge.

Ideally, the mortise is centered on the stile, so it shouldn't matter which face you lay on the table to set the blade height. But just in case the mortise is off-center, I work from the face side of the stile to begin with. (This is the side that was marked with an arrow.)

Place the face side of the stile down on the table and raise the blade until the highest point of one tooth lines up with the cheek of the mortise *(Step 1)*.

TRIAL CUT. Since the mortise is used as a gauge, this setting should be right on the money. But it's always best to make a trial cut on a piece of scrap to check it out *(Step 2)*.

Place the trial cut next to the cheek of the mortise to see if the depth of cut lines up with the mortise *(Step 3)*. It

may take several trial cuts to get the correct height for the saw blade.

SHOULDER SETTING. As mentioned earlier, the tenon is cut by making multiple passes over the blade. The important thing here is to stop right at the proper shoulder line — on all pieces. To do this, I use the fence on the table saw as a stop to limit the length of the tenon.

Note: There is a rule in woodworking that the fence and the miter gauge cannot be used together. This is true if you're making a *through* cut that will leave a chunk of waste between the blade and fence. But in this case there's no waste for the blade to throw, so the fence can be used as a stop.

For the sample frame, the shoulder setting is 1" (which is the length of the tenon). Adjust the fence so it's 1" from the *outside* (left) edge of the blade.

CUT FACE OF TENON. At this point, the depth of cut is established, and the fence is set for the shoulder distance. Now the tenons are ready to be cut.

Start by placing the rail with the face side down on the table saw.

Note: Since the depth of cut was established with the face side of the stile down, the rail should also be cut with the same face down.

Cut the tenon (with multiple passes) by guiding the rail with the miter gauge. The last pass will be the shoulder cut (when the end of the rail is against the fence) *(Step 4)*.

SMOOTH THE FACE. As the face of the tenon is cut, the saw blade will leave a rather rough surface. To smooth the face (after it's completely cut), position

the rail over the apex (highest point) of the blade. Then gently move it back and forth over the blade while slowly moving the miter gauge forward and back. The high points of the blade will remove the roughness from the entire face of the tenon *(Step 5)*.

CUT OTHER END. When one end of the rail is complete, turn it around (end for end) to work on the other end.

When the other end is cut, the rail should look like it has two half-laps, and the shoulder-to-shoulder distance should be what you want (8" for the sample frame) *(Step 6)*.

CUT OTHER SIDE. Before cutting the opposite faces, duplicate these cuts on a piece of scrap. Then flip the scrap over and make a narrow cut out at the end to make a sample tenon *(Step 7)*.

If the sample tenon fits the mortise after this cut, go ahead and cut the other two faces of the tenon.

If the sample tenon is either too tight or too loose, it means the mortise is not centered. In this case you have to cut the tenon off-center by the same amount as the mortise.

To do this, adjust the height of the saw blade and make trial cuts on the scrap piece until the tenon fits snugly in the mortise. (It's better to have the fit a little on the tight side than too loose.)

THIRD AND FOURTH SHOULDERS. The tenon's thickness should be perfect. All that's left is to cut the third and fourth shoulders so the tenon fits the length of the mortise.

I sneak up on this cut by making trial cuts out at the end of the tenon *(Step 8)*. When the third shoulder lines up, flip the rail over and cut the fourth shoulder.

FINAL FITTING. Now for the final fitting. If you want to leave the ends of the mortise round, you have to round over the corners of the tenon. I do this with a rasp *(Step 9)*.

As you're fitting the tenon into the mortise, the ideal situation is that the tenon will slide in with hand pressure only. However, there's usually a little chunk of something in the way.

Before I get out the chisel, I try to gently tap the tenon home with a hammer. If this doesn't work, don't try to pound the tenon in (this may split the cheeks of the mortise). Instead, use a chisel to clean out the mortise, or pare down the face of the tenon.

Since this joint is blind, you can't see what's going on when it's assembled, and problems are difficult to find and correct. Intuition is the best tool. I try to imagine myself inside the joint looking for problem areas. Then I take it slow. A little bit of correcting can go a long way.

Once the tenon does slide in, check to see if the shoulders rest firmly on the edge of the stile. If there's a little gap, check around the base of the tenon to see if there's a little chunk of waste that needs to be chiseled away.

If the base of the tenon is clear and the shoulders still don't rest on the edge of the stile, the tenon is probably just a hair too long. Trim about $1/16''$ off the end of the tenon and try the fit again.

GLUING UP THE FRAME

At this point all four joints for the frame should fit perfectly. Now for the big question: Is the frame square and flat? To check out the frame, dry-assemble (no clamps or glue) the rails and stiles.

CHECK FOR TWIST. Lay the frame on a flat surface and try to rock it at opposite corners to see if it's twisted. Twist is the worst thing to contend with. But it usually doesn't occur if the wood is straight.

Once again, use intuition to correct any problems — and take it slow.

CHECK WITH CLAMPS. When everything goes together like it's supposed to, the frame can be dry-clamped (no glue yet) to test the effect the clamps have on the squareness of the frame.

(You only need a bar or pipe clamp at each end — clamping the stiles against the shoulders on the rails.)

Place the clamps on a flat surface and position the rails and stiles. Tighten the clamps, but don't apply too much pressure (this can twist the frame). Use a try square to check the frame for square.

GLUE UP. If it all checks out, loosen the clamps and apply a little glue in the mortise (I use a Q-tip). And brush a little on the tenon. Then tighten the clamps. Rushing at this stage can goof up a lot of work. Take as much time as needed to make sure the frame is square as the clamps are tightened.

Wait about 2 hours for the glue to set and remove the clamps. You should have a perfect mortise and tenon frame.

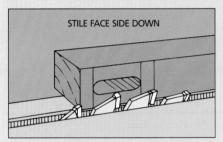

1 To set depth of cut, place stile face down on table. Raise blade so highest tooth lines up with the bottom cheek.

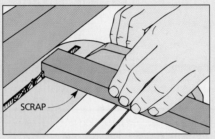

2 Use a piece of scrap to test the depth of cut. Make a cut at the end, guiding the scrap with the miter gauge.

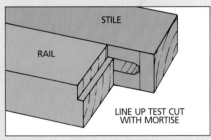

3 To check depth setting, place the trial cut next to the mortise (both facing up) to see if cut lines up with cheek.

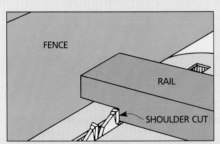

4 Set fence so distance to the outside of the blade equals tenon's length. Make repeated passes to cut face of tenon.

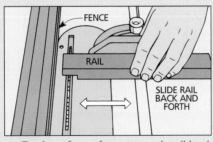

5 To clean face of tenon, push rail back and forth over top of blade while moving miter gauge forward and back.

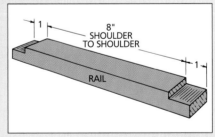

6 Turn rail end-for-end and make same cut at other end. Check the shoulder-to-shoulder distance between tenons.

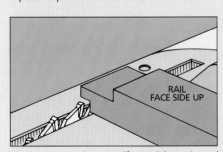

7 Now turn it over (face side up) and repeat Steps 4 and 5, starting at end of tenon and ending at shoulder of cut.

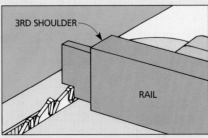

8 To cut 3rd and 4th shoulders, turn rail on edge and sneak up on cuts until tenon's width matches mortise's length.

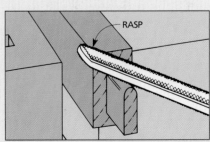

9 If ends of mortise were left round, round corners of tenon to match. Use a rasp to round over corners.

Tabletop Case

A beveled glass top lets you see your treasured possessions in this handsome display case.
And the drawer is enhanced with half-blind dovetails and a medallion-style detail carving.

Not too long ago, I happened to be visiting a historical museum. There were many impressive exhibits, but of all the objects in the place, my eye was drawn to some artifacts that were displayed in a handsome wood case with a beveled glass top.

That display case was the inspiration for this scaled-down version. It's small enough to sit on top of a coffee table or desk and is designed to hold a few of your favorite keepsakes. A drawer allows you to easily rearrange the items on display.

This case does more than just show off your prized possessions, it gives you a chance to try your hand at a few special woodworking techniques.

TECHNIQUES. The drawer is joined with half-blind dovetails, and the drawer front contains an optional, hand-carved medallion. (Also included are separate technique articles on both of these. See pages 24 and 26.)

OPTIONS. A couple other options are making machine-cut dovetails, and using a drawer pull instead of a knob.

In addition, the protective drawer liner (see inset photo) is optional.

MATERIALS. The wooden parts for the case are made from ½" and ¾" walnut, with a ¼" plywood bottom.

There isn't much hardware needed

for this project. You'll need to order the beveled glass from a local glass shop (be sure to have it in hand before beginning the project).

You'll also need a knob or pull for the drawer front, and if you choose to make the protective liner, you'll need a piece of polyester batting, fabric and a stapler.

EXPLODED VIEW

OVERALL DIMENSIONS:
17W x 17D x 4½H

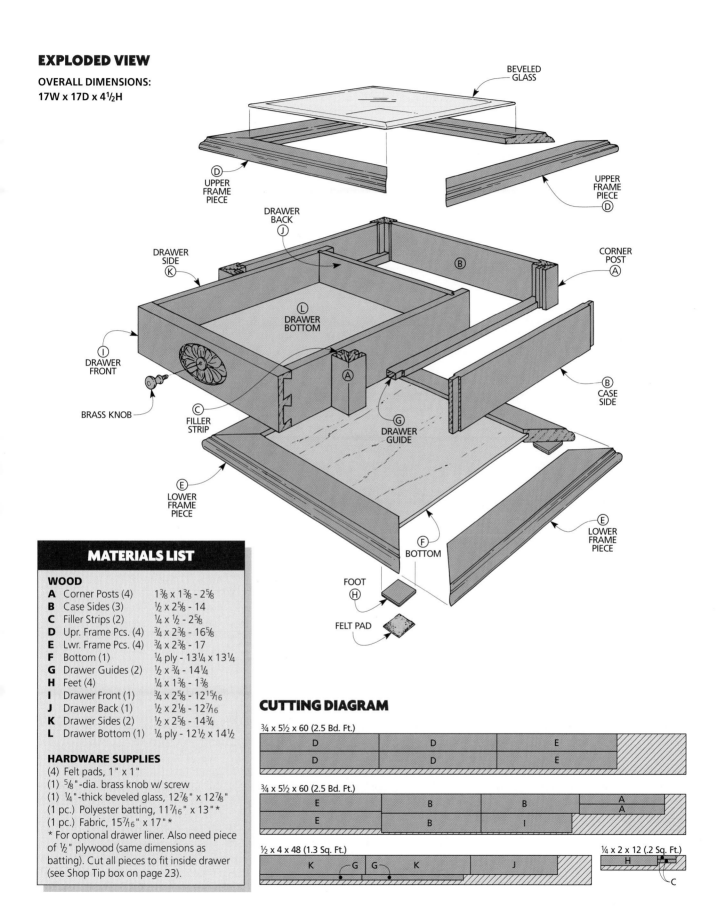

BEVELED GLASS

Ⓓ UPPER FRAME PIECE

UPPER FRAME PIECE Ⓓ

DRAWER BACK Ⓙ

DRAWER SIDE Ⓚ

Ⓑ

CORNER POST Ⓐ

Ⓛ DRAWER BOTTOM

Ⓘ DRAWER FRONT

Ⓐ

Ⓑ CASE SIDE

BRASS KNOB

Ⓒ FILLER STRIP

Ⓖ DRAWER GUIDE

Ⓔ LOWER FRAME PIECE

Ⓕ BOTTOM

Ⓔ LOWER FRAME PIECE

Ⓗ FOOT

FELT PAD

MATERIALS LIST

WOOD
A	Corner Posts (4)	1⅜ x 1⅜ - 2⅝
B	Case Sides (3)	½ x 2⅝ - 14
C	Filler Strips (2)	¼ x ½ - 2⅝
D	Upr. Frame Pcs. (4)	¾ x 2⅜ - 16⅝
E	Lwr. Frame Pcs. (4)	¾ x 2⅜ - 17
F	Bottom (1)	¼ ply - 13¼ x 13¼
G	Drawer Guides (2)	½ x ¾ - 14¼
H	Feet (4)	¼ x 1⅜ - 1⅜
I	Drawer Front (1)	¾ x 2⅝ - 12¹⁵⁄₁₆
J	Drawer Back (1)	½ x 2⅛ - 12⁷⁄₁₆
K	Drawer Sides (2)	½ x 2⅝ - 14¾
L	Drawer Bottom (1)	¼ ply - 12½ x 14½

HARDWARE SUPPLIES
(4) Felt pads, 1" x 1"
(1) ⅝"-dia. brass knob w/ screw
(1) ¼"-thick beveled glass, 12⅞" x 12⅞"
(1 pc.) Polyester batting, 11⁷⁄₁₆" x 13"*
(1 pc.) Fabric, 15⁷⁄₁₆" x 17"*
* For optional drawer liner. Also need piece of ½" plywood (same dimensions as batting). Cut all pieces to fit inside drawer (see Shop Tip box on page 23).

CUTTING DIAGRAM

¾ x 5½ x 60 (2.5 Bd. Ft.)

D	D	E
D	D	E

¾ x 5½ x 60 (2.5 Bd. Ft.)

| E | B | B | A |
| E | B | I | A |

½ x 4 x 48 (1.3 Sq. Ft.)

| K | G G | K | J |

¼ x 2 x 12 (.2 Sq. Ft.)

H		
		C

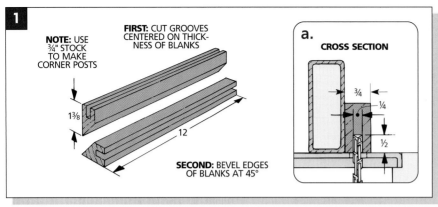

1

NOTE: USE ¾" STOCK TO MAKE CORNER POSTS

FIRST: CUT GROOVES CENTERED ON THICK-NESS OF BLANKS

1⅜

12

SECOND: BEVEL EDGES OF BLANKS AT 45°

a.

CROSS SECTION

¾   ¼

½

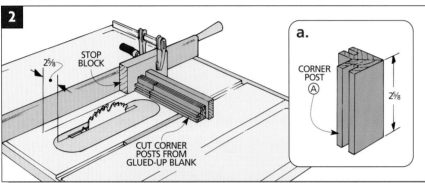

2

STOP BLOCK

2⅝

CUT CORNER POSTS FROM GLUED-UP BLANK

a.

CORNER POST Ⓐ

2⅝

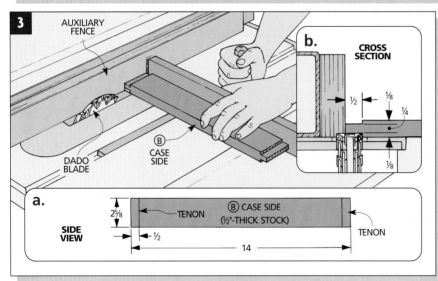

3

AUXILIARY FENCE

DADO BLADE

Ⓑ CASE SIDE

b.

CROSS SECTION

½   ⅛

¼

⅛

a.

2⅝

TENON

SIDE VIEW

½

Ⓑ CASE SIDE
(½"-THICK STOCK)

TENON

14

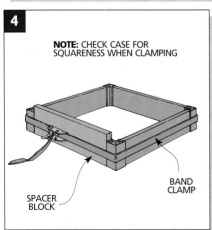

4

NOTE: CHECK CASE FOR SQUARENESS WHEN CLAMPING

BAND CLAMP

SPACER BLOCK

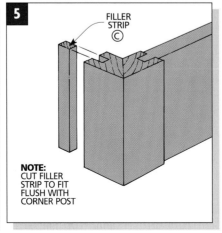

5

FILLER STRIP Ⓒ

NOTE: CUT FILLER STRIP TO FIT FLUSH WITH CORNER POST

CORNER POSTS

The finished tabletop case may look fancy with the half-blind dovetails and detail carving, but building this project is fairly simple.

Basically, the case consists of three sides joined together by four corner posts. This assembly will then be sandwiched between a top and bottom frame (see the Exploded View on page 19).

MAKE BLANKS. I started building the case by making the four corner posts (A). Each of these posts is made up of two pieces. These pieces are grooved, beveled, and glued together at a right angle. But because the posts are fairly short (2⅝"), I decided it would be safer to start with two extra-long pieces and cut them to length later *(Fig. 1)*.

After ripping the two ¾"-thick blanks to width, cut a centered groove on one edge of each piece to accept the case side *(Fig. 1a)*.

Then rip the opposite edge at a 45° bevel and glue the two pieces together. After the glue dries, cut the posts to length *(Fig. 2)*.

SIDES

The corner posts are connected by three case sides (B) (refer to the Exploded View). The fourth side is left open to receive the drawer.

TENONS. After cutting these pieces to finished size (2⅝" x 14"), I cut ½"-long tenons on each end to fit in the grooves cut in the corner posts *(Fig. 3)*.

Once I finished cutting all the tenons, I glued the three case sides to the corner posts *(Fig. 4)*. (Make sure the tenons fit snugly in the post grooves.) To help keep the box square during glue up, I used a spacer block cut out of scrap wood to fit between the front corner posts.

FILLER STRIPS. When the glue is dry and the spacer block is removed, the corner post grooves facing the drawer opening are exposed. To conceal these grooves, I cut a couple of filler strips (C) and glued them in place *(Fig. 5)*.

FRAMES

The upper and lower frames are the final pieces that make up the case. The upper frame will hold the piece of beveled glass, and the lower frame will hold a plywood bottom.

UPPER FRAME. Start by ripping the four upper frame pieces (D) to width ($2^3/8$"). But don't cut them to length yet. First cut a $3/16$" x $1/2$" rabbet on each piece to hold the beveled glass *(Fig. 6a)*.

Now cut the frame pieces to final length ($16^5/8$"), mitering the ends at 45°. Then glue up the frame and set it aside for now.

LOWER FRAME. To make the lower frame, start by ripping four lower frame pieces (E) to width. Instead of a rabbet, these pieces receive a $1/2$"-deep groove to hold a $1/4$"-thick plywood bottom *(Fig. 7a)*. The lower frame pieces are also mitered, but they're slightly longer than the upper frame pieces (17").

Finally, cut the plywood bottom (F) to fit ($13^1/4$" square in my case) and glue up the frame *(Fig. 7)*.

PROFILE. To complete the frames, I first routed a decorative profile on the top outer edge of each frame using a point-cutting ogee bit *(Figs. 8 and 8a)*. (For sources of this special profile bit, see page 126.) Then I rounded over the bottom edges of the frames with a $1/8$" roundover bit *(Fig. 9a)*.

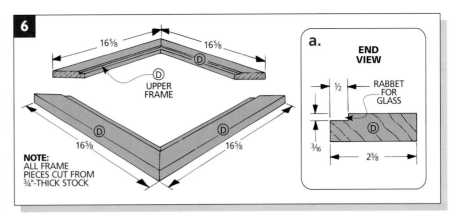

6

$16^5/8$ $16^5/8$

D

UPPER FRAME

$16^5/8$ $16^5/8$

NOTE: ALL FRAME PIECES CUT FROM $3/4$"-THICK STOCK

a.

END VIEW

$1/2$ RABBET FOR GLASS

$3/16$ D $2^3/8$

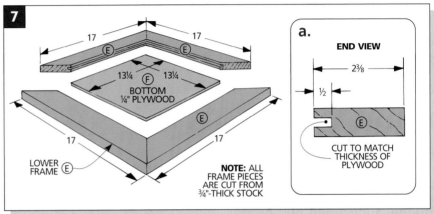

7

17   17

E   E

$13^1/4$ F $13^1/4$

BOTTOM $1/4$" PLYWOOD

E

17   17

LOWER FRAME   E

NOTE: ALL FRAME PIECES ARE CUT FROM $3/4$"-THICK STOCK

a.

END VIEW

$2^3/8$

$1/2$ E

CUT TO MATCH THICKNESS OF PLYWOOD

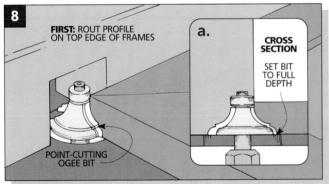

8

FIRST: ROUT PROFILE ON TOP EDGE OF FRAMES

POINT-CUTTING OGEE BIT

a.

CROSS SECTION

SET BIT TO FULL DEPTH

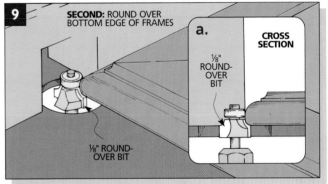

9

SECOND: ROUND OVER BOTTOM EDGE OF FRAMES

$1/8$" ROUND-OVER BIT

a.

CROSS SECTION

$1/8$" ROUND-OVER BIT

ASSEMBLY

With the upper and lower frames glued up, the next step is assembling the case. But I didn't rush into this part of the process. In order to keep the frames aligned with the corner posts and sides during the glue-up stage, I used a couple of tricks.

CENTERLINES. First, I drew centerlines on the sides as well as the frame pieces. This way all I had to do was line up the marks to center the frames.

In addition, I used small brads to keep the pieces aligned while applying clamp pressure. To do this, just nail a brad halfway into the top and bottom of each corner post, and then cut off the heads *(Fig. 10a)*.

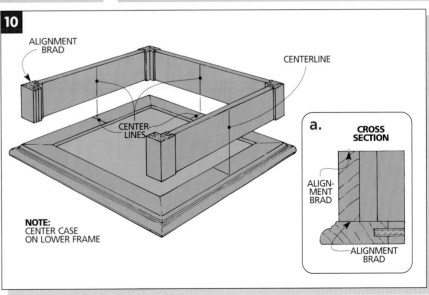

10

ALIGNMENT BRAD

CENTERLINE

CENTER-LINES

NOTE: CENTER CASE ON LOWER FRAME

a.

CROSS SECTION

ALIGN-MENT BRAD

ALIGNMENT BRAD

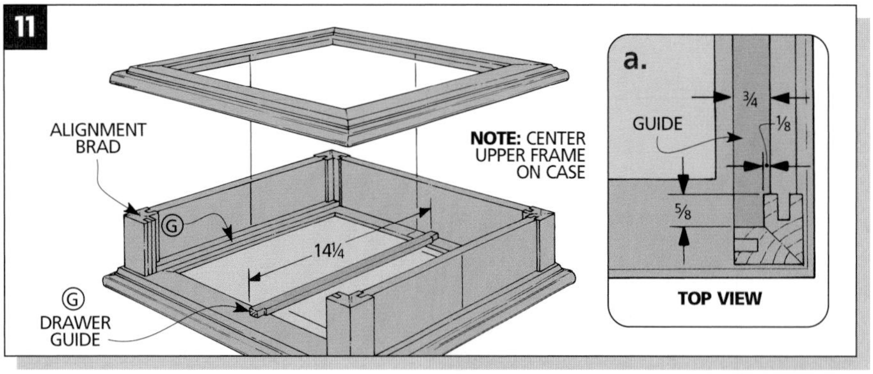
11
ALIGNMENT BRAD
NOTE: CENTER UPPER FRAME ON CASE
14¼
G
DRAWER GUIDE
a.
GUIDE
¾
⅛
⅝
TOP VIEW

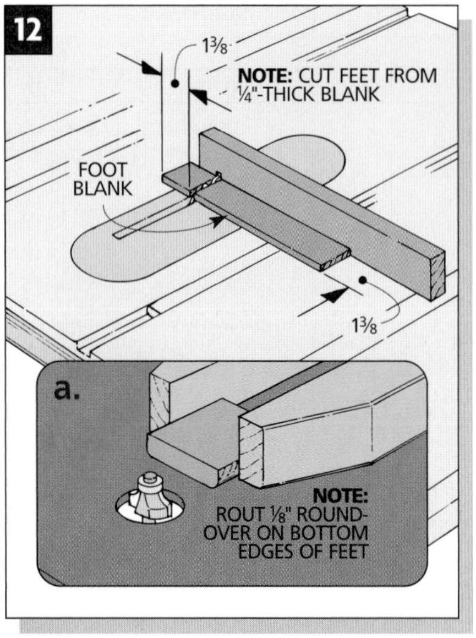
12
1⅜
NOTE: CUT FEET FROM ¼"-THICK BLANK
FOOT BLANK
1⅜
a.
NOTE: ROUT ⅛" ROUND-OVER ON BOTTOM EDGES OF FEET

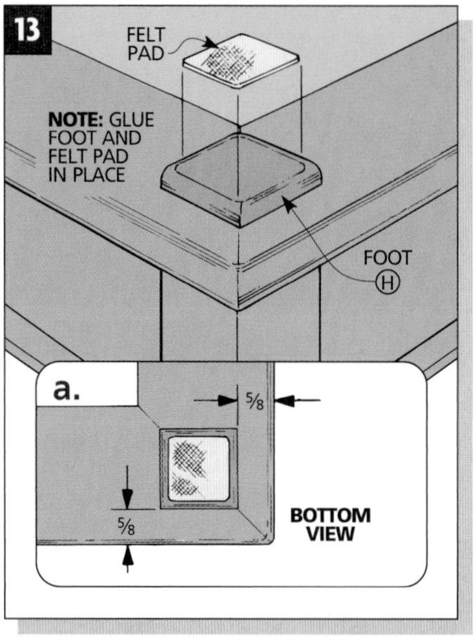
13
FELT PAD
NOTE: GLUE FOOT AND FELT PAD IN PLACE
FOOT
H
a.
⅝
⅝
BOTTOM VIEW

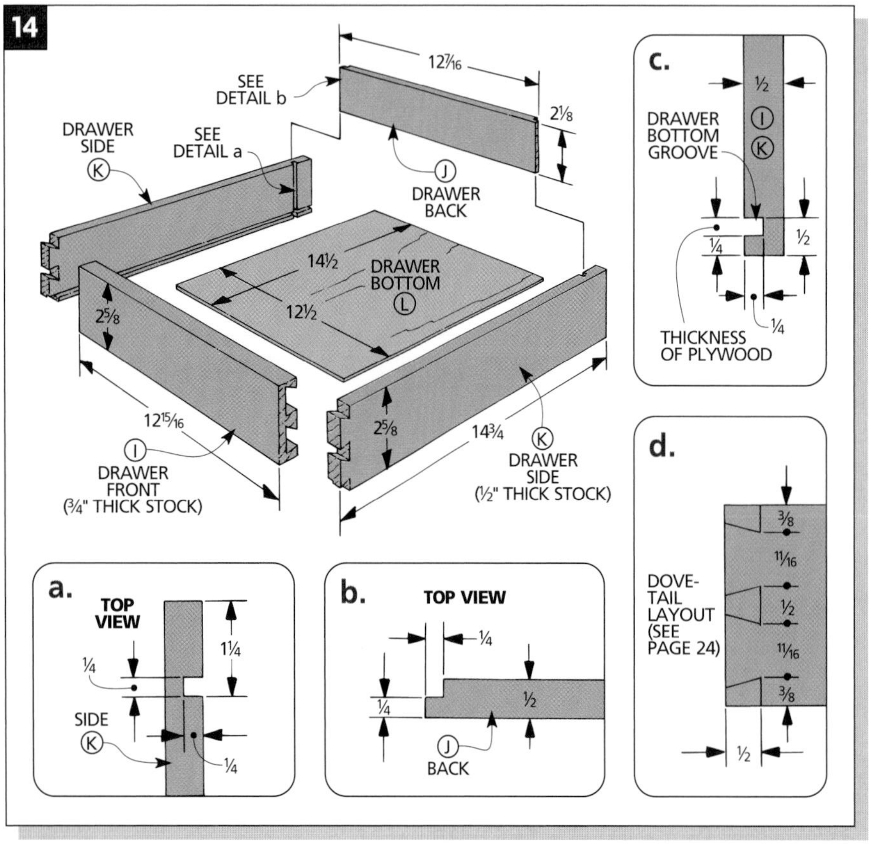
14
12⁷⁄₁₆
SEE DETAIL b
DRAWER SIDE
K
SEE DETAIL a
2⅛
J
DRAWER BACK
14½
DRAWER BOTTOM
L
12½
2⅝
12¹⁵⁄₁₆
I
DRAWER FRONT
(¾" THICK STOCK)
2⅝
14¾
K
DRAWER SIDE
(½" THICK STOCK)
c.
½
DRAWER BOTTOM GROOVE
I
K
¼
½
¼
THICKNESS OF PLYWOOD
d.
⅜
¹¹⁄₁₆
DOVE-TAIL LAYOUT (SEE PAGE 24)
½
¹¹⁄₁₆
⅜
½
a.
TOP VIEW
¼
1¼
SIDE
K
¼
b.
TOP VIEW
¼
½
¼
J
BACK

ASSEMBLY. I glued the case together in two steps. First, I glued the sides to the bottom frame.

Then, before gluing on the top frame, I cut a couple of $1/2$"-thick drawer guides (G) and glued them to the bottom frame on the inside of the case. These guides are just a couple of pieces of $1/2$" stock that are notched at both ends to fit around the corner blocks *(Figs. 11 and 11a).*

FEET. Once the top frame is glued in place, the next step is to add four feet (H) to the bottom of the case. These feet are $1^3/8$" square pieces of $1/4$"-thick stock that are rounded over on the edges *(Figs. 12 and 13).*

Safety Note: I used a small hand-screw clamp to hold each foot while routing the edges *(Fig 12a).*

The feet are aligned as shown and glued to the bottom of the case, and then a small square of felt is glued onto each foot for a pad *(Fig. 13a).*

DRAWER

The drawer is probably the most striking feature of this tabletop display case. It's joined with half-blind dovetails and has a medallion-style carving centered on the front.

Note: If you're not comfortable with making the carving, you can substitute an elegant brass bail-style pull (see the photo below).

I started by cutting out the pieces for the drawer front (I), drawer back (J),

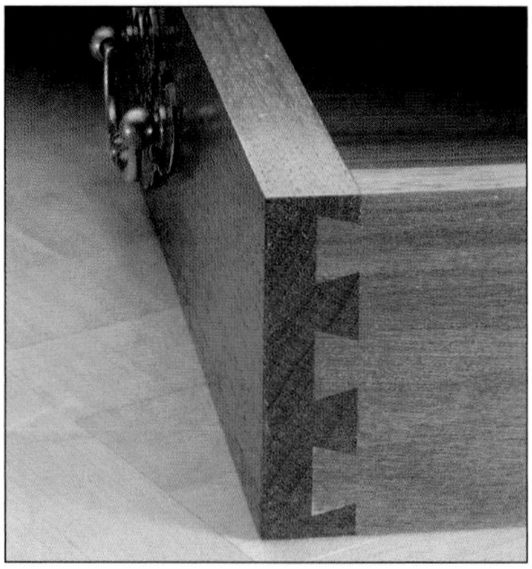

The drawer design has a couple of built-in options. You don't need to add the hand-cut half-blind dovetails or the detail carving to the case's drawer if you don't want to. As another choice, you can build the drawer with machine-cut dovetails and a brass bail pull.

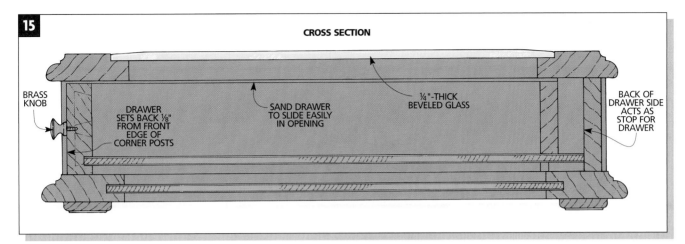

15

CROSS SECTION

BRASS KNOB

DRAWER SETS BACK ⅛" FROM FRONT EDGE OF CORNER POSTS

SAND DRAWER TO SLIDE EASILY IN OPENING

¼"-THICK BEVELED GLASS

BACK OF DRAWER SIDE ACTS AS STOP FOR DRAWER

and drawer sides (K). Then I cut a ¼"-deep groove on the inside face of the drawer front and sides to hold a ¼"-thick plywood bottom (see *Fig. 14c* for groove dimensions).

Next, I cut a dado near the end of each drawer side to hold the drawer back *(Fig. 14a)*. Then I cut a tongue on each end of the drawer back to fit snug in the dadoes *(Fig. 14b)*.

CARVING. The drawer front is joined to the sides with half-blind dovetails. But before cutting the dovetails, I carved the floral pattern on the front of the drawer (see the separate article beginning on page 26).

By doing the carving first, if I made a mistake, all I had to do was start over with a new blank.

HALF-BLIND DOVETAILS. With the carving completed, I began on the half-blind dovetails. I laid out and cut these dovetails by hand (see page 24-25 for

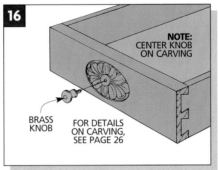

16

NOTE: CENTER KNOB ON CARVING

BRASS KNOB

FOR DETAILS ON CARVING, SEE PAGE 26

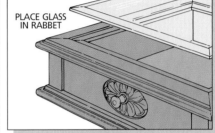

17

PLACE GLASS IN RABBET

details). But the drawer is also sized to allow you to use machine-cut dovetails if you prefer (see the photo on the opposite page).

Once all the joints were fitted together, I cut a drawer bottom (L) out of ¼" plywood. Then I glued up all the drawer parts.

FINISH. When the drawer was complete, I applied a couple coats of a wipe-on oil finish to all the wooden parts of

the case and drawer.

After the finish was dry, I attached a small brass knob to the drawer front. The knob should be centered on the carving *(Fig. 16)*.

Then I added an optional cushioned insert to the inside of the drawer (see the Designer's Notebook below).

Finally, to complete the case I carefully placed the beveled glass top in the rabbets in the top frame *(Fig. 17)*. ■

DESIGNER'S NOTEBOOK

DRAWER LINER

■ To protect objects placed in the tabletop case and add a little decoration, I made an optional liner for the drawer bottom. To make this protective liner, start by cutting a piece of ½" plywood slightly (¼") smaller than the inside dimensions of the drawer.

■ The next step is to cut a piece of polyester batting to the same width and length as the plywood.

■ Once you have cut the plywood and batting, cut a piece of fabric 4" larger in each direction.

■ Now place the fabric face down and roughly center the batting and plywood on top of it. Then, gently press the plywood down, and wrap one side of the fabric over the edge, tacking it in place with a staple. Work your way around,

stapling the fabric in place.

When you get to the corners, fold down and staple the flaps of fabric so that they don't cause wrinkles.

■ Finally, just slip the liner into the drawer and press it down.

JOINERY . . . . *Half-Blind Dovetails*

When it comes to drawer joints, nothing can beat a dovetail for strength and beauty. But on a formal-looking project like the Tabletop Case (see page 18), I didn't want the ends of the dovetails to be visible from the front. So I decided to use half-blind dovetails instead.

With a half-blind dovetail, the pins of the joint aren't cut completely through the drawer front. This way, the drawer front overlaps the ends of the tails, concealing them from view.

At first glance, you might think that cutting half-blind dovetails would be more difficult than cutting standard through dovetails. But the steps are basically the same. And since you only see the joint from one side, you don't have to be quite as concerned with getting a perfect fit.

TAILS

When I make half-blind dovetails, I start by cutting the tails. Since they are cut all

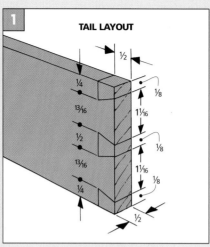

1 TAIL LAYOUT

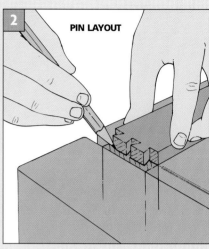

2 PIN LAYOUT

the way through, I can use the completed tails to lay out the pins.

First, lay out the tails on the drawer side *(Steps 1 and 2 and Fig. 1)*. To avoid confusion, I mark the waste sections between the tails with an 'X.'

Removing the waste is a simple two-step process. First, I use a fine-toothed hand saw to cut along the waste side of

the layout lines *(Step 3)*. Then I use a chisel to carefully clean out the waste *(Steps 4 and 5)*.

After removing all the waste, clean up the sides of the tails by making light, paring cuts with the chisel *(Step 6)*. The goal here is to keep the shoulders and sides of the tails square with the face of the workpiece.

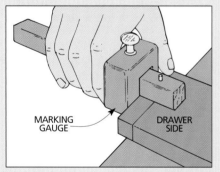

1 To begin, mark the length of the tails on the face and edges of the drawer side. To do this, score a line with a marking gauge or razor knife.

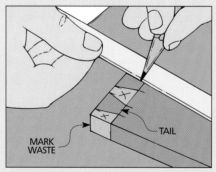

2 Use a ruler and straightedge to lay out the tails according to the measurements shown in Fig. 1 above. Mark the waste with an 'X.'

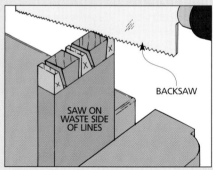

3 After laying out the angles, use a fine-toothed back saw to cut along the waste side of each layout line. Be careful not to cut too deep.

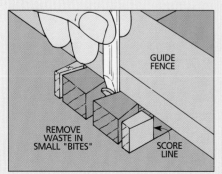

4 The waste between the tails can be chiseled out next. To ensure a square cut, clamp a guide fence to the workpiece at the score line.

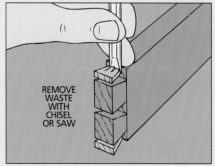

5 Now remove the two sections of waste on the outside edges of the workpiece. But take care not to cut into the tails themselves.

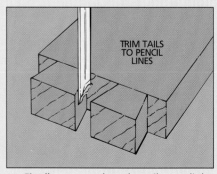

6 Finally, to complete the tails, use light, paring cuts to clean up the sides. Be sure to keep the sides and shoulders square to the face.

PINS

After the tails are cut, laying out the pins is a snap. Just place the tails over the end of the drawer front and trace the outline (Fig. 2). Then scribe a baseline on the inside face of the drawer front to indicate the thickness of the sides (Step 7).

Now use a square and a pencil to extend the layout lines down the face of the workpiece (Step 8).

When cutting and chiseling out the waste around the pins, the trick is to cut along the inside edge of the penciled layout lines. If you remove too much material, you'll have a loose-fitting joint.

To remove the waste, I start by making diagonal cuts on the waste side of the lines (Step 9). When doing this, hold the saw at a steep angle until you reach the scribed baseline, and then level it out to finish the cut.

After making these cuts, carefully chisel out the waste, working from the end and inside face of the drawer front (Steps 10 and 11).

After most of the waste is removed, you can start cleaning up the shoulders and sides of all the pins (Steps 12 and 13).

Check the fit and make any necessary adjustments by lightly paring the sides or shoulders of the pins (Step 14).

Note: Since the joint will be visible only from the side, I like to undercut the sides of the pins slightly to ensure a close fit (Step 15).

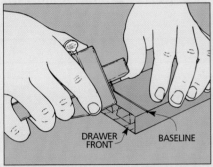

7 After tracing outline of tails on drawer front, use marking gauge to scribe baseline that equals thickness of side.

8 With a square and pencil, extend layout lines of pins down face of drawer front and mark waste sections.

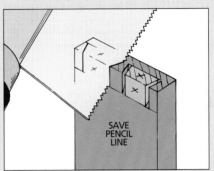

9 Staying well to the waste side of the layout lines, remove waste by making angled cuts in the end of the workpiece.

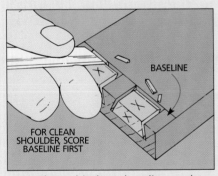

10 Place chisel on baseline and tap straight down with mallet. Pare away small 'V' section in front of baseline.

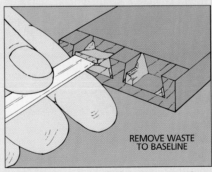

11 Next, taking light cuts, continue removing waste between pins until you reach the baseline on end of board.

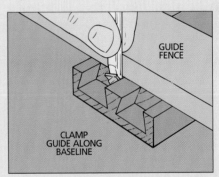

12 Again, clamp guide fence in place and square up shoulders by chopping straight down with chisel and mallet.

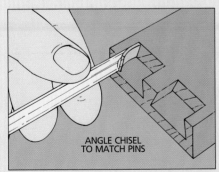

13 Now, clean out the remaining waste on the sides of the pins by holding the chisel at an angle to follow the layout lines.

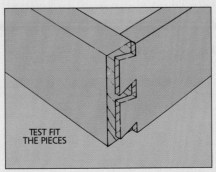

14 Test the fit of the joint to determine which areas need to be trimmed further. Be careful not to trim too much at one time.

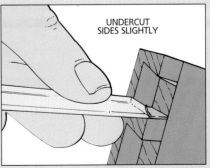

15 Finally, if the fit is too tight, undercut the sides of the pins slightly until the tails fit nicely into the sockets created by the pins.

Most of the carving I've done in my life has been with a whittling knife on a stick. So when the idea of including a carving on the display case first came up, I was a little skeptical. After all, skilled carvers can spend years perfecting their technique.

Fortunately, the floral design we used for the tabletop case on page 18 doesn't take long to master. And it doesn't require a drawer full of expensive carving tools either.

PRACTICE. Even though this design isn't too difficult, carving is not a skill that many people are born with. So it's probably a good idea to make two or three attempts at this carving before you start on your actual drawer front. You'll be surprised at how much your work improves with each trial run.

OVAL TEMPLATE. The first step is to make the oval outline of the design. To create a nice, smooth oval, I used a template and a router fitted with a guide bushing and a 1/8"-diameter straight bit.

To make the template, first I transferred the pattern (shown full-size at upper right on opposite page) to a piece of 1/4"-thick hardboard. An easy way to do this is to make a photocopy of the design and use a hot iron to transfer the toner to the hardboard *(Step 1)*. (I used the same method to transfer the pattern to the drawer front.) Then I cut out the

oval and sanded the inside edge smooth.

To complete the template, I attached a couple of cleats to the sides so that it would straddle the drawer front.

Using carpet tape to hold the template in place, I set the router bit to cut a 1/8"-deep groove and routed the outline of the oval *(Step 2)*.

Once the oval is established, score the outlines of the individual petals to a depth of about 1/16" *(Step 3)*. This helps prevent you from accidentally cutting into the design or chipping out a splinter as you chisel the background.

CREATING THE RELIEF. Next, I began removing the background material all

around the outline of the floral pattern using a round-nose chisel *(Step 4)*. Continue removing the background material and deepening the outline around the design until the entire background is recessed to the same depth as the router cut (1/8").

SHAPING THE PETALS. With the background material removed, I set about shaping the petals. Here is where you start getting down to some real carving. I started by deepening the outline around each petal. To do this, I made a deep, slicing cut along the outside of each petal and around the center of the flower *(Step 5)*.

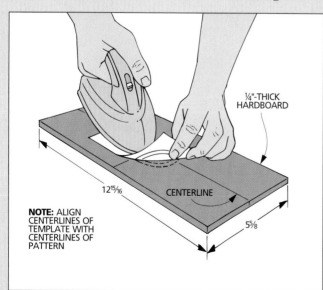

1 After making two photocopies of the full-size floral pattern, use an iron to transfer one copy to the hardboard template and the other copy to the drawer front.

Labels: 1/4"-THICK HARDBOARD, CENTERLINE, 12 15/16, 5 5/8, **NOTE:** ALIGN CENTERLINES OF TEMPLATE WITH CENTERLINES OF PATTERN

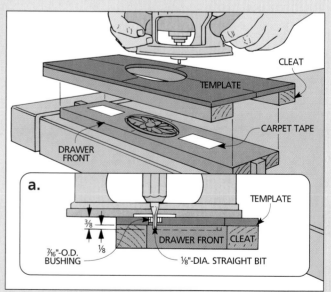

2 Cut out the oval (template outline) and sand the inside edges smooth. Then attach it to the drawer front with carpet tape and rout the oval outline (tinted area in pattern on next page).

Labels: CLEAT, TEMPLATE, CARPET TAPE, DRAWER FRONT, **a.**, TEMPLATE, 3/8, 1/8, DRAWER FRONT, CLEAT, 7/16"-O.D. BUSHING, 1/8"-DIA. STRAIGHT BIT

To give the petals some dimension, I hollowed them out with shallow cuts, starting at the edge and cutting down and toward the vein of each petal *(Step 6)*.

As you continue to remove material from the petals, the initial vein cuts will disappear. To avoid chipout, it's important to redefine these veins as you cut deeper and deeper into the petals. To do this, I re-cut each vein with a V-groove chisel *(Step 7)*.

Now just keep alternating between *Steps 6 and 7*.

Continue hollowing out the petals until the veins are almost as deep as the carving background.

STIPPLED BACKGROUND. Once I had finished shaping the petals, I cleaned up the outline of the design with a sharp chisel. Then using a nail set, I stippled

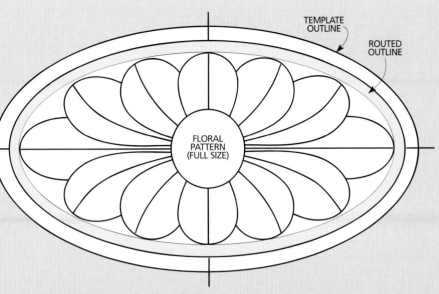

TEMPLATE OUTLINE

ROUTED OUTLINE

FLORAL PATTERN (FULL SIZE)

the background around the design *(Step 8)*. This evens out any roughness in the background and helps to accentuate the carving.

To finish up, I smoothed out the tool marks by lightly sanding each petal. To

do this, I just wrapped a small piece of 400-grit sandpaper around my finger and sanded each petal.

Then finally, I wiped the carving with a tack cloth to remove any traces of sanding dust.

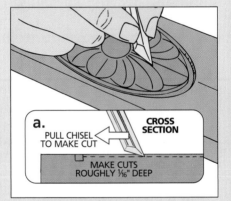

a.
PULL CHISEL TO MAKE CUT
CROSS SECTION
MAKE CUTS ROUGHLY 1/16" DEEP

3 Score all the lines of the floral design with a chip carving knife or skew chisel. To help maintain control while cutting, use light pressure.

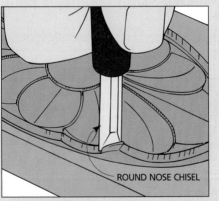

ROUND NOSE CHISEL

4 Next, start chiseling out the background material. Be careful and take shallow cuts to avoid chipping out a large splinter of wood.

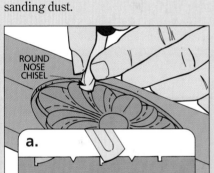

ROUND NOSE CHISEL

a.
CROSS SECTION

5 To make the petals appear distinct from one another, make a beveled, slicing cut around the outside edge of each petal.

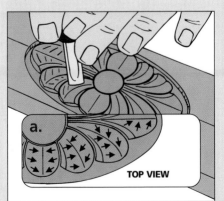

a.
TOP VIEW

6 Start hollowing out the petals. Working toward the center of each petal, make shallow cuts down into the veins to avoid chipout.

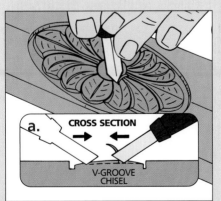

a.
CROSS SECTION
V-GROOVE CHISEL

7 As you hollow out the petals, redefine the veins using a V-groove chisel. Working from both ends of the petal, cut each vein in two passes.

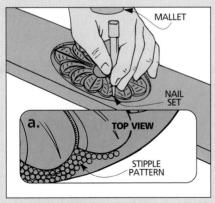

MALLET
NAIL SET
a.
TOP VIEW
STIPPLE PATTERN

8 Using a nail set and a hammer, stipple the background of the design. Use even-pressured blows to create a uniform-looking background.

Contemporary Cabinet

This contemporary cabinet only takes two and a half sheets of plywood and some hardwood edging to build, but the shelves are deep enough to display books, pictures and collectibles.

When you build a large project like this contemporary cabinet, plywood is an ideal material to use. It's flat, dimensionally stable, and comes in sheets large enough so you can avoid the tedious process of edge-gluing a lot of boards together.

However, plywood has two main disadvantages. The edges have to be covered to hide the plies. And, the project has to be designed around the fact that plywood comes in 4 x 8 sheets.

To get the most efficient use of each sheet, I had to juggle the size of all the pieces to fit a certain cutting diagram. I also had to watch the grain direction — especially with the doors (I tried to arrange the pieces on the sheet to get the nicest grain pattern on the doors).

JOINERY. I decided to use tongue and groove joints throughout this project, beginning with the primary joint that fastens the fixed shelves to the case sides.

Here, I cut a $1/4$"-wide dado across the inside face of each side, then cut tongues on the ends of the shelves.

But why cut a $1/4$"-wide dado? Why not make it $3/4$" wide to match the thickness of the plywood?

I used $3/4$" oak plywood, which is rarely $3/4$" thick — it's usually slightly less. It can also have slight variations in thickness throughout the sheet (usually due to the final sanding). So rather than take a chance on a sloppy fit (or a joint line that looks wavy), I cut a $1/4$"-wide dado, and then cut a tongue to fit.

EDGING. In addition to using tongue and grooves as the primary joinery to assemble the case, I also used it to attach edging strips to the case sides and shelves. Although they could be glued on with butt joints, using tongue and groove joints helps align the edging. (For more on this, see pages 35–36.)

FINISH. When the case was done, I decided to apply two coats of a golden oak stain. Then I finished it off with two coats of a semi-gloss varnish.

EXPLODED VIEW

OVERALL DIMENSIONS:
30W x 16D x 80H

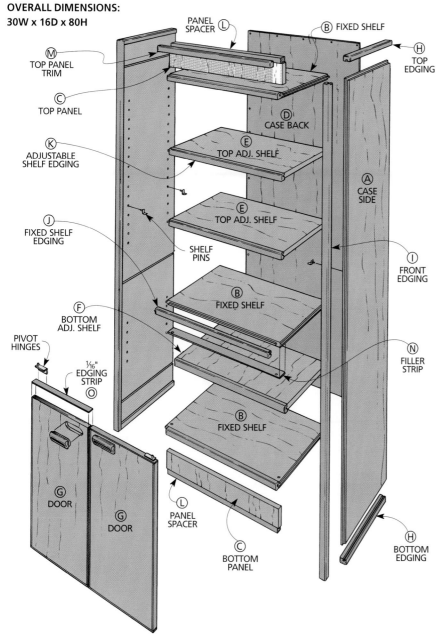

- Ⓜ TOP PANEL TRIM
- Ⓒ TOP PANEL
- Ⓚ ADJUSTABLE SHELF EDGING
- Ⓙ FIXED SHELF EDGING
- SHELF PINS
- Ⓕ BOTTOM ADJ. SHELF
- PIVOT HINGES
- 1/16" EDGING STRIP Ⓞ
- Ⓖ DOOR
- Ⓖ DOOR
- Ⓛ PANEL SPACER
- Ⓒ BOTTOM PANEL
- Ⓛ PANEL SPACER
- Ⓑ FIXED SHELF
- Ⓗ TOP EDGING
- Ⓓ CASE BACK
- Ⓔ TOP ADJ. SHELF
- Ⓔ TOP ADJ. SHELF
- Ⓐ CASE SIDE
- Ⓑ FIXED SHELF
- Ⓘ FRONT EDGING
- Ⓝ FILLER STRIP
- Ⓑ FIXED SHELF
- Ⓗ BOTTOM EDGING

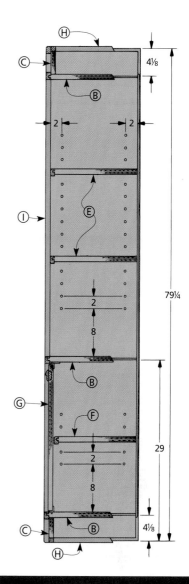

CUTTING DIAGRAM

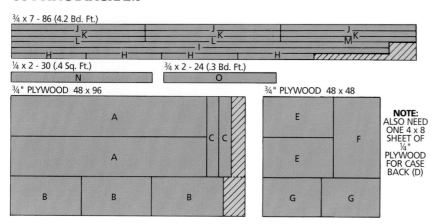

3/4 x 7 - 86 (4.2 Bd. Ft.)

L K J L K J L K M

H H H H

1/4 x 2 - 30 (.4 Sq. Ft.)
N

3/4 x 2 - 24 (.3 Bd. Ft.)
O

3/4" PLYWOOD 48 x 96
A / C C / A / B B B

3/4" PLYWOOD 48 x 48
E / F / E / G G

NOTE: ALSO NEED ONE 4 x 8 SHEET OF 1/4" PLYWOOD FOR CASE BACK (D)

MATERIALS LIST

CASE

A	Case Sides (2)	$3/4$ ply - $15^{5}/_{8}$ x $79^{1}/_{4}$
B	Fixed Shelves (3)	$3/4$ ply - $15^{3}/_{8}$ x $29^{1}/_{4}$
C	Top/Btm. Panels (2)	$3/4$ ply - $28^{1}/_{2}$ x $3^{1}/_{2}$
D	Case Back (1)	$1/4$ ply - $29^{1}/_{2}$ x $71^{1}/_{2}$
E	Top Adj. Shelves (2)	$3/4$ ply - $14^{3}/_{8}$ x $28^{3}/_{8}$
F	Btm. Adj. Shelf (1)	$3/4$ ply - $28^{3}/_{8}$ x $13^{1}/_{2}$
G	Doors (2)	$3/4$ ply - $13^{11}/_{16}$ x $23^{1}/_{2}$

SOLID TRIM EDGING

H	Top/Bottom (4)	$3/4$ x 1 - $15^{1}/_{4}$
I	Front Sides (2)	$3/4$ x 1 - 80
J	Fixed Shelves (3)	$3/4$ x 1 - 28
K	Adj. Shelves (3)	$3/4$ x 1 - $28^{3}/_{8}$
L	Panel Spacers (2)	$3/4$ x $3/4$ - 28
M	Top Panel Trim (1)	$3/4$ x 1 - 28
N	Filler Strip (1)	$1/4$ x $1^{1}/_{2}$ - $28^{1}/_{2}$
O	Edging Strips (1)	$1/16$ x $3/4$ - 13 lineal ft.

HARDWARE SUPPLIES

(32) No. 6 x $3/4$" Fh woodscrews
(12) $1/4$" brass shelf supports
(2) Recessed red oak door pulls
(2 pr.) Pivot hinges
(1) Double plate magnetic catch
(2) Adjustable levelers

CASE SIDES

I started work on this cabinet by making two case sides (A). Although the sides are just two pieces of plywood, they present a problem. Each side has three sets of dadoes for the fixed shelves (B) — and these dadoes have to be perfectly aligned so the shelves lay flat and parallel. The trick is to cut the dadoes across one wide blank of plywood. Then cut the blank in half to get two identical pieces that can be used as the case sides (Fig. 1).

CUT TO SIZE. To do this, first cut a large blank to a rough width of 32", and a finished length of 79¼" (Fig. 1). (Remember, this wide blank will be ripped in half later.)

TONGUES. Before the blank is ripped in half, there are two things that have to be done to it. First, tongues are cut on all four edges (Figs. 1 and 2a). These tongues are used to attach hardwood edging (refer to Fig. 6 on page 32). (See the Technique on page 35 for more on adding edging to plywood with tongue and groove joints.)

DADOES FOR SHELVES. Next, I routed three dadoes for the fixed shelves (B) across the large blank (Figs. 1 and 2b). To do this, mark the location of the three dadoes. Then clamp a fence to the plywood blank and rout each dado. (See the Shop Tip below for a simple gauge to help align the fence.)

CUT CASE SIDES. Now, to get the two case sides (A), I ripped the plywood blank into two pieces. Each piece was 15⅝" wide.

Note: When ripping the second piece to width, make sure you trim the edge *without* the tongue.

BACK PANEL RABBET. The last thing to do is to rout a rabbet on the back edge

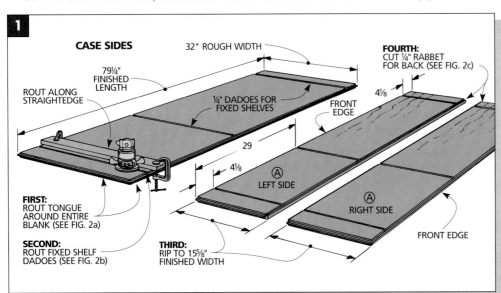

1

CASE SIDES

79¼" FINISHED LENGTH

32" ROUGH WIDTH

ROUT ALONG STRAIGHTEDGE

¼" DADOES FOR FIXED SHELVES

FRONT EDGE

FOURTH: CUT ¼" RABBET FOR BACK (SEE FIG. 2c)

4⅛"

29

4⅛"

(A) LEFT SIDE

(A) RIGHT SIDE

FRONT EDGE

FIRST: ROUT TONGUE AROUND ENTIRE BLANK (SEE FIG. 2a)

SECOND: ROUT FIXED SHELF DADOES (SEE FIG. 2b)

THIRD: RIP TO 15⅝" FINISHED WIDTH

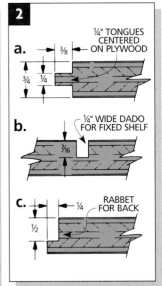

2

a. ¼" TONGUES CENTERED ON PLYWOOD
⅜ ¾ ¼

b. ¼" WIDE DADO FOR FIXED SHELF
7/16

c. RABBET FOR BACK
¼ ½

SHOP TIP .... Router Fence Alignment

When routing a dado across a wide panel, I mark the location of the dado first. Then I clamp a fence parallel to the layout lines to guide the router.

The problem is figuring out the exact location of the fence. You have to measure the distance from the edge of the router base to the cutting edge of the bit, then transfer this measurement to the workpiece. Somewhere there's likely to be an error.

To be a little more accurate, I made a simple gauge. It's a piece of scrap with a dado cut across it to align the fence parallel to the layout lines (Fig. 2).

To make the gauge, clamp a piece of scrap to the bench and clamp a higher fence at one end (Fig. 1). Now mount the bit in the router and run the router base against the high fence to rout a dado across the scrap.

To use the gauge, turn it over on the workpiece so the dado aligns with the layout lines. Then butt the fence against the end of the gauge and clamp it down (Fig. 2). Now rout along the edge of the fence. The dado should match the layout lines.

Since router bases can be mounted off center in relation to the bit, always keep the router facing the same direction that it was when you routed the gauge.

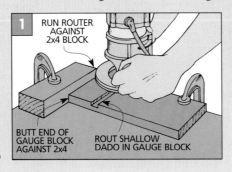

1 RUN ROUTER AGAINST 2x4 BLOCK

BUTT END OF GAUGE BLOCK AGAINST 2x4

ROUT SHALLOW DADO IN GAUGE BLOCK

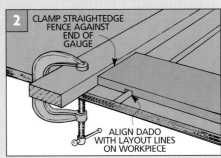

2 CLAMP STRAIGHTEDGE FENCE AGAINST END OF GAUGE

ALIGN DADO WITH LAYOUT LINES ON WORKPIECE

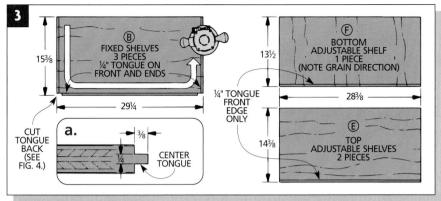

3

15⅜ — FIXED SHELVES (B) 3 PIECES ¼" TONGUE ON FRONT AND ENDS

— 29¼ —

CUT TONGUE BACK (SEE FIG. 4.)

a. ⅜ / ¼ CENTER TONGUE

¼" TONGUE FRONT EDGE ONLY

13½ — BOTTOM ADJUSTABLE SHELF (F) 1 PIECE (NOTE GRAIN DIRECTION)

— 28⅜ —

14⅜ — TOP ADJUSTABLE SHELVES (E) 2 PIECES

4

PIVOT HINGE

1¹¹⁄₃₂"-DIA. ¼" DEEP — BUSHING — ⅞

¼

CUT TONGUE BACK ½" ON BOTH ENDS, ALL FIXED SHELVES ½

NOTE: DRILL HINGE HOLES IN BOTTOM FIXED SHELF ONLY

---

of each case side to attach the case back (added later) *(Fig. 2c)*.

SHELVES

After the case sides are finished, work can begin on the shelves. There are three fixed shelves (B), two top adjustable shelves (E), and one bottom adjustable shelf (F). I started by cutting all six of these shelves to size *(Fig. 3)*.

TONGUES. After the shelves are cut to size, tongues are routed on the *front edges* of all the shelves for the edging strips *(Fig. 3a)*. Next, rout tongues on both *ends* of the fixed shelves (B) only. These tongues fit into the dadoes in the case sides *(Fig. 1)*.

There's one more step on the tongues. The tongues on the front edge of the fixed shelves (B) have to be trimmed back to allow space for the edging that's applied to the case sides. Trim the tongues ½" on both ends *(Fig. 4)*.

HOLES FOR PIVOT HINGES. Later, when the doors are hung, I used pivot hinges to mount them (refer to *Fig. 4*).

The only problem with these hinges is that you have to drill the holes in the bottom fixed shelf (B) before the case is assembled. If you don't drill these holes now, you can't get the drill close to the corner after assembly.

Also, these holes must be drilled in the right location for the doors to swing properly *(Fig. 4)*. After marking the locations as shown, drill the holes at both ends of the shelf to accept the bushings for the hinges.

ASSEMBLE THE CASE

Once the shelves were made, I began to assemble the case. I started by getting three clamps in position on the floor, spacing them so they would be in line with the dadoes *(Fig. 5)*. Then stand the sides on edge with the fixed shelves (B) loosely in place. (You may want to call in an assistant at this point.)

Note: To get even clamping pressure across the whole joint, I made some tapered clamping blocks. (For more information, see the Shop Tip

below.) When using these blocks, I put a small piece of double-sided carpet tape on the clamp heads to hold the blocks in place.

When the clamps and tapered blocks are in place, remove one shelf and apply glue in the dado. Then clamp the shelf in place, checking for square against the sides with a framing square. Clamp the other two fixed shelves using the same procedure.

As the clamps are tightened, make sure the front shoulders of the tongues on the shelves are flush with the shoulders of the tongues on the case sides.

SHOP TIP

Tapered Blocks

To get even pressure on the entire joint, I made tapered clamping blocks from 2x2 scrap. Use a plane (or belt sander) to create a bowed shape. About ¹⁄₁₆" per foot is enough. It just has to bow enough so the middle touches before the ends.

BOW CREATES PRESSURE IN MIDDLE OF JOINT

CROSS SECTION

TAPER EXAGGERATED FOR CLARITY ¹⁄₁₆" PER FOOT

5

CHECK CASE WITH SQUARE

TOP SHELF (B)

(B) MIDDLE SHELF

(B) BOTTOM SHELF

PIPE CLAMPS

TAPER CLAMPING BLOCKS, SIX PIECES

LAY OUT PIPE CLAMPS ON FLAT SURFACE

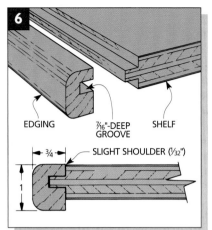

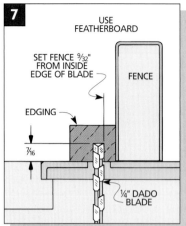

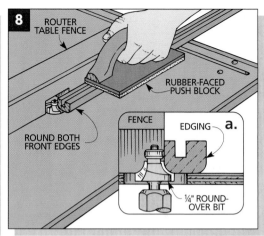

EDGING

While the case was drying, I cut 12 edging strips: four strips for the top and bottom case edges (H), two for the front edges (I), and six for the shelves (J, K).

CUT EDGING. Start by ripping 1"-wide strips from $3/4$"-thick stock. Then cut the twelve pieces to rough length.

OFF-CENTER GROOVE. Next, cut grooves in each strip to fit over the tongues on the case sides and shelves *(Fig. 6)*. Since the edging is 1"-wide and the plywood is only $3/4$" thick, the grooves are cut slightly off-center. This produces a lip on the inside of the case sides and on the bottom of the shelves.

To cut the groove, I used a dado blade on the table saw set $7/16$" deep *(Fig. 7)*. (The groove is $1/16$" deeper than the tongue to allow a glue relief.) Position the groove so the edging will extend about $1/32$" above the face of the plywood *(Fig. 6)*. Later, you can trim this shoulder flush with the plywood. (I used a flush trim jig. See page 37.)

PROFILE EDGES. After the grooves are cut, round over the front edges of all the edging strips with a $1/4$" roundover bit on the router table *(Fig. 8a)*.

Note: Since the edging strips are narrow, I used a rubber-faced push block to guide them *(Fig. 8)*.

CUT TO LENGTH. After making the edging strips, I cut them all to length. First cut the top and bottom strips (H) so the ends align with the shoulders of the tongues on the sides *(Fig. 9a)*.

Next, cut the front strips (I) that go on the front edges of the sides. Then round over the ends. Also, since the groove extends through the top end, cut a plug to fit this hole *(Fig. 9a)*.

Now, cut the shelf edging (J, K) to length, round over the ends, and glue it onto the shelves. Note that the lip on the top shelf faces up. The lips on the middle and bottom shelves face down.

SHELF HOLES

Once the edge strips were glued on, I drilled holes for the pin supports used to mount the top adjustable shelves (E). To position the holes, I cut a drilling template to fit between the top and middle shelves *(Fig. 9)*. Then I drilled $1/4$" holes, spaced as shown on page 29. (A piece of pegboard can also work as a template. Make sure you keep the same end down and mark which holes to drill into.)

After drilling the holes in the upper part of the wall unit, trim the template down to drill the holes in the lower part.

BACK, TOP, & BASE

The basic cabinet is completed by adding the case back and the top and bottom panels.

Cut the back (D) out of $1/4$" plywood so it fits snugly between the rabbets on the back of the case sides, and flush with the top and bottom fixed shelves *(Fig. 10)*. Then screw it into the rabbets.

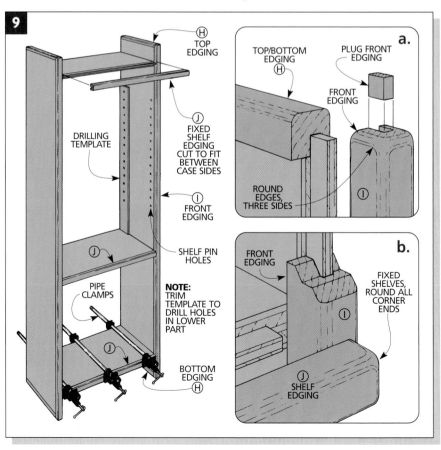

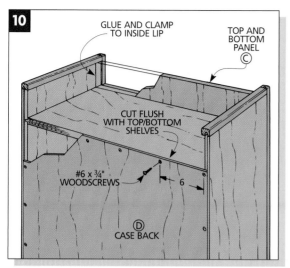

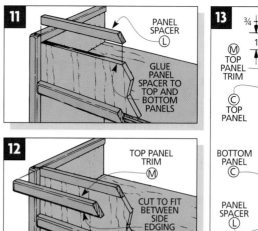

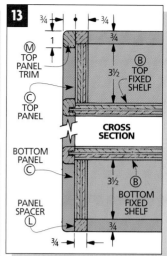

TOP AND BOTTOM PANELS. Next come the top and bottom panels (C). The panels are glued to fit behind the lips of the edging strips *(Fig. 10)*. Note that the grain direction runs vertically.

SPACERS. To complete these panels, I added edging pieces made to look like all the other edging. To do this, first add spacers (L) to the top edge of the top panel and bottom edge of the bottom panel *(Figs. 11 and 13)*.

Now, on the top panel only, cut a top panel trim strip (M) 1" wide (to duplicate the look of the edging) and round over the front edges and ends with a $\frac{1}{4}$" roundover bit. Then glue this trim strip to the front of the spacer *(Fig. 12)*.

DOORS

The cabinet is complete at this point and could be used as it is. However, I added doors (G) to the bottom.

DOOR SIZES. To find the height of the doors, first measure between the edging strips on the two lower shelves.

Then subtract $\frac{1}{4}$" for the $\frac{1}{8}$" space above and below, and subtract another $\frac{1}{8}$" for the $\frac{1}{16}$"-thick edging strips (O) that trim the doors.

To determine the width of the doors, measure between the edging strips on the case sides, subtract $\frac{3}{8}$" (for the $\frac{1}{8}$" spaces on each side of the doors and the one between the doors), and subtract $\frac{1}{4}$" for the edging strips. Then divide by two and cut the doors to width.

EDGING STRIPS. After cutting the

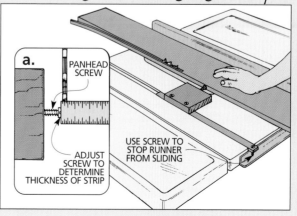

doors to size, I cut $\frac{1}{16}$"-thick edging strips to cover all four edges of the doors. (See the Shop Tip box below.)

After the strips are cut, glue and clamp the strips on the side edges of the doors first. Then add the strips on the top and bottom edges. Finally, trim the edges flush with the faces of the doors.

SHOP TIP . . . . *Cutting Thin Edging Strips*

To cut thin strips safely, I rip them off the waste side of the stock. And to cut them to a uniform thickness, I use a simple stop system. On the edge of this stop there's a "fine tuning" screw.

To use the stop, first move it alongside the blade and adjust the screw until the distance between the saw blade and the screw equals the thickness

of the strip you're trying to cut off.

Now secure the stop 3" in front of the blade.

Next, slide the workpiece against the screw. And then slide the fence against the workpiece. Lock down the fence and cut off a strip. To cut strips exactly the same width, slide the workpiece and fence against the screw again and reset the fence.

The last steps are to mount the hardware on the wall unit.

PULLS. I started by cutting recesses and mounting the pulls. Since I only had two recesses to rout, I did them freehand. The pulls have a $3/32$"-wide lip around the outside — that's enough room to allow some minor variations.

I began by laying out the position of the recesses on the workpiece (refer to *Fig. 14*). Now, set a pull inside the lines and draw the round ends *(Fig. 15)*.

To rout most of the recess, mount a straight bit and set it to depth to align with the *thickest* part of the pull *(Fig. 16)*.

Note: On the door pulls I used, the back was sanded at an angle. So the distance from the lip to the back of the pull was inconsistent.

Now, turn on the router and plunge the bit into the center of the layout lines. Slowly clean out the waste in a clockwise direction from the center to the layout lines *(Fig. 17)*.

After most of the waste is cleared out with a router, switch to a chisel to clean out to the layout line *(Fig. 18)*. The lip is wider on the ends of the pull, so you don't have to chisel out a perfect radius.

HINGES. The doors are mounted between the two lower shelves with pivot hinges. The holes for these hinges are already drilled in the bottom shelf.

For the top holes, add a filler strip (N) first *(Fig. 19)*. Cut this strip to fit, then drill the holes in the same position as on the bottom shelf *(Fig. 19a)*.

Then mount the hinges and screw them to the doors *(Fig. 20)*. I also mounted a magnetic catch underneath the middle fixed shelf *(Fig. 21)*.

LEVELERS. Although the wall unit may be perfectly level, the floor it rests on may not be — especially if there's a tack strip under the carpet near the wall. To level it, I added two adjustable levelers behind the bottom panel *(Fig. 22)*. The adjustment for these levelers is through a hole in the bottom shelf. Finally, there's a plug that comes with the leveler to cover this hole. ∎

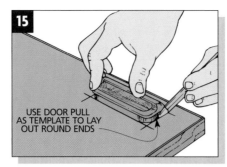

15 USE DOOR PULL AS TEMPLATE TO LAY OUT ROUND ENDS

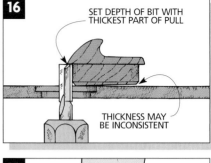

16 SET DEPTH OF BIT WITH THICKEST PART OF PULL
THICKNESS MAY BE INCONSISTENT

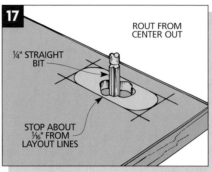

17 ROUT FROM CENTER OUT
$1/4$" STRAIGHT BIT
STOP ABOUT $1/16$" FROM LAYOUT LINES

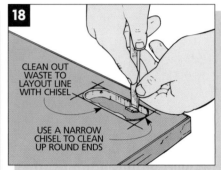

18 CLEAN OUT WASTE TO LAYOUT LINE WITH CHISEL
USE A NARROW CHISEL TO CLEAN UP ROUND ENDS

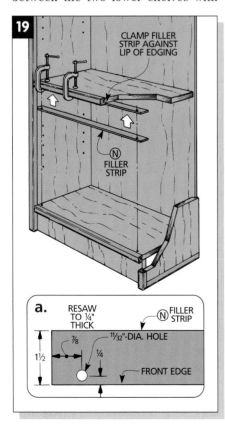

19 CLAMP FILLER STRIP AGAINST LIP OF EDGING
FILLER STRIP (N)

a. RESAW TO $1/4$" THICK
FILLER STRIP (N)
$7/8$
$11/32$"-DIA. HOLE
$1/4$
$1\frac{1}{2}$
FRONT EDGE

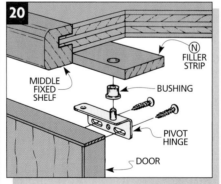

20 MIDDLE FIXED SHELF
FILLER STRIP (N)
BUSHING
PIVOT HINGE
DOOR

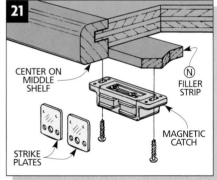

21 CENTER ON MIDDLE SHELF
FILLER STRIP (N)
MAGNETIC CATCH
STRIKE PLATES

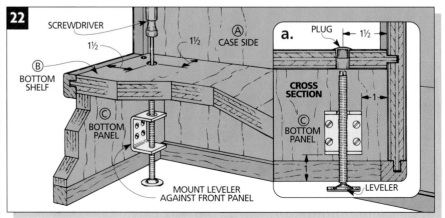

22 SCREWDRIVER
$1\frac{1}{2}$
$1\frac{1}{2}$
(A) CASE SIDE
(B) BOTTOM SHELF
(C) BOTTOM PANEL
MOUNT LEVELER AGAINST FRONT PANEL
a. PLUG $1\frac{1}{2}$
CROSS SECTION
(C) BOTTOM PANEL
1
LEVELER

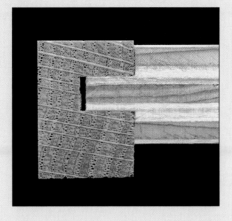

Unfortunately, the beauty of plywood is only skin deep. It's nice to work with plywood when a project calls for large pieces, but you have to cover the edges to hide the plies.

Covering the edges is usually thought of as just cosmetic. But besides hiding the ply layers, there's a design reason for adding edging to plywood.

On many projects the plywood will look too thin if edging isn't added. For example, on the contemporary cabinet the sides are over 6 feet high, yet only $3/4$" thick — a little out of proportion.

The solution is to add solid edging to the plywood. By adding a 1"-wide strip to the plywood, the piece looks thicker and more in proportion. (It also allows you to round over the edges.)

TONGUE & GROOVE

When I want to apply solid-wood edging strips to plywood, I use a tongue and groove joint. But why not just glue the strips right on the edge? The answer has to do with alignment.

ALIGNMENT. Dealing with long strips and getting their edges aligned with the face of the plywood panel can lead to headaches. As the clamps are tightened, the edging will tend to slip on the glue.

If the edging slips down below the face of the plywood, you'll see the exposed edge. To prevent this, I align the edging just slightly ($1/32$") above the face of the plywood (see photo above).

This little lip ensures the edging strip covers the edge of the plywood completely, even if there are variations in the thickness of the plywood. Also, by creating this lip, you don't have to try to get the edging to fit exactly flush with

the face of the plywood. After the edging is glued on, you can come back and trim off the lip so it's perfectly flush.

Trimming off this lip is easier than it sounds. On small pieces, I use a hand plane or scraper. If I'm working with large pieces, I use a router with a flush trim bit (see page 37).

TONGUE OR GROOVE FIRST? The easiest way to align the edging to get this $1/32$" lip is to use a tongue and groove joint. That is, cut a tongue on the edge of the plywood, and cut a groove down the edging strip to fit over the tongue. But which do you cut first?

PROBLEMS. Most of the fitting problems stem from cutting the groove, because you have to be concerned about both the width of the groove (to fit the tongue) and the position of the groove (to form the lip).

So, go ahead and cut the grooves in all the edging strips first, right? Well, you could do that, but once the grooves are cut, you're committed to the position of the groove. That is, you won't know if it's in the right position to create that little lip until after the tongue is cut.

So, cut the tongues first? Well, if you

cut the tongues first, and then cut the grooves later with a dado blade, you have to make sure the tongue fits the exact width of the groove — but the groove isn't cut yet, so you can't check.

It's a problem either way. So I cut both of them first. That is, I start by cutting a tongue on the plywood but I also set up the dado blade and cut a groove in a test piece to test the fit of the tongue.

CUTTING THE TONGUE

Although the tongue can be cut on a table saw, I think you get the best results with a router. Router bits don't usually splinter the plywood as much.

If I'm working with small pieces, I use a router table, sliding the workpiece against the fence. With large pieces I use a hand-held router. It's easier to handle a router on a large piece of plywood than handling a sheet on a router table.

ROUT RABBETS. To make a tongue, just rout a rabbet on each face of the plywood. Since you're working from both faces with an identical setting on the router, the resulting tongue will be perfectly centered on the thickness.

ROUTER BIT. Okay, let's back up a minute. Since you're going to be routing rabbets, there are two ways to go about it: use a rabbet bit with a ball-bearing pilot or, use a straight bit with an edge guide attachment on the router.

RABBET BIT. The rabbet bit *(Fig. 1)* is the quickest to set up, but may not give the best results. Often the pilot hits a void in the core plies or runs over a splinter on the edge, which puts a little bump in the shoulder of the rabbet.

EDGE GUIDE. Although it takes longer to set up, I like to use a straight bit with an edge guide on the router *(Fig. 2)*.

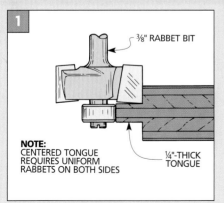

1 $3/8$" RABBET BIT
NOTE: CENTERED TONGUE REQUIRES UNIFORM RABBETS ON BOTH SIDES — $1/4$"-THICK TONGUE

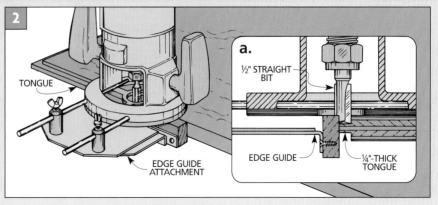

2 TONGUE — EDGE GUIDE ATTACHMENT
a. $1/2$" STRAIGHT BIT — EDGE GUIDE — $1/4$"-THICK TONGUE

When using an edge guide and a straight bit, the edge guide smoothes over any bumps or dips in the plywood edge. (For a ³⁄₈"-wide rabbet, I use a ¹⁄₂" straight bit so I'm sure to clear away all the waste in one pass.)

To make the tongue on the edge of the plywood, set up the edge guide to rout a ³⁄₈"-wide rabbet. Then the depth has to be set. This is when you need the test piece with the groove in it.

Use a dado blade on the table saw to cut a groove in a piece of scrap hardwood. Then set the depth of cut on the router and rout rabbets on both faces of a piece of scrap plywood.

Note: Make sure the scrap is from the same sheet as the "real" pieces.

Gradually adjust the depth of cut, making cuts on both faces until the resulting tongue fits the groove. When the tongue fits the groove, rout rabbets on both faces of the "real" pieces.

As each tongue is completed, use the test piece to check the fit in the groove. Run the test piece down the length of the tongue to see if there's a tight area. If you hit a thick spot, rout back over that area, or clean it up with a chisel.

CUTTING THE GROOVE

After the tongue is formed on the edges of the plywood, I cut the edging strips to width and to rough length (about 2" long). Then I set up the table saw to cut the groove in the edging. There are three things to consider here.

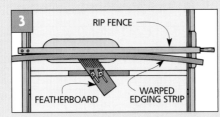

First, the width of the groove must match the thickness of the tongue you've just cut. That's taken care of with the test groove.

Second, the depth of the groove should be a little (¹⁄₁₆") deeper than the length of the tongue. This allows the shoulders to "bottom out" before the tongue hits the bottom of the groove.

Finally, the groove has to be located so the face of the edging sticks up about ¹⁄₃₂" above the face of the plywood.

POSITION GROOVE. To get the groove in that particular position, it's basically a matter of sneaking up on the cut. To get close, measure the size of the shoulder above the tongue. Then set the fence that distance from the blade, plus ¹⁄₃₂".

Now make a test cut, cutting a groove in a piece of scrap first. Then hold the groove on the tongue on the edge of the plywood. You should be able to feel the slight lip on the top edge. Slide it along all the tongues to make sure you feel the lip everywhere. If you don't, move the fence away from the blade just a hair more and cut another test groove.

The idea is to feel that little ¹⁄₃₂" lip. When the groove on the test piece checks out, you can work on the real edging strips.

WARPED PIECES. As you start, look for any warp in the edging strips. It makes things a little more difficult if a strip is warped, but it will still work because the tongue and groove joint will force the strip into position.

If you do find a strip that's warped, face the bowed edge toward the fence (*Fig. 3*). Then use a featherboard to force the strip against the fence as the groove is cut.

TEST FIT. As each groove is cut, test its fit on the plywood edge. If it's too tight, don't change the fence until grooves are cut in all the pieces. Then move the fence away from the blade slightly and make another pass. This widens the groove, but keeps the same lip on the top edge.

After the grooves are cut, the edging strips can be glued and clamped to the edge of the plywood (see below).

HOW TO CLAMP EDGING TO PLYWOOD

The problem with most pipe clamps (and bar clamps) is that they apply pressure too high up. The pressure is applied in line with the screw on the clamp head, which on most pipe clamps is centered about ⁵⁄₈" to ³⁄₄" above the surface of the pipe.

This can be a problem when you're gluing 1"-wide edging to ³⁄₄"-thick plywood, or even in the usual practice of edge-gluing ³⁄₄"-thick stock together.

If I'm gluing an edging strip to plywood, I lay the clamps on a flat surface and push the workpieces down against the pipes. However, as the clamps are tightened, the clamping pressure will be applied at the top edge of the edging strip (*Fig. 1*). This causes the edging strip to twist so the bottom edge pulls away from the plywood.

One solution is to make a clamping board with round edges. The round edges redistribute the force of the clamp so its centered on the thickness of the clamping board (*Fig. 2*).

To clamp edging to ³⁄₄" plywood, I rip a clamping board out of ¹⁄₄"-thick stock and round over all four edges with a ³⁄₈" roundover bit (or use a ³⁄₄" dowel).

THIN STRIPS. When gluing on thin strips (such as the ¹⁄₁₆"-thick strips on the doors of the contemporary cabinet), I make a slight alteration. These strips are so thin that if all the pressure is at the center, the top and bottom won't get enough pressure.

So, I make the clamping board with only one round edge which is placed against the clamp head. The flat edge goes against the thin strip (*Fig. 3*).

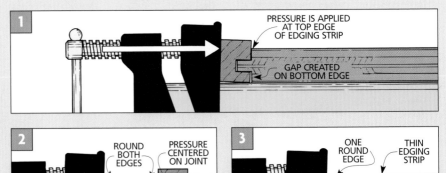

SHOP JIG .... Flush Trim Jig

Whenever you use wooden edging strips on plywood (or plastic laminate), you have the problem of trimming the edging down so it's flush. Using a router with a flush trim bit is probably the easiest method. But, there can be a problem. It's difficult to balance the router on the narrow edging strip without having it tip and creating an angled cut.

So I designed a flush trim jig. It's actually an "outrigger" that's screwed to the bottom of the router.

NEW BASE. To make the jig, begin by making a base plate (A) from 1/4" hardboard. First, cut the base plate 7" x 7" *(Fig. 1)*. Then use your router's plastic base plate as a template to lay out the bit hole and the screw holes.

Now drill the holes, counterboring the screw holes to keep the screws below the surface of the plate *(Fig. 2)*.

SUPPORT RAILS. After making the base plate, I cut two support rails (B) to

size from 3/4" stock *(Fig. 3)*. Also, cut two 1/8" kerfs 3/4" from the end of these rails. These kerfs are used to mount the end support (C) and permit alignment of the bit.

Now, screw the support rails to the base plate *(Fig. 3)*. Then screw the base plate to the router using the original router screws *(Fig. 4)*. To keep the chips from flying in my face, I added a 1/4" plastic chip shield *(Fig. 4)*.

END SUPPORT. The last piece to make is the end support (C). This controls the angle of the router bit and acts as a handle. Cut this piece to fit between the support rails *(Fig. 5)*. Then glue a 1 1/4"-wide grip on the top edge.

SET UP JIG. To set up for routing, mount a flush trim bit in the router. Then hold a square along the cutting edge of the bit and align the bottom edge of the end support *(Fig. 5)*. When the end support is aligned, tighten panhead screws into the kerfs.

USING THE JIG. To use the jig, adjust the bit depth so the cutting edge is only on the edging. Then place the jig on the workpiece so it rides on the bit's pilot and the end support *(Fig. 6)*.

Turn on the router and pull it toward you, concentrating on keeping pressure down on the handle, not on the router. If the bit is cutting at an angle, raise or lower the support *(Fig. 6)*.

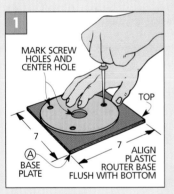

1
MARK SCREW HOLES AND CENTER HOLE
TOP
7
7
Ⓐ BASE PLATE
ALIGN PLASTIC ROUTER BASE FLUSH WITH BOTTOM

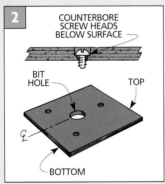

2
COUNTERBORE SCREW HEADS BELOW SURFACE
BIT HOLE
TOP
C̶L
BOTTOM

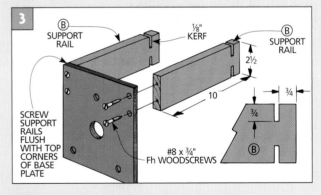

3
Ⓑ SUPPORT RAIL
1/8" KERF
Ⓑ SUPPORT RAIL
2 1/2
10
3/4
3/4
SCREW SUPPORT RAILS FLUSH WITH TOP CORNERS OF BASE PLATE
#8 x 3/4" Fh WOODSCREWS
Ⓑ

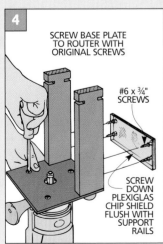

4
SCREW BASE PLATE TO ROUTER WITH ORIGINAL SCREWS
#6 x 3/4" SCREWS
SCREW DOWN PLEXIGLAS CHIP SHIELD FLUSH WITH SUPPORT RAILS

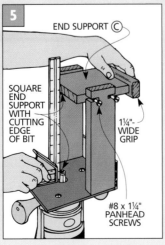

5
END SUPPORT Ⓒ
SQUARE END SUPPORT WITH CUTTING EDGE OF BIT
1 1/4"-WIDE GRIP
#8 x 1 1/4" PANHEAD SCREWS

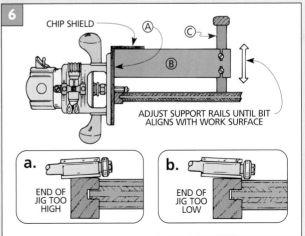

6
CHIP SHIELD
Ⓐ
Ⓒ
Ⓑ
ADJUST SUPPORT RAILS UNTIL BIT ALIGNS WITH WORK SURFACE
a. END OF JIG TOO HIGH
b. END OF JIG TOO LOW

Curio Cabinet

Glass shelves and panels give this curio cabinet an open, inviting look. But the decorative moldings are what give it character, and the techniques used to make them will please any woodworker.

There are two completely different ways to look at a curio cabinet. To someone who has valuable collectibles, a cabinet like this one is a nice way to show them off, while at the same time keeping them out of harm's reach.

A woodworker, however, might very well ignore the items on display and concentrate on the construction of the cabinet itself.

He/she wouldn't open the door to get a better view of the collectibles, but rather to see how the glass was installed, or to see if the joint lines on the back of the door fit as well as those on the front.

To simplify things, the construction of this curio cabinet is based on only two techniques: building frames and cutting molding strips. But to complicate things, the sequence of construction is a little backwards.

DENTIL MOLDING. The reason for starting the construction process with the decorative molding instead of the frames is really very simple. It has to do with making the dentil molding look perfectly symmetrical.

Dentil molding is nothing more than a strip of wood cut with uniform kerfs to create a series of evenly spaced blocks. For dentil molding to look its best, the blocks at the corners and ends of the molding strip must be the same length as the rest. Therefore, the dimensions of the cabinet itself must be designed around this molding.

Complete instructions for two ways of cutting dentil molding are given on page 119.

CUT TO FIT. Because your dentil molding may vary from the pieces I cut, plan to use the measurements in the drawings only as a guide, based on the length of the molding strips. Then be sure you measure and cut all other pieces accordingly. This includes the glass panels and shelves, which will have to be ordered or cut to size *after* the cabinet frame and doors are finished.

TECHNIQUES. Aside from cutting the dentil molding, several other woodworking techniques are used on this curio cabinet.

For example, the web frames are assembled using stub tenon and groove joinery. The side frames and door frames are joined with molded-edge mortise and tenon joints. (Detailed instructions and tips on cutting a mortise and tenon joint are given on pages 13 to 17.)

A variety of other moldings are also cut, but all are made on the router table with three standard bits.

OPTIONS. You don't have to build this cabinet exactly as shown. One option is to replace the plywood back with a mirror to provide a better view of your display items. Refer to the Shop Tip box on page 42 for more on this.

On the other hand, if you don't want a cabinet this tall, or if you're short of floor space, you might choose to build a shorter, hanging version of the cabinet. This option is shown in the Designer's Notebook on pages 46-47.

MATERIALS. I made all the wood parts of this cabinet out of walnut.

The frame pieces, moldings and filler strips are all made of $3/4$" stock, while the back pieces and top panel are made of $1/4$" plywood. The web frame panels are $3/4$" plywood.

Very little hardware is needed for this project, as strong joinery and glue are enough to keep it together. Woodscrews, however, will be used to hold the plywood backs in place while gluing, and brads will fasten the glass stops in place.

I used offset hinges and store-bought knobs with screws for the two doors. For information on mail order sources, see page 126.

EXPLODED VIEW

OVERALL DIMENSIONS:
24¾"W x 15⅞"D x 73⅜"H

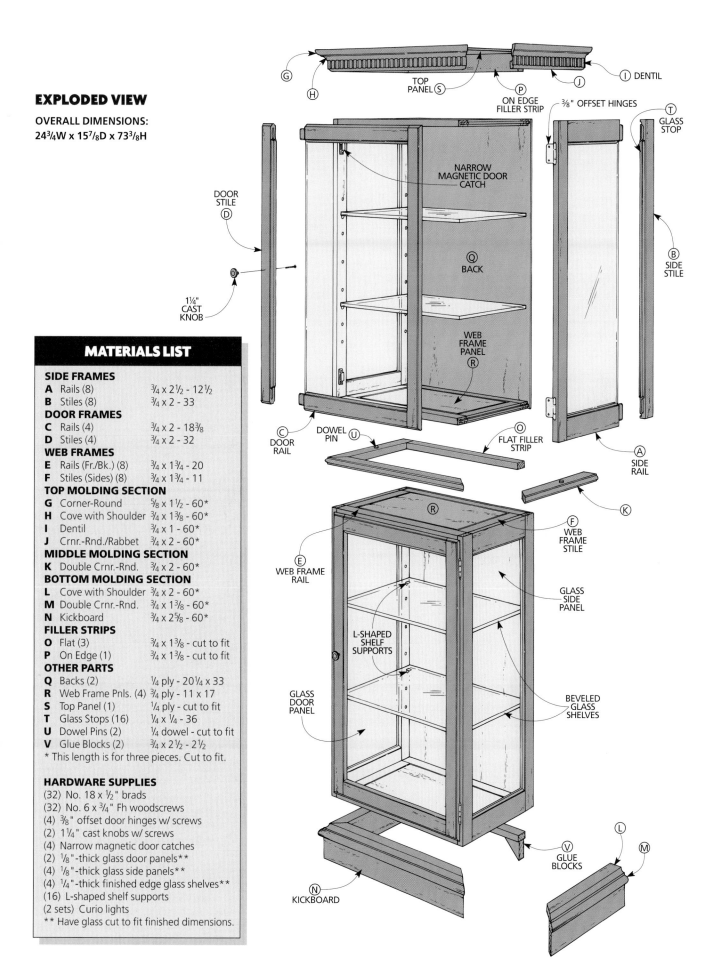

DENTIL

TOP PANEL S

ON EDGE FILLER STRIP

⅜" OFFSET HINGES

T GLASS STOP

G H

J

I

P

NARROW MAGNETIC DOOR CATCH

DOOR STILE D

Q BACK

B SIDE STILE

1¼" CAST KNOB

WEB FRAME PANEL R

C DOOR RAIL

DOWEL PIN U

O FLAT FILLER STRIP

A SIDE RAIL

R

F WEB FRAME STILE

K

E WEB FRAME RAIL

GLASS SIDE PANEL

L-SHAPED SHELF SUPPORTS

GLASS DOOR PANEL

BEVELED GLASS SHELVES

GLUE BLOCKS V

L

M

N KICKBOARD

MATERIALS LIST

SIDE FRAMES
A Rails (8) ¾ x 2½ - 12½
B Stiles (8) ¾ x 2 - 33

DOOR FRAMES
C Rails (4) ¾ x 2 - 18⅜
D Stiles (4) ¾ x 2 - 32

WEB FRAMES
E Rails (Fr./Bk.) (8) ¾ x 1¾ - 20
F Stiles (Sides) (8) ¾ x 1¾ - 11

TOP MOLDING SECTION
G Corner-Round ⅝ x 1½ - 60*
H Cove with Shoulder ¾ x 1⅜ - 60*
I Dentil ¾ x 1 - 60*
J Crnr.-Rnd./Rabbet ¾ x 2 - 60*

MIDDLE MOLDING SECTION
K Double Crnr.-Rnd. ¾ x 2 - 60*

BOTTOM MOLDING SECTION
L Cove with Shoulder ¾ x 2 - 60*
M Double Crnr.-Rnd. ¾ x 1⅜ - 60*
N Kickboard ¾ x 2⅝ - 60*

FILLER STRIPS
O Flat (3) ¾ x 1⅜ - cut to fit
P On Edge (1) ¾ x 1⅜ - cut to fit

OTHER PARTS
Q Backs (2) ¼ ply - 20¼ x 33
R Web Frame Pnls. (4) ¾ ply - 11 x 17
S Top Panel (1) ¼ ply - cut to fit
T Glass Stops (16) ¼ x ¼ - 36
U Dowel Pins (2) ¼ dowel - cut to fit
V Glue Blocks (2) ¾ x 2½ - 2½
* This length is for three pieces. Cut to fit.

HARDWARE SUPPLIES
(32) No. 18 x ½" brads
(32) No. 6 x ¾" Fh woodscrews
(4) ⅜" offset door hinges w/ screws
(2) 1¼" cast knobs w/ screws
(4) Narrow magnetic door catches
(2) ⅛"-thick glass door panels**
(4) ⅛"-thick glass side panels**
(4) ¼"-thick finished edge glass shelves**
(16) L-shaped shelf supports
(2 sets) Curio lights
** Have glass cut to fit finished dimensions.

CUTTING DIAGRAM

¾ x 7¼ - 60 (3 Bd. Ft. each)

¾ x 7¼ - 48 (2.4 Bd. Ft. each)

NOTE: CUT DOWEL PINS (U) FROM ¼" DOWEL.

¾ x 7¼ - 72 (3.6 Bd. Ft. each)

48 x 48
¼" PLYWOOD

24 x 48
¾" PLYWOOD

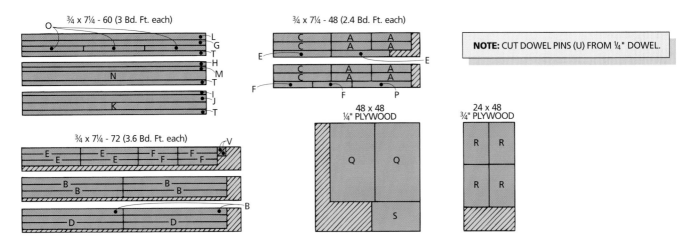

FRONT DENTIL HAS 30 FULL-WIDTH BLOCKS

MITER AT END OF BLOCK

CUT MOLDING TO FIT DENTIL

RABBET TO FIT DENTIL

MOLDING OVERHANGS CASE ⁷⁄₁₆" ON EACH SIDE

SHOULDER TO SHOULDER DISTANCE

¼" CORNER-ROUND WITH ³⁄₃₂" SHOULDER

DENTIL

Most of the visual impact of this cabinet is the result of the molding — especially the dentil (I). This is made by cutting a series of ¼"-wide kerfs along a board to produce the ½"-wide blocks (see "Making Dentil Molding" on page 119).

THE PROBLEM. The dentil strip looks best if there's a full-width block at each end *(Fig. 1)*. But if the cabinet is built first, it's almost impossible to cut the dentil with the proper spacing.

THE SOLUTION. So I cut the dentil first, and used it as a guide for the rest of the cabinet. The dentil for the front is the key. This should be 22¼" long — if everything works out perfectly.

But the actual length of the dentil that you cut may be slightly different when measured from the full-width blocks at each end. (There should be a total of 30 full-width blocks.)

The dentil strips for the sides of the cabinet are not quite so critical. I cut them to rough length at first. Then, during the final assembly stages, they can be trimmed to fit the cabinet. But for the most pleasing visual effect, they should also end with full-width blocks at both the front and back corners.

OTHER MOLDING STRIP. After the dentil is made, one more molding strip (J) is cut to fit below the dentil. The top edge of this strip is rabbeted to accept the dentil. Then a corner-round profile is cut on the bottom edge with a ¼" roundover bit, leaving a ³⁄₃₂" shoulder *(Fig. 2)*.

To get the final length of this strip, use the "heel-to-heel" length of the dentil (the distance between the heels of the miter on the back of the dentil). Cut

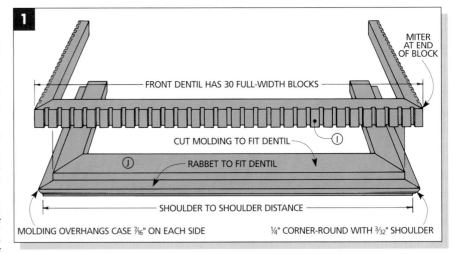

¼" CORNER-ROUND WITH ³⁄₃₂" SHOULDER

KERFS ⅛" DEEP

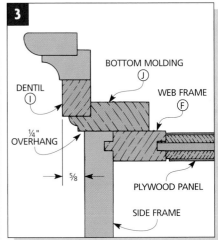

BOTTOM MOLDING

DENTIL

WEB FRAME

¼" OVERHANG

PLYWOOD PANEL

SIDE FRAME

it to length *(Fig. 2)*. When this molding strip and the dentil are cut to final length, you can start on the web frames.

WEB FRAMES

The cabinet is built as two separate units. And in keeping with the odd con-

struction sequence, I built each unit inside out. I started with the web frames (the top and bottom of each unit).

There are four web frames in all (two for each unit). The key one is the top web frame (for the top unit). It must be sized according to the final length of the dentil and molding piece that were just cut. Then the other three web frames are cut to match the top one.

RAILS AND STILES. The rails (E) (front and back pieces) and the stiles (F) (side pieces) are ripped to a width of $1^{3}/_{4}$" *(Fig. 4)*. The lengths take some figuring.

To get the length of the rails, measure the distance between the shoulders of the corner-round on the bottom edge of molding piece (J) ($21^{1}/_{2}$") *(Fig. 1)*. Subtract a total of $1^{1}/_{2}$" to allow $3/_{4}$" on each end. This $3/_{4}$" is for the $1/_{4}$" overhang, plus $3/_{4}$" for the thickness of the side frames, minus $1/_{4}$" for the tongue on the edge of the web frame *(Fig. 3)*.

The stiles are 11" long to make the web frame 14" deep *(Fig. 4)*. (This length allows for a $10^{1}/_{2}$" shoulder-to-shoulder distance plus the two stub tenons.)

GROOVES. $1/_{4}$" x $1/_{4}$" grooves are cut along the inside edges of all 16 pieces. This groove holds the plywood panel, and is also used to join the web frames.

To join the frames, cut stub tenons on the ends of the stiles to fit the thickness and depth of the groove *(Fig. 4a)*.

PLYWOOD PANELS. Dry-assemble the web frames and measure between the bottoms of the grooves to get the size of the plywood panels (R). Cut the panels to size and cut rabbets on the top and bottom faces, leaving tongues to fit the grooves. I also cut a $1/_{16}$" x $1/_{16}$" decorative rabbet along the "show" face of each panel (Side Cross Section in *Fig. 4*). Now the rails, stiles and panels are glued together to form the web frames.

Later, tongues will be cut on the outside edges of these frames to fit into the sides of the cabinet (refer to *Fig. 8*).

SIDE FRAMES

The four side frames (two for each unit) are joined with molded-edge mortise and tenon joints. The molded edges add a little class, and also serve as glass stops.

WIDTH AND LENGTH. First rip the stiles (B) 2" wide and 33" long *(Fig. 5)*. The rails (A) are ripped to a width of $2^{1}/_{2}$" and a length of $12^{1}/_{2}$".

Note: The total width of these frames is equal to the web frames, 14". So the shoulder-to-shoulder length of the rails is $10^{1}/_{2}$". Then add 2" for the two 1"-long tenons to get the final length of $12^{1}/_{2}$".

MOLDED EDGE. Cut a shouldered $1/_{4}$" corner-round profile on the inside edge of each piece. Set the depth of cut of the router bit to leave a $3/_{32}$" shoulder on the face side of each piece *(Fig. 5)*.

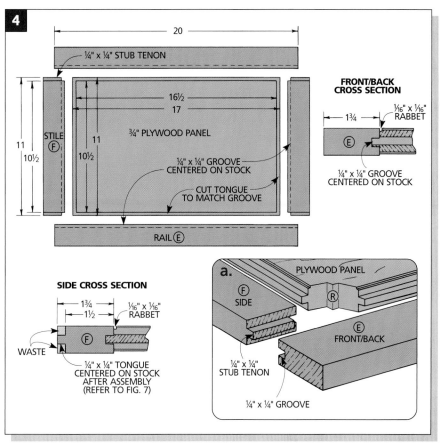

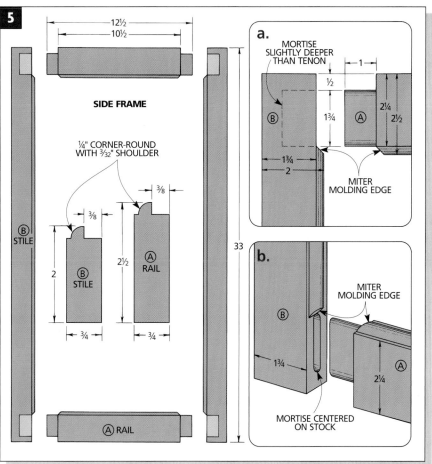

RABBET. After the molded edge has been routed on each rail and stile of the side frames, cut a rabbet on the back side of the molding so the shoulder of the rabbet lines up with the shoulder of the corner-round (refer to *Fig. 5*).

The depth of this rabbet should be $3/8$" (to accept a piece of single-pane glass and a $1/4$"-thick glass stop).

MORTISE AND TENON. Once the rabbet has been cut on each piece, the mortises and tenons can be cut.

ASSEMBLE AND RABBET. After all of the joints have been cut, assemble the four frames.

Note: To miter the molding edges, build the jig shown on page 94.

Then cut a $1/4$" x $3/8$" rabbet along the back edge of each assembled frame to accept the plywood back *(Fig. 7)*.

Note: I decided to use $1/4$" walnut-veneer plywood for the backs of the curio cabinet. But you are not limited to plywood as your only option. Another choice is to use a mirror. See the Designer's Notebook below.

HOLES FOR SHELVES. Later, two plate glass shelves will be mounted in each unit. These shelves are supported with L-shaped shelf pins that are mounted in $1/4$" holes.

It's important that these holes are in exactly the same position on all four stiles of each unit. So to make sure they all aligned properly, I made a simple drilling jig. Just mark and drill the holes on a piece of scrap, spacing them as shown in *Fig. 6*. Then use this jig to drill

consistent holes in all eight stiles.

Note: You can use a piece of pegboard in place of the jig, as long as you keep the same end down and mark the holes you're drilling into.

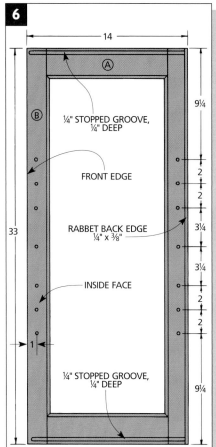

6

14

Ⓐ

Ⓑ

$1/4$" STOPPED GROOVE, $1/4$" DEEP

FRONT EDGE

RABBET BACK EDGE $1/4$" x $3/8$"

INSIDE FACE

$1/4$" STOPPED GROOVE, $1/4$" DEEP

$9^{1}/4$

33

2
2
$3^{1}/4$
$3^{1}/4$
2
2

1

$9^{1}/4$

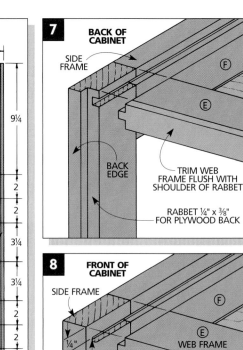

7

BACK OF CABINET

SIDE FRAME

Ⓕ

Ⓔ

BACK EDGE

TRIM WEB FRAME FLUSH WITH SHOULDER OF RABBET

RABBET $1/4$" x $3/8$" FOR PLYWOOD BACK

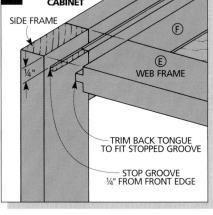

8

FRONT OF CABINET

SIDE FRAME

Ⓕ

Ⓔ

WEB FRAME

$1/4$"

TRIM BACK TONGUE TO FIT STOPPED GROOVE

STOP GROOVE $1/4$" FROM FRONT EDGE

ADDING THE WEB FRAMES

Now the side frames and web frames can be joined together to make the two basic units of the cabinet.

ROUT GROOVES. To join the frames, use a router to cut $1/4$"-wide grooves on the inside faces of the side frames. These grooves are $1/4$" from the top and bottom edges of the frame, and stop $1/4$" from the front edge *(Fig. 8)*.

CUT TONGUES. After cutting the grooves, cut two rabbets on the edges of the web frames to form tongues that fit in the grooves *(Fig. 8)*.

Note: This may take some experimenting on scrap to make sure the top face of the web frame lines up with the top edge of side frame.

TRIM WEB FRAMES. After the tongue and groove joints are cut, the back edge of the web frames needs to be trimmed down a bit so it's in line with the shoulder of the rabbet on the back edge of the side frames *(Fig. 7)*.

ASSEMBLY. Finally, dry-assemble the web frames and side frames to get the dimensions for the plywood backs, and cut the backs to size. Then glue and

DESIGNER'S NOTEBOOK

MIRROR BACK

■ If you want to give a more complete view of your collectibles, you can replace the plywood back with a mirrored one.

Note: If you do this, do *not* cut the rabbets in the side frames until you have the back materials in hand.

■ First, have the mirror cut $1/8$" smaller than you would have cut the plywood back. Then cut the backing for the mirror (I used $1/8$" hardboard to keep the cabinet sturdy) a little larger, to fit tight.

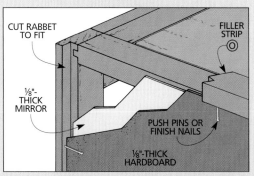

CUT RABBET TO FIT

FILLER STRIP Ⓞ

$1/8$"-THICK MIRROR

PUSH PINS OR FINISH NAILS

$1/8$"-THICK HARDBOARD

■ Find the total thickness of the mirror and backing, and add $1/8$" for the pins or nails used to hold them in place. This will be the depth of the rabbets in the side frames.

clamp the frames together to form the two units. (Screw the plywood back in place to hold everything square while the glue dries.)

DOOR FRAMES

After the two units are assembled, the frames for the doors can be built. These frames are sized to overlap the opening $1/4$" on all four edges.

STILES AND RAILS. The first step in making these frames is to rip the stiles (D) and rails (C) to a width of 2" *(Fig. 9)*. The length of the stiles is equal to the opening in the assembled cabinet, plus $1/2$" (to allow for a $1/4$" overlap on the top and the bottom).

To figure out the length of the rails, measure the width of the opening in the cabinet. (Mine was $19^3/8$".) Then add $1/2$" for the overlap (to get the total width of the door frame). Subtract $3^1/2$" for the two $1^3/4$"-wide stiles to get the shoulder-to-shoulder length of the rails. And finally, add 2" for the two 1"-long tenons *(Fig. 9)*. (My rails were $18^3/8$".)

From here on the procedure for the door frames is just like the side frames: cut the shouldered corner-round on the inside edge, then cut a rabbet for the glass, and finally cut the mortise and tenon joints *(Fig. 10)*.

Next, assemble the door frames *(Fig. 11)*. They should be a total of $1/2$" wider and higher than the opening in the cabinet.

RABBET. Now you can cut a $3/8$" x $3/8$" rabbet on the outside edge of the frame to form a lip *(Fig. 12)*.

Note: The rabbet is $3/8$" wide to allow for the $1/4$" overlap, plus a $1/8$" clearance between the rabbet and the frame.

CORNER-ROUND. Finally, cut a shouldered corner-round above the rabbet *(Fig. 13)*. This matches the cuts on the inside edges, and makes a nice lip around the outside of the door.

DOOR HINGES. The doors are mounted to the cabinet with $3/8$"-offset hinges. Normally these hinges would be mounted without cutting hinge mortises. However, this would create a small gap on the side between the door and the cabinet.

To eliminate this gap, I decided to cut a mortise on both faces of the side frame to accept the *inside* flap of the hinge *(Fig. 14)*. The other flap is mounted directly to the door (no mortise is needed here) *(Fig. 15)*.

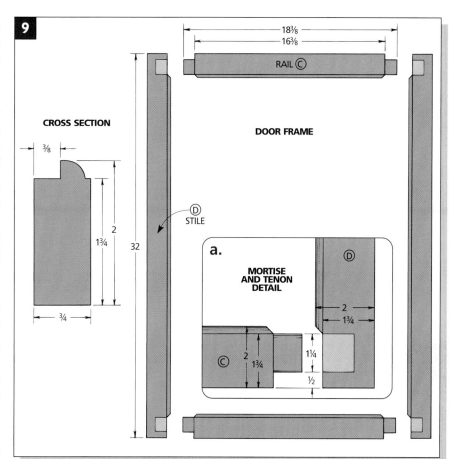

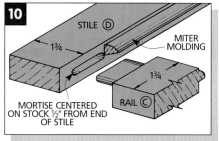

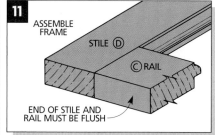

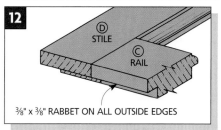

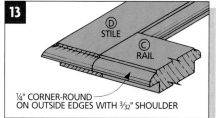

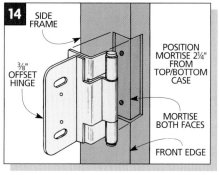

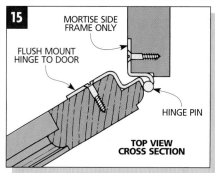

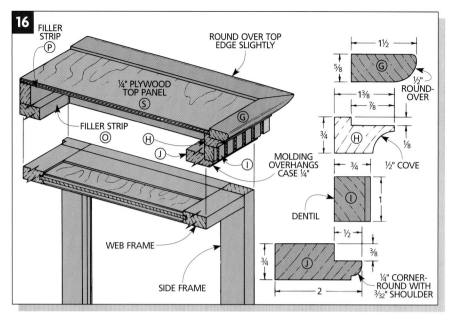

16

FILLER STRIP (P)

ROUND OVER TOP EDGE SLIGHTLY

¼" PLYWOOD TOP PANEL (S)

FILLER STRIP (O)

(H)

(J)

(I)

(G)

MOLDING OVERHANGS CASE ¼"

WEB FRAME

SIDE FRAME

DENTIL

1½

⅝ (G)

½" ROUND-OVER

1⅜

⅞

¾ (H) ⅛

¾ ½" COVE

(I) 1

½

¾ (J) ⅜

2 ¼" CORNER-ROUND WITH ³⁄₃₂" SHOULDER

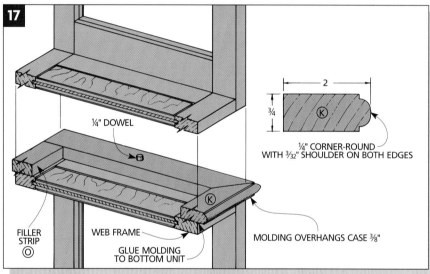

17

¼" DOWEL

FILLER STRIP (O)

WEB FRAME

GLUE MOLDING TO BOTTOM UNIT

2

¾ (K)

¼" CORNER-ROUND WITH ³⁄₃₂" SHOULDER ON BOTH EDGES

(K)

MOLDING OVERHANGS CASE ⅜"

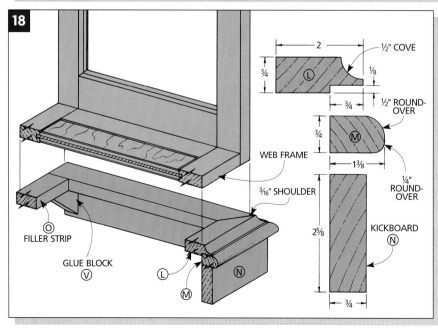

18

WEB FRAME

³⁄₁₆" SHOULDER

FILLER STRIP (O)

GLUE BLOCK (V)

(L)

(N)

(M)

2 ½" COVE

¾ (L) ⅛

¾ ½" ROUND-OVER

¾ (M)

1⅜ ¼" ROUND-OVER

KICKBOARD (N)

2⅝

¾

MOLDINGS

At this point, the two basic units for the cabinet are built. All that remain are the molding pieces that make the cabinet shine *(Fig. 16)*. They look impressive, but I was able to cut all of these moldings on a router table, using only three standard bits: a ¼" roundover bit, a ½" roundover bit, and a ½" cove bit.

Note: When routing the profiles for these moldings, remember that it's best to sneak up on the depth of cut. That is, don't try to cut the final profile in one pass. You don't want to rush into a mistake and have to start with a new piece of wood. Instead, make several passes, raising the bit each time until you reach the full depth of cut.

MOLDINGS AT THE TOP

There are four different molding strips that make up the top of this cabinet. Two of these were already made, at the beginning of the project: the dentil (I), and molding strip (J).

MOLDING STRIP (J). I started by gluing and clamping molding strip (J) to the front edge of the cabinet. This front strip was already mitered to length so the shoulders of the corner-round overhang the side frames by ¼" on each end. The two strips for the sides were cut to rough length.

Now they can be trimmed to final length so they're flush with the back edge of the cabinet *(Fig. 19)*.

DENTIL. Next, the front dentil strip (I) is glued in the rabbets of molding strip (J). Then the side dentil strips are cut to length and glued in place.

MOLDING STRIP (H). To make the third molding strip (H), rip a piece of stock to a rough width of 1½". Then cut a ⁷⁄₈"-wide by ⅛"-deep rabbet on the top edge of this piece, and a ½" cove right below the rabbet *(Fig. 16)*.

Then rip this piece to final width so the back edge is flush with the back of the dentil, and the front edge (at the bottom of the cove) overhangs the dentil ⅛".

MOLDING STRIP (G). The molding strip (G) at the very top of the cabinet is made by first resawing (ripping on edge) a piece of stock to a thickness of ⁵⁄₈" *(Fig. 16)*.

Then one edge is rounded with a ½" roundover bit, and the top edge is rounded slightly by sanding. Then this strip is glued and clamped in the rabbet of molding strip (H).

TOP PANEL. To finish off the top of the cabinet, I added two filler strips (O and P) along the back of the cabinet *(Fig. 16)*. Then I cut a $1/4$"-thick plywood top panel (S) to fit on top, and tacked it in place *(Fig. 19)*.

MOLDING BETWEEN UNITS

At this point, the top unit is complete. So next I worked on the pieces that go between the two units.

I added a single molding strip (K) to the top of the bottom unit. This strip is made by cutting a shouldered $1/4$" corner-round on the top and bottom edges of the stock *(Fig. 17)*.

The piece for the front of the cabinet is cut to length so the shoulder of the corner-round overhangs the front and sides of the cabinet $3/8$". Then the two side pieces are added, and a filler strip (O) is cut for the back.

POSITION DOWEL PINS. Since the two units are not permanently joined together (so they can be moved easily), I added two small dowel pins (U) to position them *(Fig. 17)*.

To do this, first drill a $1/4$" hole centered on the bottom edge of each side frame of the top unit.

Then mark the position of a second (matching) hole on molding strip (K). When this second hole is drilled, insert the dowel pins and make sure the top unit is positioned on molding strip (K) just like the bottom unit is.

BOTTOM MOLDINGS & KICKBOARD

Once the area between the units is complete, work can begin on the bottom unit. There are two molding strips and a kickboard at the bottom of the cabinet.

MOLDING STRIP (L). Molding strip (L) is made by cutting a $3/4$"-wide by $1/8$"-deep rabbet on the edge of a piece of stock *(Fig. 18)*. Then a $1/2$" cove cut is made above the rabbet.

Glue and clamp this molding strip to the cabinet so there's a $3/16$" flat space between the web frame and the cove. Then add these molding strips to the sides, and cut another flat filler strip (O) to fit along the back edge of the cabinet *(Fig. 18)*.

MOLDING STRIP (M). Molding strip (M) is ripped to width so it's $5/8$" wider

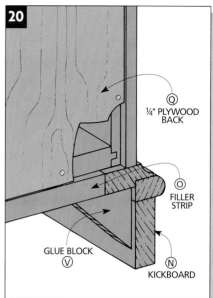

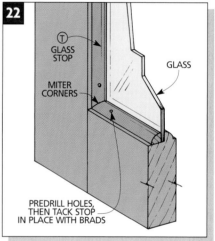

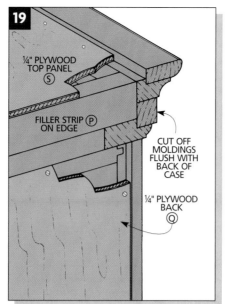

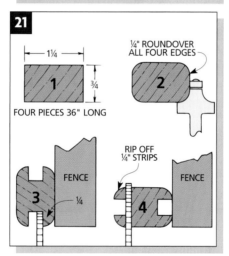

than the rabbet in molding strip (L). Then the top edge of this strip is rounded with a $1/2$" roundover bit, and the bottom edge is rounded with a $1/4$" roundover bit.

KICKBOARD. Finally, the kickboard (N) is cut to size and glued and clamped to the bottom side of molding strip (M).

To hold the kickboard steady, I glued and screwed a triangular glue block (V) on each of the two back corners *(Fig. 20)*.

FINISHING STEPS

Before any of the glass was installed, I finished this cabinet with three coats of a tung oil varnish.

This oil finish has just enough varnish in it to protect the cabinet, but it's also easy to apply and wipe smooth so I wouldn't have any problems with drip marks on the moldings.

GLASS. Finally, I installed the glass in the sides and doors. (I measured the openings and asked a local glass store to cut single-pane glass to fit.) The glass is held in place with custom-made quarter-round stops. (See *Fig. 21* for the cutting procedure.) To install these stops, I chucked a No. 18 x $1/2$" brad in a drill and predrilled the holes.

GLASS SHELVES. I also had the four plate glass shelves cut to size (with nicely beveled edges).

Note: The width of the shelves should be about $1/8$" less than the inside dimensions of the cabinet to allow for the L-shaped shelf supports.

CURIO LIGHTS. Finally, I installed special curio lights, screwing them to the top of each unit. (For sources of lights, see page 126.)

Now it's just a matter of arranging your favorite collectibles (and showing off your favorite cabinet). ∎

DESIGNER'S NOTEBOOK

This shallow Keepsake Cabinet is designed to hang on a wall and display small collectibles. Some of the parts change, but the basic construction is the same as the Curio Cabinet.

CONSTRUCTION NOTES:

■ This Keepsake Cabinet allows you to use all of the same building techniques as the Curio Cabinet, but it takes up less space. In addition to changing the sizes of some parts (refer to the Materials List below), you'll also need a couple mounting cleats to hang the cabinet on the wall.

Note: Again, have the glass panels and shelves cut to size *after* you have the final dimensions of your cabinet.

■ All of the parts across the front of the cabinet are the same length as on the Curio Cabinet. The parts that change in size are those that affect the overall *depth* of the cabinet.

The main case of the cabinet shown here is 8" deep. That means that both the web frames and the side frames need to be built to a width of 8".

■ To change the size of the web frames, just shorten up the sides (F) to a length of 5" *(Fig. 1)*. Then cut the width of the ³/₄" plywood panel (R) to 5" wide.

■ To change the size of the side frames, cut the side rails (A) to an overall length of 6¹/₂" *(Fig. 2)*. All of the joinery remains the same.

■ Now the top and bottom molding pieces (G, H, I, J, L, M) can be cut to fit the new dimensions.

■ The ¹/₄" plywood top panel (S) will also have to be cut narrower to fit the new dimensions.

■ Since you're only building one cabinet you won't need the middle molding pieces (K) or the dowel pins (U) that position the two cabinets on top of each other. And since the cabinet hangs on the wall, there isn't any need for the kickboard or glue blocks (N, V).

■ The other major difference for this design is the system that's used to mount the cabinet to a wall. A case with this much glass will be heavy, so just screwing through the plywood isn't strong enough. Instead, I glued two ¹/₂"-thick mounting cleats (W) to the back of the cabinet *(Fig. 3* and the cross section on the opposite page). These cleats are 2" wide with a corner-round profile added to match the rest of the cabinet design.

KEEPSAKE CABINET

■ To mount the cabinet on the wall, I drilled countersunk holes in each cleat for No. 8 brass screws. If possible, drive these screws into wall studs. If not, use heavy-duty wall anchors or molly bolts to mount the cabinet securely *(Fig. 3)*.

MATERIALS LIST

CHANGED PARTS
A Side Rails (4)   ³/₄ x 2¹/₂ - 6¹/₂
F Web Frm. Sides (4)   ³/₄ x 1³/₄ - 5
R Web Frm. Panels (4) ³/₄ ply - 5 x 17

NEW PARTS
W Mounting Cleats (2) ¹/₂ x 2 - 19¹/₂

Note: Do not need parts K, N, U, V. Only need two parts O. Top panel (S) and all molding pieces are cut to fit new dimensions. Only need half as many of all other wood parts.

HARDWARE SUPPLIES
(16) No. 18 x ¹/₂" brads
(16) No. 6 x ³/₄" flathead woodscrews
(2) ³/₈" offset door hinges w/ screws
(1) 1¹/₄" cast knob w/ screw
(2) Narrow magnetic door catches
(1) ¹/₈"-thick glass door panel
(2) ¹/₈"-thick glass side panels
(2) ¹/₄"-thick finished edge glass shelves
(8) L-shaped shelf supports
(4) No. 8 x 3" flathead woodscrews

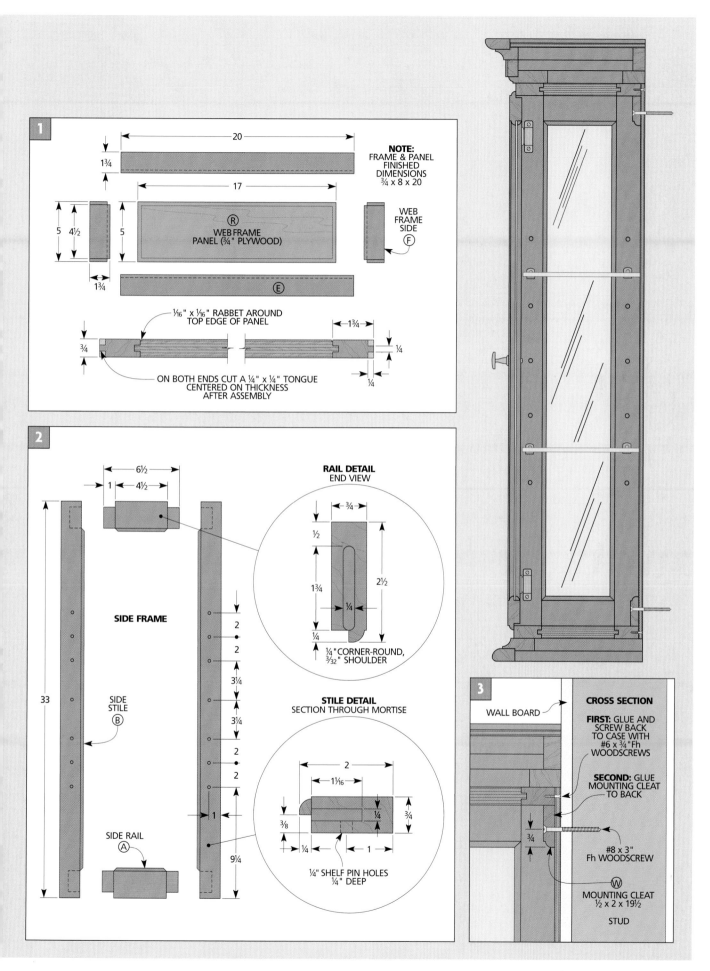

1

20

1¾

NOTE:
FRAME & PANEL
FINISHED
DIMENSIONS
¾ x 8 x 20

17

5   4½

5

Ⓡ
WEB FRAME
PANEL (¾" PLYWOOD)

WEB
FRAME
SIDE
Ⓕ

1¾

1¾

Ⓔ

¹⁄₁₆" x ¹⁄₁₆" RABBET AROUND
TOP EDGE OF PANEL

¾

1¾

¼

¼

ON BOTH ENDS CUT A ¼" x ¼" TONGUE
CENTERED ON THICKNESS
AFTER ASSEMBLY

2

6½

1   4½

RAIL DETAIL
END VIEW

¾

½

1¾

2½

¼

¼

¼"CORNER-ROUND,
³⁄₃₂" SHOULDER

SIDE FRAME

33

SIDE
STILE
Ⓑ

SIDE RAIL
Ⓐ

2

2

3¼

3¼

2

2

1

9¼

STILE DETAIL
SECTION THROUGH MORTISE

2

1¹⁄₁₆

¼

¾

⅜

¼

1

¼" SHELF PIN HOLES
¼" DEEP

3

WALL BOARD

CROSS SECTION

FIRST: GLUE AND
SCREW BACK
TO CASE WITH
#6 x ¾"Fh
WOODSCREWS

SECOND: GLUE
MOUNTING CLEAT
TO BACK

¾

#8 x 3"
Fh WOODSCREW

Ⓦ

MOUNTING CLEAT
½ x 2 x 19½

STUD

STORAGE PROJECTS

A classic cabinet can be a beautiful and practical addition to any room. These projects are designed to meet a variety of storage situations, and they are sure to give years of useful service. They also offer a wide variety of joinery and finish options to help sharpen your skills.

For example, the strong, clean lines of the storage pedestal are borrowed from classic architecture. And in the tradition of master cabinetmakers, there's a cleverly hidden door that conceals a compartment for CDs, videos or other valuables.

The charming apothecary cabinet features an array of easy-to-make drawers. While it fits easily on a countertop, it will help you organize any number of small items.

Two hanging cabinets provide storage where you need it. With several design and finish options to choose from, the cottage wall cabinet is suitable for any room in the house.

Finally, the Scandinavian cabinet makes good use of space that might otherwise go to waste. You can choose between the traditional version with a panel door or one with a glass front that displays the very things it protects.

Storage Pedestal

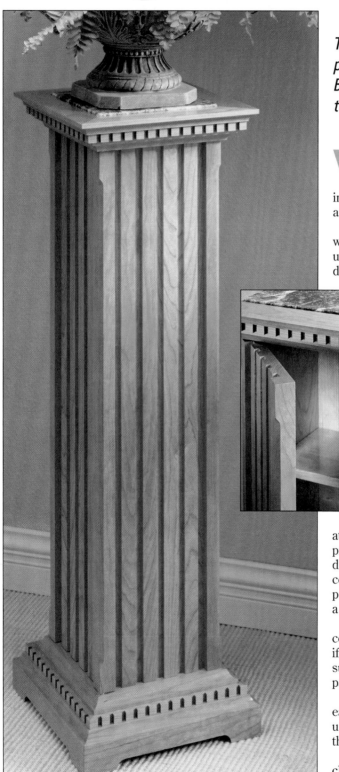

The fluted panels and dentil molding make this pedestal look like a piece of classic architecture. Behind the hidden door you'll find storage space that you can customize to your needs.

When you first look at this pedestal, there seems to be nothing out of the ordinary. It has all the features that make for a classic-looking pedestal and an interesting project to build — a fluted case, dentil molding, and even a piece of marble tile on top.

SECRET STORAGE. But there's more to this project than what you can see. In fact, it's what you *can't* see that makes it unique. On the inside, there's a secret storage compartment designed to hold videos, compact discs, whatever you like.

HIDDEN DOOR. The real trick when designing the "secret" compartment was coming up with a way to get into it — an "invisible" door. But a door isn't an easy thing to hide. You have to make sure the hardware is completely out of view, with no visible hinges or knobs.

A brass knuckle, even a small one as on a knife hinge, would have been a dead giveaway. And I ruled out the European-style concealed hinges right away too. They're completely hidden, but they take up room inside the case and can get in the way. And I wanted both the outside and inside to look as clean as possible.

PINS. I'll admit it took a couple of attempts to "hide" the door, but the solution ended up being pretty simple. The door pivots open and closed on two $\frac{1}{8}$"-dia. steel pins. The pins are offset in the post at the left front corner to allow the door to swing clear. These thicker corner posts have another benefit: The front right post also serves as a handle for the door, eliminating the need for a knob or pull.

OPTIONS. Besides the secret compartment, there are a couple of optional features you might want to consider. First, if you don't want to use marble tile in the top, you can easily substitute a wood panel. See the Designer's Notebook on page 57 for more about doing this.

There's also an option for modular cases that hold 12 CDs each. You can stack four of these cases inside the pedestal, or use a combination of shelves and CD cases. For more about this option, see the Designer's Notebook on page 58.

WOOD. The pedestal shown in the photo was built from cherry and then finished with several coats of an oil/urethane combination.

EXPLODED VIEW

OVERALL DIMENSIONS:
11½W x 11½D x 36H

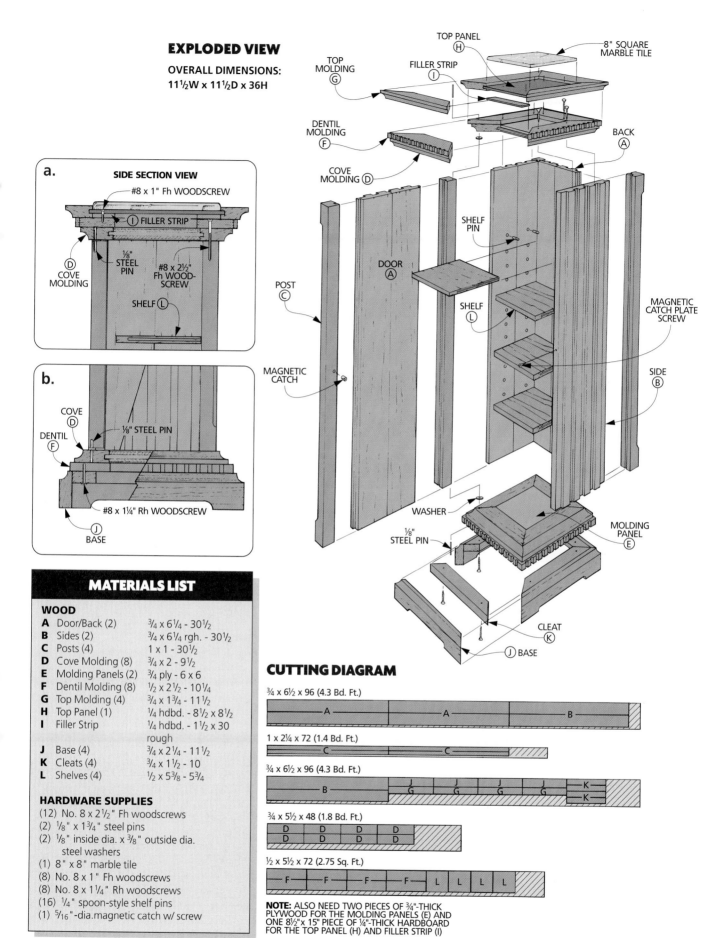

a. SIDE SECTION VIEW

- #8 x 1" Fh WOODSCREW
- (I) FILLER STRIP
- (D) COVE MOLDING
- ⅛" STEEL PIN
- #8 x 2½" Fh WOODSCREW
- SHELF (L)

b.

- COVE (D)
- ⅛" STEEL PIN
- DENTIL (F)
- #8 x 1¼" Rh WOODSCREW
- (J) BASE

Labels in main view:
- TOP PANEL (H)
- 8" SQUARE MARBLE TILE
- TOP MOLDING (G)
- FILLER STRIP (I)
- DENTIL MOLDING (F)
- COVE MOLDING (D)
- BACK (A)
- SHELF PIN
- POST (C)
- DOOR (A)
- SHELF (L)
- MAGNETIC CATCH PLATE SCREW
- MAGNETIC CATCH
- SIDE (B)
- MOLDING PANEL (E)
- WASHER
- ⅛" STEEL PIN
- CLEAT (K)
- (J) BASE

MATERIALS LIST

WOOD

A	Door/Back (2)	¾ x 6¼ - 30½
B	Sides (2)	¾ x 6¼ rgh. - 30½
C	Posts (4)	1 x 1 - 30½
D	Cove Molding (8)	¾ x 2 - 9½
E	Molding Panels (2)	¾ ply - 6 x 6
F	Dentil Molding (8)	½ x 2½ - 10¼
G	Top Molding (4)	¾ x 1¾ - 11½
H	Top Panel (1)	¼ hdbd. - 8½ x 8½
I	Filler Strip	¼ hdbd. - 1½ x 30 rough
J	Base (4)	¾ x 2¼ - 11½
K	Cleats (4)	¾ x 1½ - 10
L	Shelves (4)	½ x 5⅜ - 5¾

HARDWARE SUPPLIES

(12) No. 8 x 2½" Fh woodscrews
(2) ⅛" x 1¾" steel pins
(2) ⅛" inside dia. x ⅜" outside dia. steel washers
(1) 8" x 8" marble tile
(8) No. 8 x 1" Fh woodscrews
(8) No. 8 x 1¼" Rh woodscrews
(16) ¼" spoon-style shelf pins
(1) 5/16"-dia. magnetic catch w/ screw

CUTTING DIAGRAM

¾ x 6½ x 96 (4.3 Bd. Ft.)
| A | A | B |

1 x 2¼ x 72 (1.4 Bd. Ft.)
| C | C |

¾ x 6½ x 96 (4.3 Bd. Ft.)
| B | J J J J | K |
| | G G G G | K |

¾ x 5½ x 48 (1.8 Bd. Ft.)
| D | D | D | D |
| D | D | D | D |

½ x 5½ x 72 (2.75 Sq. Ft.)
| F | F | F | F | L | L | L | L |

NOTE: ALSO NEED TWO PIECES OF ¾"-THICK PLYWOOD FOR THE MOLDING PANELS (E) AND ONE 8½"x 15" PIECE OF ¼"-THICK HARDBOARD FOR THE TOP PANEL (H) AND FILLER STRIP (I)

The pedestal case consists of four ³/₄"-thick fluted panels with a 1"-square post at each corner *(Fig. 1)*. Three of these panels will be glued to the back two posts so you end up with a U-shaped case assembly. Then the remaining pieces are glued together to create the door in front. However, to make things as simple as possible, each of the panels and posts starts off exactly the same.

PANELS. I glued up each of the panels out of two pieces, selecting stock with grain that was as straight as possible.

After the glue is dry, you can cut the door and back (both A) and sides (B) to a final width of 6¹/₄" and *rough* length of 31" *(Fig. 1)*.

Note: The sides will be trimmed 6¹/₈" wide later, but for now, it's easier to leave all the panels the same.

FLUTES. After the panels were sized, I cut the flutes. I used a ¹/₂"-dia. straight bit in the router table rather than a dado blade because I wanted smooth, flat-bottomed flutes *(Fig. 3)*.

First, lay out the flutes on the end of only one of the panels *(Fig. 2)*. Then line up the bit with the layout marks and cut the flutes on all the panels.

Note that the flutes on the outside are a little wider than ¹/₂" (to create tongues later), so they require two passes. Start with the outside pass first *(Fig. 3a)*. Then rout to the layout line on the second pass, because if you start at the layout line and work out, you might run into some chipout.

TONGUES. With the flutes routed, the next step is to create tongues on the edges of the panels *(Fig. 4)*. (These hold the corner posts that are added later.) To create each tongue, I routed a rabbet on the inside face of each panel. The width of the tongue should be ¹/₈".

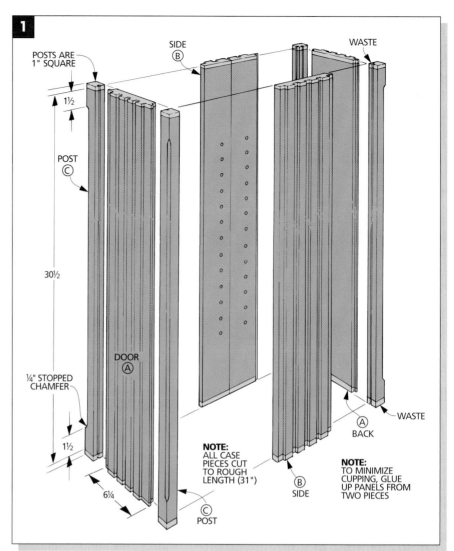

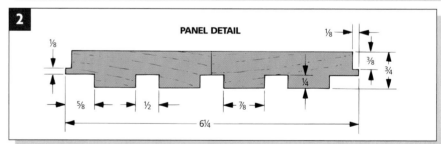

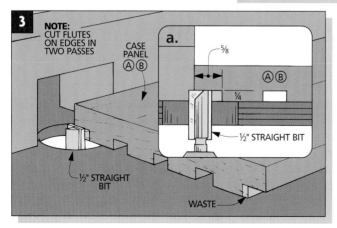

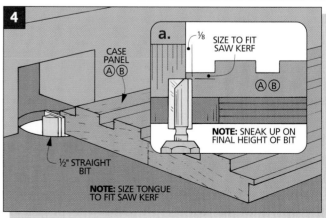

To determine the final thickness of the tongue, sneak up on the height of the bit until the remaining tongue fits into a kerf left by your saw blade *(Fig. 4a)*.

POSTS. At this point, you can begin working on the four posts (C) for the corners *(Fig. 1)*. These pieces are planed and ripped 1" square and cut to the same rough length as the panels.

Next, cut $\frac{1}{8}$"-deep grooves on the inside faces of the posts *(Fig. 5)*. These grooves hold the tongues on the panels. They're positioned so the inside faces of the panels will be flush with the inside faces of the posts *(Figs. 5a and 5b)*.

The thing to keep in mind is not all four posts are exactly the same. The *door* posts have only one groove each to hold the door panel *(Fig. 6a)*. However, each *back* post has two grooves — one to hold the back panel and one for a side panel. The fence position is the same for both grooves, but to cut them close to the inside corner of the post, you'll need to flip and rotate the pieces.

PANEL AND POST ASSEMBLY. Now the posts can be glued to each side of the door and back panels *(Fig. 6)*. When doing this, make sure that the inside faces of the posts and panels are flush.

Don't worry too much about getting the ends exactly even during assembly. After the glue is dry, the next step is to trim a little off each end, cutting the panel assemblies (and side panels) to finished length ($30\frac{1}{2}$") *(Figs. 1 and 7)*.

Note: These long workpieces are a bit unwieldy, so I attached an auxiliary fence to my miter gauge to add some support. And I clamped a stop block to the fence to make sure they all ended up the same length.

Next, trim off the tongue on the front edge of each side panel *(Fig. 7)*. Then two sets of holes are drilled on the inside of each side panel for the $\frac{1}{4}$"-dia. shelf pins that hold the shelves. (A hard-

board template is helpful for spacing out these $\frac{5}{16}$"-deep holes.)

Finally, I routed a stopped $\frac{1}{4}$" chamfer on the outside corner of each post *(Figs. 1 and 8)*. These chamfers stop $1\frac{1}{2}$" from the top and bottom of the post. And to do this, I simply marked start and stop lines on the router fence.

CASE ASSEMBLY. Now the case can be assembled *(Fig. 9)*. The trick when

clamping up this U-shaped assembly is keeping it square. So I cut two spacers out of $\frac{3}{4}$" plywood to match the inside of the case (6" x 6"). Then, to prevent the spacers from being glued into the assembly, I cut off the corners.

Note: When the glue is dry, don't throw the spacers away. They'll come in handy when attaching the molding that's added next.

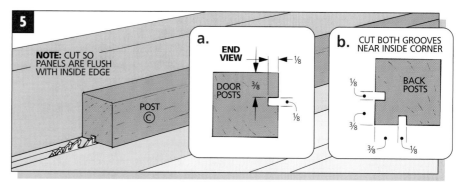

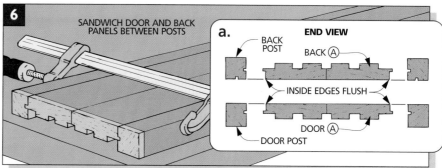

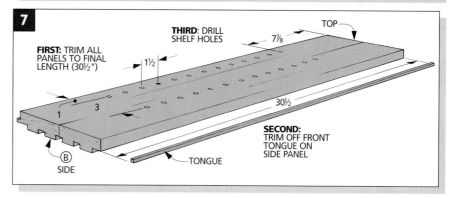

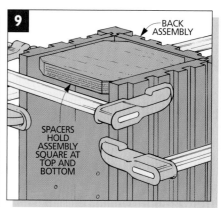

With the pedestal case complete, two layers of molding can be added to the top and bottom of the case. The top and bottom layers are identical, and they're not just decorative. They trap the door with two steel pins that allow the door to swing open and shut.

COVE MOLDING. The layers of molding closest to the top and bottom of the case are two $3/4$"-thick frames with a cove molding profile routed on all four sides (Fig. 10).

To create the cove molding (D), I started with 2"-wide blanks and mitered them to length so I'd end up with two frames that were $9^1/2$" square. This allows the frames to overhang the posts $3/4$" (Fig. 10a). Then to hold a panel, I cut $1/4$"-wide grooves $1/4$" deep and centered on their inside edges.

The $3/4$"-thick plywood molding panels (E) that fit in the grooves form the top and bottom of the case interior. So cut the $1/4$" tongues, positioning them so the inside face of the panel is flush with the inside face of the frame.

Now, before routing the cove on the molding pieces, I glued the frames together around each panel. (It's hard to glue the mitered pieces together if the profile is already routed.) Then when the glue is dry, you can rout a $1/2$" cove (Fig. 11).

DENTIL MOLDING. The next layers to add are the dentil molding (Fig. 10). These $1/2$"-thick frames are built the same way as the cove molding (but there are no plywood panels).

First, I mitered $2^1/2$"-wide blanks to length to create two $10^1/4$"-square dentil molding (F) frames (Figs. 10 and 12). (This allows a $3/8$" overhang.)

Then after the frames are glued up, the dentils can be laid out on one edge of one of the frames (Fig. 12a). The dentils are cut with a $1/4$"-wide dado blade. A wooden auxiliary fence on the miter gauge helps steady the frame and prevent tear-out. It also provides a place to clamp a stop block. With each stop block setting, cut one dentil on each edge of both frames. Then reset the fence and repeat.

When the dentil molding is cut, you can glue the cove and dentil molding frames together (Fig. 13). But before screwing the molding assemblies to the top and bottom of the pedestal case, I added the door.

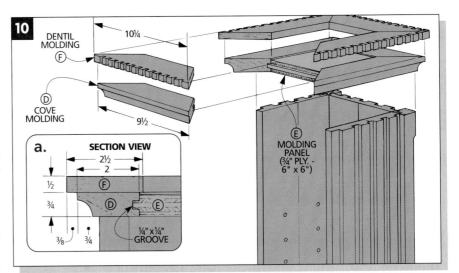

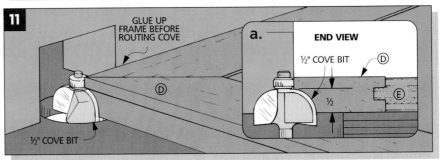

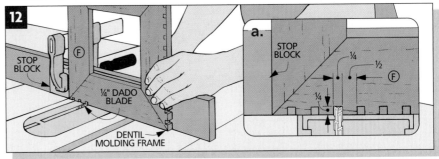

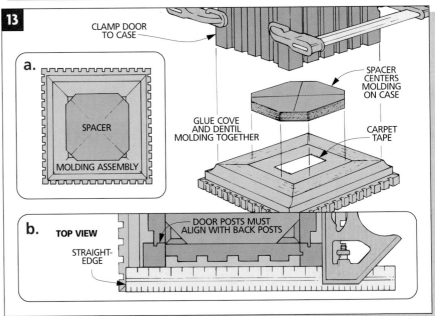

ADDING THE DOOR

The door is sandwiched between the two molding assemblies and pivots on steel pins. To keep the door from rubbing at the bottom and keep it from sagging, I placed thin washers between the door and the top and bottom moldings.

The first step is to clamp the door to the front of the case *(Fig. 13)*. Just make sure that the posts in front and back line up *(Fig. 13b)*.

MOLDINGS. The molding assemblies should be set in place so they're centered at the top and bottom of the case. Here's where the spacers used earlier really come in handy. Using carpet tape, I stuck one to the inside face of each assembly *(Fig. 13)*. Now when set in the case, the spacer centers the molding and keeps it from shifting.

PILOT HOLES. With the molding temporarily in place, I traced the left corner of the door onto the top and bottom moldings *(Fig. 14)*. By measuring in $3/16''$, you'll have the exact position of the pilot holes for the steel pins *(Fig. 14a)*.

Now lift the molding assemblies off the case and drill the holes. To make sure these holes are straight, it's a good idea to use the drill press here *(Fig. 15)*. And while you're at it, you can also lay out and drill the countersunk shank holes in the back and side pieces of both molding assemblies for screwing the molding to the case *(Fig. 15a)*.

With the pilot holes drilled, it's time to "transfer" them to the door. I set the molding back on the case and used the pilot holes as a guide for drilling $1/2''$ deep into the door *(Fig. 16)*.

TRIM DOOR. There's still one more thing to do before you can attach the molding and door. The door needs to be trimmed slightly so it won't rub against the molding *(Fig. 17)*. I trimmed my door just slightly less than the thickness of the two steel washers used later for spacers. (You want a tight fit so the door doesn't sag.)

MOUNT DOOR. After the door was trimmed, I clamped it to the case, making sure the gaps at the top and bottom were the same. Then I slipped a washer between the molding and the door at the top and bottom and added a pin to each hole *(Fig. 18a)*. Trim the pins flush with the molding. And don't worry about gluing them – when the top and base of the pedestal are added later, they will trap the pins.

Finally, with the door in place, I screwed the molding assemblies to the case *(Fig. 18)*, then removed the plywood spacers.

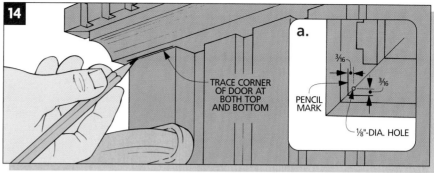

14 TRACE CORNER OF DOOR AT BOTH TOP AND BOTTOM

a. $3/16$ $3/16$ PENCIL MARK $1/8''$-DIA. HOLE

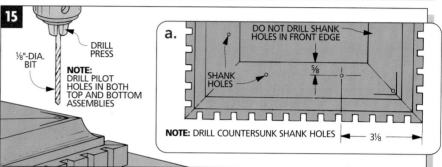

15 $1/8''$-DIA. BIT DRILL PRESS **NOTE:** DRILL PILOT HOLES IN BOTH TOP AND BOTTOM ASSEMBLIES

a. DO NOT DRILL SHANK HOLES IN FRONT EDGE SHANK HOLES $5/8$ **NOTE:** DRILL COUNTERSUNK SHANK HOLES $3\ 1/8$

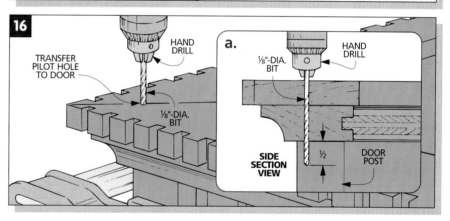

16 TRANSFER PILOT HOLE TO DOOR HAND DRILL $1/8''$-DIA. BIT

a. $1/8''$-DIA. BIT HAND DRILL SIDE SECTION VIEW $1/2$ DOOR POST

17 TO CREATE CLEARANCE FOR DOOR TRIM SLIGHTLY LESS THAN THE THICKNESS OF TWO WASHERS AUX. FENCE DOOR

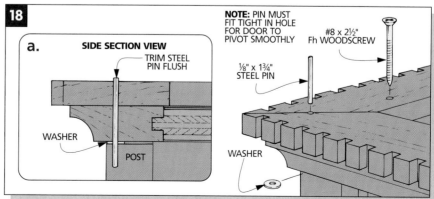

18 **a.** SIDE SECTION VIEW TRIM STEEL PIN FLUSH WASHER POST

NOTE: PIN MUST FIT TIGHT IN HOLE FOR DOOR TO PIVOT SMOOTHLY #8 x 2 1/2'' Fh WOODSCREW $1/8''$ x $1\ 3/4''$ STEEL PIN WASHER

Once the molding is screwed in place, all that's left is to add the top and base of the pedestal and the shelves *(Fig. 19)*.

TOP FRAME. The top is similar to the cove molding already attached. But it has a hardboard panel that supports a piece of 8"-square marble tile. (You can add a hardwood panel instead of the marble. See the Designer's Notebook on the next page.) Be aware that marble tile isn't always exactly 8" square, so make sure you have your tile on hand before building the top.

I sized the top molding (G) pieces so the finished frame wraps tight around the tile on the inside and overhangs the dentil ⅝" on the outside *(Fig. 19a)*. (My top frame pieces were 1¾" wide and 11½" long.)

Then cut a groove inside each frame piece and cut a ¼" hardboard top panel (H) to fit inside. Position the grooves so the marble tile will stand slightly proud of the frame *(Fig. 19a)*.

After gluing the frame around the hardboard, I routed a ½" cove. Then glue some hardboard filler strips (I) under the top panel and screw the top to the dentil molding (F).

BASE. Like the top, the base also has a cove profile. But it has a foot profile along the bottom too *(Fig. 19d)*.

After the base (J) pieces are cut to width (2¼"), glue a 1½"-wide cleat (K) to the inside edge of each piece, flush with the top edge of the base. Then miter these pieces to the same length as the top pieces (11½").

Next, I cut a foot profile on each with a band saw. After the base pieces have been glued into a frame, rout a ½" cove profile around the top edge *(Fig. 19c)*. Now the base assembly can be screwed to the bottom of the pedestal.

MAGNETIC CATCH. To hold the door closed, I added a magnetic catch at the center of the door post *(Fig. 19b)*. To avoid a gap between the door and case, countersink the hole so the catch is flush. For the strikeplate, I used a brass-plated steel screw.

SHELVES. Finally, cut four shelves (L) to fit inside the case. (Or you can add CD cases. See the Designer's Notebook on page 58 for details about making these.) I used spoon-style pins to support the shelves, but hid the pins in grooves. (Refer to the Shop Tip on the opposite page for more about this.) ∎

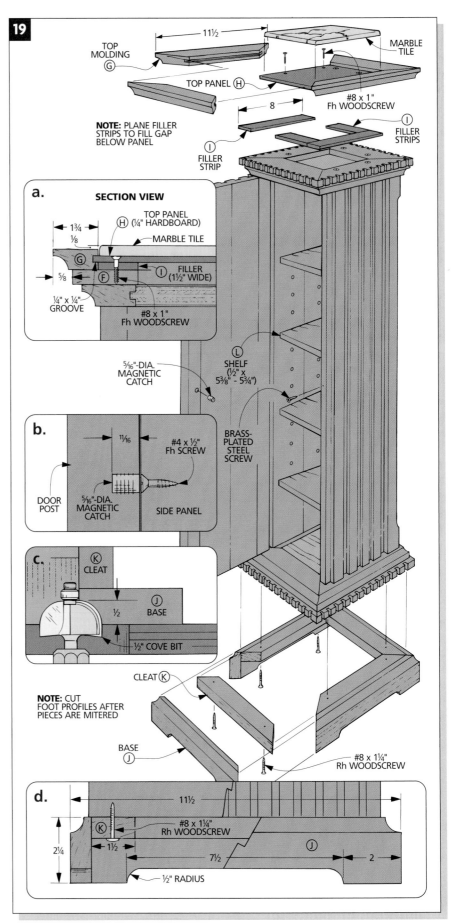

Whenever I use spoon-style shelf pins, I can usually count on the weight of the shelf to help hold it in place. But the shelves used with the storage pedestal are so small and light, I was concerned they might get knocked off the pins every time an item was removed from the shelf.

So instead of just setting the shelf on the shelf pins, I routed stopped slots on the edges of the shelves to allow them to fit over the pins *(Detail a)*. This slot helps "lock" the shelves onto the pins.

To do this, I clamped a stop block to the fence of my router table. Then, I mounted a ⅛" straight bit in the router and positioned the fence so the bit was centered on the thickness of the shelves. (Test the setup on some scrap.)

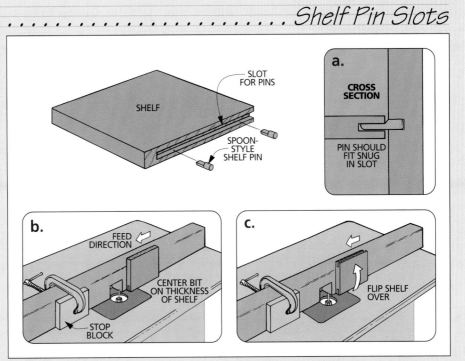

If the bit isn't centered, one side of the shelf will be higher than the other.

With the router set up, I routed stopped slots on the edges of each shelf *(Details b and c)*. Cut the slot just a hair deeper than the length of the flat portion of the pin *(Detail a)*.

Note: Some shelf pins may fit a little too snug in a ⅛"-wide slot. If this is the case, file down the pins slightly until they fit.

DESIGNER'S NOTEBOOK

HARDWOOD TOP

■ Start by gluing up a hardwood blank. Its thickness should be the depth of the opening in the top plus ⅛" or so (see drawing). (For a different look, try a contrasting wood for the panel instead of using the same type of wood used for the pedestal.)

■ To allow for a lip that overhangs the top molding, trim the panel ½" wider and longer than the opening.

■ With the panel cut to size, rabbet the bottom edge so the panel fits into the opening with a ¹⁄₁₆" gap at each edge (see drawing).

■ Next, rout a ⅛" roundover along the top of all four edges of the panel.

■ Finally, set the panel into the opening. To allow for expansion, do not glue it in.

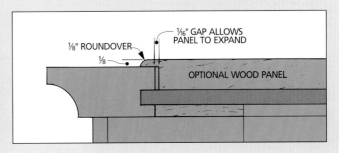

DESIGNER'S NOTEBOOK

The inside of the pedestal is the perfect place to store your favorite CDs. These cases hold them securely, and they can be used in combination with the shelves for even more versatility.

CONSTRUCTION NOTES:

■ These cases are sized to stack four high inside the pedestal with no gap at the top. So cut the sides (M) so you can stack four of them inside *your* pedestal.

■ First, cut two sides (M) for each case to size from $3/4$"-thick stock *(Fig. 1)*. (Mine were $4^3/4$" x $7^5/8$".)

■ To make it easier to slip CDs into the case, tilt the saw blade 45° and bevel the front edge of each side piece *(Fig. 2)*.

■ The CDs fit into $7/16$"-wide dadoes cut in the sides. Lay out these dadoes on one of the pieces, starting at the center. At the ends, there will be $1/2$" left over for the rabbets that hold the top and bottom in place.

■ When the dadoes are laid out, raise the dado blade to make a $1/4$"-deep cut, and use a stop block to make sure all the dadoes align *(Fig. 3)*.

■ After the dadoes are cut, raise the blade and cut the $1/2$"-deep rabbets on the ends *(Fig. 3a)*.

■ Now all that's left to do is cut a top and bottom (N) to fit in the rabbets *(Fig. 1)*. These pieces match the width of the sides ($4^3/4$"). And their length should allow the assembled case to slide into

the pedestal without any gaps on the sides. (Mine were $5^1/2$" long.)

■ The four pieces of each case can now be glued together *(Fig. 1)*.

■ Apply a finish to match the pedestal.

CD PEDESTAL

MATERIALS LIST

NEW PARTS

M	CD Case Sides (8)	$3/4$ x $4^3/4$ - $7^5/8$
N	Case Top/Btm. (8)	$1/2$ x $4^3/4$ - $5^1/2$

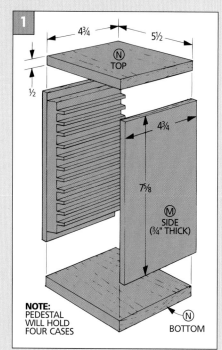

1
$4^3/4$ $5^1/2$
N TOP
$1/2$
$4^3/4$
$7^5/8$
M SIDE ($3/4$" THICK)
NOTE: PEDESTAL WILL HOLD FOUR CASES
N BOTTOM

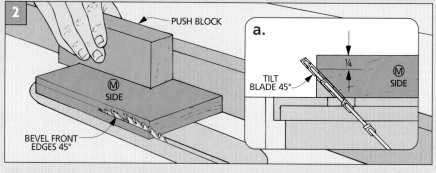

2
PUSH BLOCK
M SIDE
BEVEL FRONT EDGES 45°

a.
$1/4$
TILT BLADE 45°
M SIDE

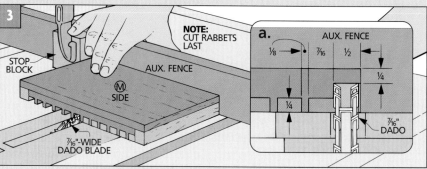

3
NOTE: CUT RABBETS LAST
STOP BLOCK
AUX. FENCE
M SIDE
$7/16$"-WIDE DADO BLADE

a.
AUX. FENCE
$1/8$ $7/16$ $1/2$
$1/4$
$1/4$
$1/4$
$7/16$" DADO

Apothecary Cabinet

From fishing flies to sewing supplies, there are dozens of ways to use this box full of boxes.
And there's no complicated joinery to worry about — just rabbets, dadoes, and a few basic setups.

There's a certain fascination with drawers. For many people it's "What can they hold?" In the case of this cherry apothecary cabinet, just about anything smaller than a shoe.

But the drawers might raise a different question from a woodworker. Such as "How do they work?" Or, "How are they built?" The answer to both questions is the same — very simply. The drawers fit in the cabinet with no special hardware. And they're built in a low-tech way, too.

SIMPLE JOINERY. The drawers use the same joinery that holds the entire cabinet together — rabbets and dadoes.

They're a couple of the most versatile, and basic, joints in woodworking. Just a step up from butt joints.

TEST PIECES. Even though dadoes and rabbets are simple to cut (using straight bits in the router table), they must be cut perfectly. That's because when the whole cabinet is assembled there are no screws or nails to reinforce the joints. Just glue. Plus, the joints will be visible. So as you're cutting the parts for the cabinet, it may be worth the time to cut a few test pieces to use when setting up the router table.

FINISH. Ordinarily when I build a project using cherry, I leave the wood

unstained. But this project was different, and the reason was the knobs.

The knobs I thought looked best for the drawers weren't available in cherry, only birch. And if you've ever tried to stain a light wood (such as birch) to match a darker wood (cherry), you know what a challenge it can be.

CONTRAST. What I did instead was apply just an oil finish to the drawer fronts to enhance their natural color. I then stained the knobs a darker color, instead of trying to match the natural color of the drawer fronts. And finally, for contrast, I stained the rest of the cabinet the same color as the knobs.

EXPLODED VIEW

OVERALL DIMENSIONS:
14¼W x 9D x 15H

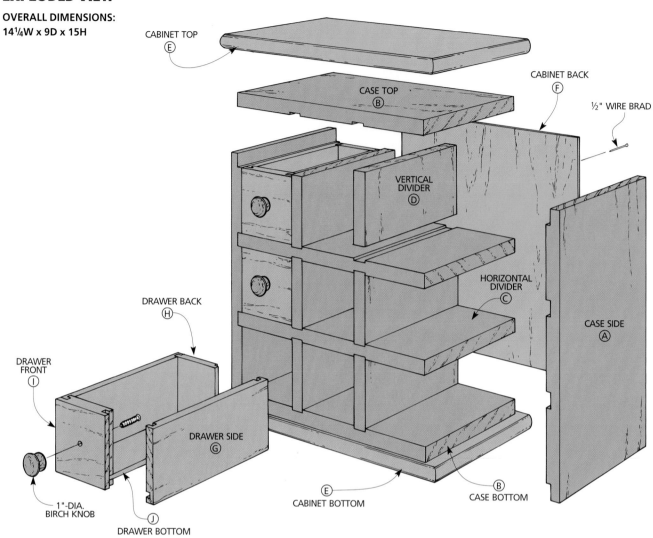

CABINET TOP
E

CABINET BACK
F

½" WIRE BRAD

CASE TOP
B

VERTICAL DIVIDER
D

HORIZONTAL DIVIDER
C

DRAWER BACK
H

CASE SIDE
A

DRAWER FRONT
I

DRAWER SIDE
G

CABINET BOTTOM
E

CASE BOTTOM
B

1"-DIA. BIRCH KNOB

DRAWER BOTTOM
J

MATERIALS LIST

WOOD

A	Case Sides (2)	¾ x 8⅝ - 13½
B	Case Top/Bottom (2)	¾ x 8⅜ - 12½
C	Horiz. Dividers (2)	¾ x 8⅜ - 12½
D	Vertical Dividers (6)	¾ x 8⅜ - 3¾
E	Cabinet Top/Btm. (2)	¾ x 9 - 14¼
F	Cabinet Back (1)	¼ ply - 12½ x 13½
G	Drawer Sides (18)	½ x 3⁷⁄₁₆ - 8⅛
H	Drawer Backs (9)	½ x 3⁷⁄₁₆ - 2¹⁵⁄₁₆
I	Drawer Fronts (9)	¾ x 3⁷⁄₁₆ - 3⁷⁄₁₆
J	Drawer Bottoms (9)	¼ ply - 2⅞ x 7⁹⁄₁₆

HARDWARE SUPPLIES

(9) 1"-dia. birch knobs w/ screws
(10) ½"-long wire brads

CUTTING DIAGRAM

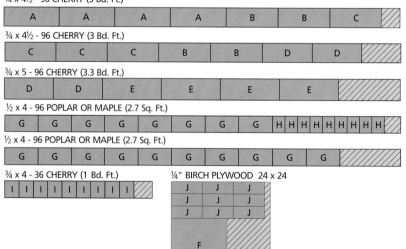

¾ x 4½ - 96 CHERRY (3 Bd. Ft.)

| A | A | A | A | B | B | C |

¾ x 4½ - 96 CHERRY (3 Bd. Ft.)

| C | C | C | B | B | D | D |

¾ x 5 - 96 CHERRY (3.3 Sq. Ft.)

| D | D | E | E | E | E |

½ x 4 - 96 POPLAR OR MAPLE (2.7 Sq. Ft.)

| G | G | G | G | G | G | G | G | H H H H H H H H H |

½ x 4 - 96 POPLAR OR MAPLE (2.7 Sq. Ft.)

| G | G | G | G | G | G | G | G | G | G |

¾ x 4 - 36 CHERRY (1 Bd. Ft.)

| I | I | I | I | I | I | I | I | I |

¼" BIRCH PLYWOOD 24 x 24

J	J	J
J	J	J
J	J	J
F		

PREPARING THE PANELS

I cut the parts for most projects only when I'm ready for them. That way I can measure the project itself and cut to fit.

This time there's a good reason to cut the parts in advance. On this project, the reason is the joinery. Since the parts fit together with dadoes and rabbets (refer to *Fig. 4*) they must start out the same thickness and size so the joints can all be cut the same.

BLANKS. I started by gluing up over-size blanks for all of the case parts.

Note: *Fig. 1* shows *finished* dimensions for each of the pieces.

THICKNESS. Before cutting the blanks to finished size, they should all be planed to the same thickness ($3/4$"). And to ensure good-fitting joinery, it helps to check the thickness of each part in a test dado. I cut this dado using a $3/4$" straight bit in the router.

DADOES & RABBETS

After the panels have all been planed to the same thickness, the individual parts for the case (A, B, and C) can be cut to finished length and width *(Fig. 1)*.

Note: Set aside the blanks for the vertical dividers (D) and the cabinet top and bottom (E) until later on.

DADOES AND RABBETS. When the case parts have been cut to finished dimensions, the dadoes and rabbets can be routed.

Because these cuts will be visible on the front of the cabinet, you want the bottoms to be perfectly flat and the sides square. So I used a $3/4$" straight bit in the router table *(Figs. 2 and 3)*. A stack dado set will also work, but only the very best will cut as accurately as a straight router bit.

SEQUENCE. All the dadoes and rabbets can be cut with the same router bit. But there are a number of different router table setups needed.

CASE SIDES. First I raised the bit $1/4$" above the table top and positioned the fence so it was flush with the back edge of the bit. Then I routed the rabbets on the top and bottom of the sides (A) *(Figs. 4 and 4a)*.

Next, I routed the dadoes across the sides *(Fig. 4b)*. These are critical cuts. With the fence adjusted to the proper distance from the router bit ($4^1/4$"), the dadoes on each workpiece will create equal-size openings when the cabinet is assembled *(Figs. 2, 3 and 4)*. Turn each side end for end between cuts.

The third setup is for cutting a $1/4$" rabbet to accept the plywood back. For this, the router table fence must be

repositioned to rout a $1/4$"-deep rabbet along the back edge of each side piece (A) *(Fig. 4)*.

TOP AND BOTTOM. Now the case sides can be set aside for a moment. For the next set of cuts, lower the router bit to $1/8$" above the table. Then cut the remaining dadoes on the case top, bottom, and horizontal dividers (B, C).

Note: The case top and bottom (B) have dadoes on *one* side only *(Fig. 4)*. The horizontal dividers (C) receive dadoes on *both* faces *(Fig. 4c)*.

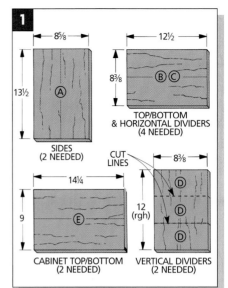

1

$8^5/8$ · $12^1/2$

$13^1/2$ · A

$8^3/8$ · B C

SIDES (2 NEEDED)

TOP/BOTTOM & HORIZONTAL DIVIDERS (4 NEEDED)

CUT LINES

$14^1/4$ · $8^3/8$

9 · E · 12 (rgh) · D D D

CABINET TOP/BOTTOM (2 NEEDED)

VERTICAL DIVIDERS (2 NEEDED)

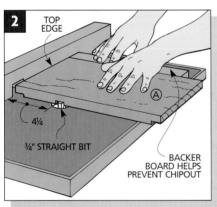

2

TOP EDGE

A

$4^1/4$

$3/4$" STRAIGHT BIT

BACKER BOARD HELPS PREVENT CHIPOUT

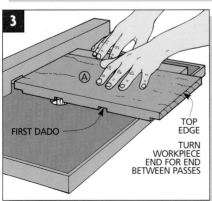

3

A

FIRST DADO

TOP EDGE

TURN WORKPIECE END FOR END BETWEEN PASSES

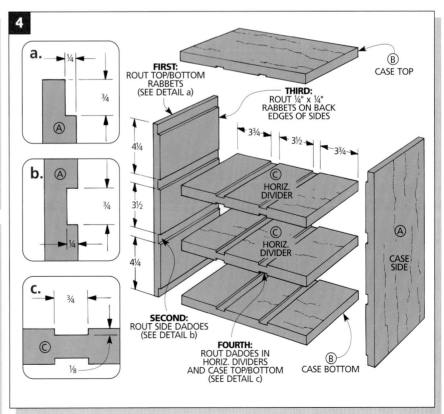

4

a. $1/4$ · $3/4$ · A · $4^1/4$

b. A · $3/4$ · $3^1/2$ · $1/4$

c. $3/4$ · C · $1/8$

FIRST: ROUT TOP/BOTTOM RABBETS (SEE DETAIL a)

CASE TOP · B

THIRD: ROUT $1/4$" x $1/4$" RABBETS ON BACK EDGES OF SIDES

$3^3/4$ · $3^1/2$ · $3^3/4$

HORIZ. DIVIDER · C

HORIZ. DIVIDER · C

A · CASE SIDE

$3^1/2$

$4^1/4$

SECOND: ROUT SIDE DADOES (SEE DETAIL b)

FOURTH: ROUT DADOES IN HORIZ. DIVIDERS AND CASE TOP/BOTTOM (SEE DETAIL c)

CASE BOTTOM · B

VERTICAL DIVIDERS

After the dadoes and rabbets have been cut on the case parts, the pieces can be dry-assembled to test the fit.

Note: The parts should be flush across the front of the assembly. The back edges of the horizontal pieces should align to the inside edges of the rabbets for the plywood back *(Fig. 8)*.

VERTICAL DIVIDERS. Now, work can begin on the vertical dividers. The first thing to do is rip the blank for the dividers to finished width (the same width as the horizontal dividers, 8³⁄₈") (refer to *Fig. 1* on page 61).

Now the vertical dividers (D) can be cut to finished length (height). But instead of cutting each piece in one pass using the miter gauge on the table saw, I did something different. (Again, the reason was to cut all the dividers exactly the same length.)

First, measure between the bottoms of each pair of dadoes *(Fig. 5)*. Then cut each blank into three oversize pieces, slightly longer than this measurement *(Fig. 6)*. Note that the grain runs *vertically* on the installed dividers.

Now the dividers can be cut to finished length using the table saw and rip fence *(Fig. 7)*.

FINAL ASSEMBLY

When the vertical dividers have all been fitted inside the case, I added a top and bottom, then a plywood back.

ASSEMBLY. First, I disassembled the case, then put it back together with glue in all the joints. It's easiest to start from the outside and work toward the center.

TOP AND BOTTOM. Next, cut the cabinet top and bottom (E) to size. These pieces have a ³⁄₈" overhang on the front and sides *(Fig. 8b)*. (They will be installed flush at the back of the case.)

Once these pieces are cut to size, I routed a bullnose profile on the sides and front (not the back) *(Fig. 8a)*.

Finally, I glued the top and bottom onto the case. A couple nipped-off brads keep the panels from slipping around when they're glued and clamped in place *(Fig. 8b)*.

BACK. Finally, cut a piece of ¹⁄₄" plywood for the cabinet back (F).

The back (F) should fit in the rabbets in the case sides, and between the top and bottom pieces (E) *(Fig. 8)*. Short brads secure it to the case.

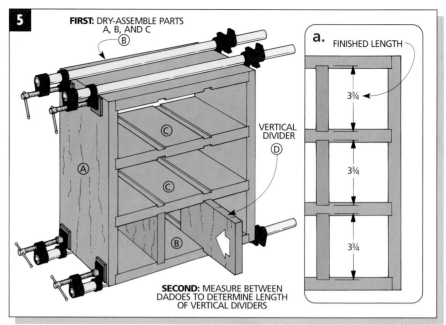

5 FIRST: DRY-ASSEMBLE PARTS A, B, AND C

VERTICAL DIVIDER (D)

SECOND: MEASURE BETWEEN DADOES TO DETERMINE LENGTH OF VERTICAL DIVIDERS

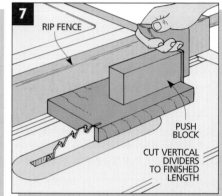

a. FINISHED LENGTH

3¾ 3¾ 3¾

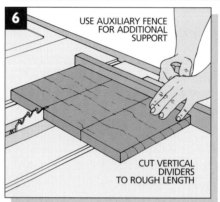

6 USE AUXILIARY FENCE FOR ADDITIONAL SUPPORT

CUT VERTICAL DIVIDERS TO ROUGH LENGTH

7 RIP FENCE

PUSH BLOCK

CUT VERTICAL DIVIDERS TO FINISHED LENGTH

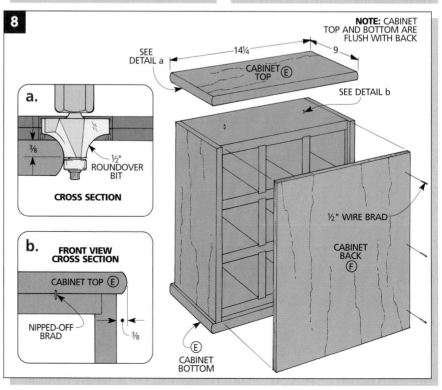

8 NOTE: CABINET TOP AND BOTTOM ARE FLUSH WITH BACK

SEE DETAIL a

14¼   9

CABINET TOP (E)

SEE DETAIL b

a.

³⁄₈

½" ROUNDOVER BIT

CROSS SECTION

b. FRONT VIEW CROSS SECTION

CABINET TOP (E)

NIPPED-OFF BRAD

³⁄₈

½" WIRE BRAD

CABINET BACK (F)

(E) CABINET BOTTOM

DRAWERS

What makes this cabinet useful are the drawers. And they're all made the same way in a series of repetitive cuts. Locking dado and rabbet joints hold the parts together (Figs. 9a and 9b).

CUT TO SIZE. The key to making multiple drawers is the setup. If the drawer openings are all the same size ($3^{1}/_{2}$" square), the parts for the drawers can be cut the same size, too (Fig. 9).

Note: The drawer sides (G) and backs (H) are cut from $1/_2$" stock. The drawer fronts (I) are cut from $3/_4$" stock.

When the parts have been cut, work can begin on the joinery.

DRAWER JOINTS. There are just a few steps required to make the joints for the drawers. And the cuts can be made with three different setups using a $1/_4$" straight bit in the router table.

To prevent the small workpieces from tipping into the bit opening in my router table, I added a "zero-clearance" overlay on top of my table. It's just a piece of $1/_4$" hardboard with a small bit opening (Fig. 10a). I held it to the top of my router table with carpet tape.

Also, for tight-fitting joints, it helps to start with test cuts on scrap wood.

DADOES AND GROOVES. The first cut to make is a $1/_4$" dado toward the front

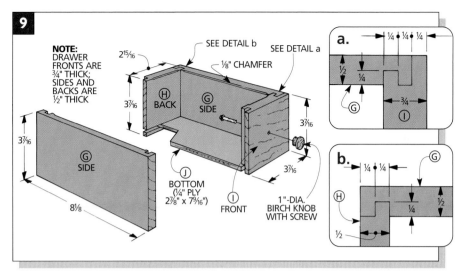

and back end of each drawer side (G) (Fig. 10). This dado is $1/_4$" deep.

Now, with the same setup, rout in each drawer part a groove for the drawer bottom (Fig. 11). For the groove on the drawer sides, plunge the piece onto the bit and rout from the front dado to the back dado (Fig. 11a).

TONGUES. Next, rout the tongues on the drawer front and back to fit the grooves in the sides. To do this, first raise the height of the bit to $1/_2$", but don't move the fence (Fig. 12a). Then hold the drawer front on edge and run it over the bit (Fig. 12).

To complete the tongues, lower the bit ($1/_4$" high) and reposition the fence (Fig. 13a). Then run the drawer fronts and backs over the bit (Fig. 13).

ASSEMBLY. Now the $1/_4$" plywood drawer bottoms (J) can be cut to fit between the grooves (Fig. 9). When the bottoms are cut, the drawer parts are glued together.

CHAMFER. Once the glue dried, I softened the top *inside* edge of each drawer by using the router table to rout a narrow ($1/_8$") chamfer. Finally, I drilled holes centered on each drawer front to attach the knobs (Fig. 9). ∎

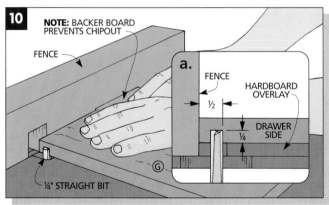

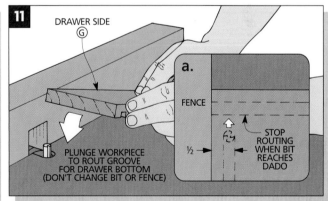

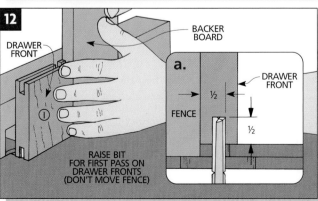

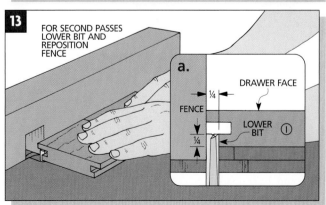

Cottage Wall Cabinet

You can build this cabinet to organize your bathroom or customize the design to help keep your messages handy along with your keys and mail. Either style looks great with our optional antique finish.

D esigning a cabinet with classic lines doesn't mean it has to be tough to build. In fact, everything on this project has been planned to be as "builder-friendly" as possible. Even the design options.

For one thing, the door is held together with stub tenon and groove joinery. This is a simple joint, and we've included step-by-step instructions to help you make it (see the Joinery article starting on page 70).

The door is also easy to install. Its rabbeted lip overhangs the case, so there's no fussing with the tiny gaps that you'd have around an inset door. Plus, I used a pair of no-mortise hinges so hanging the door is simple, too.

In fact, everything's pretty straightforward with this cabinet. Except for some routed molding and the scallops on the sides, almost all the work is done on the table saw.

WOOD. As with any project, the type of wood you use will make a big difference on the final appearance of the project. I used red oak, which is an informal wood (like pine). But you could "dress up" the cabinet by building it out of cherry or walnut.

DESIGN OPTIONS. As shown here, the cabinet is a useful addition to the bathroom. By replacing the towel bar with a row of Shaker pegs you have a piece that will complement other rooms as well. And we offer a few more options that turn the cabinet into a handy message center for the kitchen. See the Designer's Notebooks on pages 67 and 72 for more on these variations.

FINISH OPTIONS. As for the finish, there are a lot of options here, too. You can "paint" it with a couple coats of stain first. Then highlight the pores with an additional coat of a darker stain, as shown at left. (For more on this, see the Finishing box on page 69.) Or you can wipe on a few coats of an oil finish, as I did with the cabinet shown on page 67.

EXPLODED VIEW

OVERALL DIMENSIONS:
18¾"W x 8⅜"D x 37H

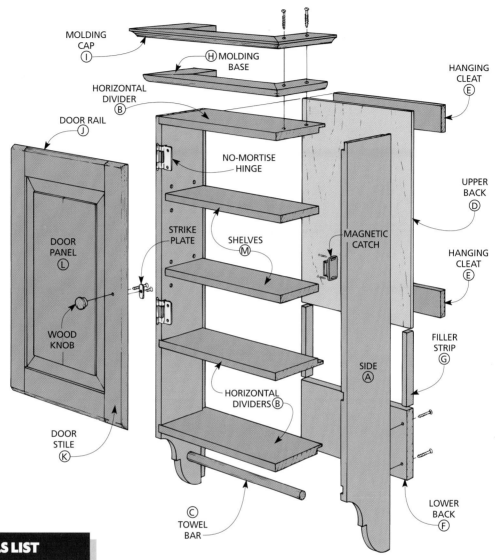

MOLDING CAP ⓘ

Ⓗ MOLDING BASE

HORIZONTAL DIVIDER Ⓑ

HANGING CLEAT Ⓔ

DOOR RAIL Ⓙ

NO-MORTISE HINGE

UPPER BACK Ⓓ

DOOR PANEL Ⓛ

STRIKE PLATE

SHELVES Ⓜ

MAGNETIC CATCH

HANGING CLEAT Ⓔ

WOOD KNOB

FILLER STRIP Ⓖ

SIDE Ⓐ

DOOR STILE Ⓚ

HORIZONTAL DIVIDERS Ⓑ

LOWER BACK Ⓕ

Ⓒ TOWEL BAR

MATERIALS LIST

WOOD

A	Sides (2)	¾ x 7 - 35½
B	Horiz. Dividers (3)	¾ x 7 - 15¼
C	Towel Bar (1)	¾ dowel - 15¼
D	Upper Back (1)	¼ ply - 15½ x 21
E	Hanging Cleats (2)	½ x 2½ - 15½
F	Lower Back (1)	¾ x 6¾ - 15½
G	Filler Strips (2)	½ x ¾ - 7
H	Molding Base (2)	¾ x 2½ - 20 rgh.
I	Molding Cap (2)	¾ x 3¼ - 20 rgh.
J	Door Rails (2)	¾ x 2¼ - 11¼
K	Door Stiles (2)	¾ x 2¼ - 20½
L	Door Panel (1)	½ x 11⅛ - 16⅝
M	Shelves (2)	¾ x 5¾ - 14⅜

HARDWARE SUPPLIES

(1 pair) Antique brass ⅜" inset hinges
(7) No. 6 x 1½" Fh woodscrews
(7) No. 8 x 2" Fh woodscrews
(1) 1¼"-dia. wood knob w/ screw
(1) Magnetic catch and strike plate
(8) Spoon-style shelf support pins

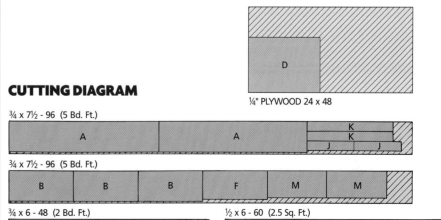

¼" PLYWOOD 24 x 48

CUTTING DIAGRAM

¾ x 7½ - 96 (5 Bd. Ft.)

¾ x 7½ - 96 (5 Bd. Ft.)

¾ x 6 - 48 (2 Bd. Ft.)

½ x 6 - 60 (2.5 Sq. Ft.)

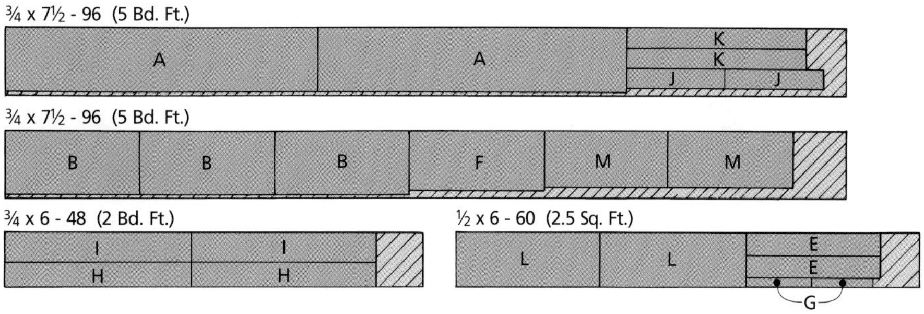

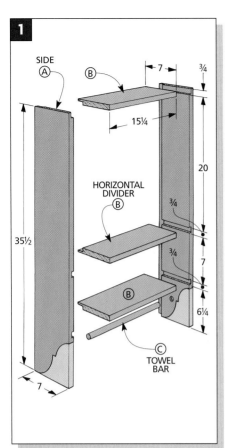

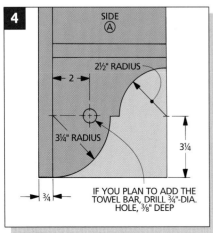

SIDE
(A)

(B)

7

3/4

15 1/4

20

HORIZONTAL
DIVIDER
(B)

3/4

35 1/2

3/4

7

(B)

6 1/4

(C)
TOWEL
BAR

7

CASE, BACKS, & MOLDING

There are really just a few parts to the case of the cottage wall cabinet — two side pieces that sandwich three horizontal dividers *(Fig. 1)*. And the joinery is simple too — just dadoes and rabbets.

SIDES AND HORIZONTAL DIVIDERS. To build the case, I started by cutting the sides (A) and horizontal dividers (B) to size from ³/₄"-thick stock *(Fig. 1)*.

DADOES AND RABBETS FOR DIVIDERS. The next step is to cut two dadoes and a rabbet in each side piece (A) *(Fig. 1)*. The dadoes are cut to fit the two horizontal dividers (B) that form the fixed shelves *(Fig. 1)*. The rabbet cut on the end holds the third divider that forms the top of the case.

Both the dadoes and rabbet are cut ³/₈" deep *(Figs. 2a and 2b)*. To help prevent chipout, it's a good idea to use an auxiliary fence on the miter gauge. And to make sure the dadoes aligned with each other, I used the rip fence as a stop.

RABBETS FOR BACKS. Next, I cut the rabbets to hold the backs of the case. This case actually has two backs — the upper back is cut from ¹/₄"-thick ply-wood, and the lower back is ³/₄"-thick solid wood (refer to *Fig. 6*).

Instead of making two separate rabbets for the different-sized backs, I cut a single, ³/₄"-deep rabbet for both, using a dado blade in the table saw.

To do this, first attach an auxiliary fence to the rip fence and set it to cut a ³/₄"-wide rabbet *(Fig. 3a)*. Then raise the blade ¹/₂" above the table and cut the rabbets along the back edges of both side pieces and all three horizontal dividers *(Figs. 1 and 3)*.

SCALLOPS ON SIDES. Now the joinery is complete, and the scallops on the bottom ends of the sides can be laid out *(Fig. 4)*. Cut the scallops with a band saw or jig saw. Then sand them smooth.

TOWEL BAR OR PEGS. If you decide to use Shaker pegs (see the Designer's Notebook on the next page), then you're ready to assemble the case.

If you are going to include the towel bar, you'll need to drill a ³/₈"-deep hole on the inside face of each side *(Fig. 4)*.

With the holes drilled, cut the towel bar (C) to length from a ³/₄"-dia. dowel.

ASSEMBLY. Now the case can be assembled *(Fig. 5)*. One thing to watch

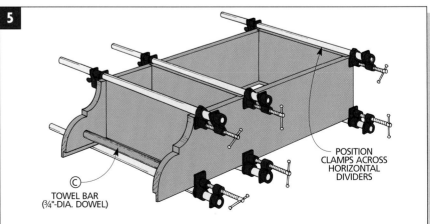

AUXILIARY
FENCE

a. **FRONT VIEW**
3/4
(A)
3/8

SIDE
(A)

b. **FRONT VIEW**
3/4
(A)
3/8

DADO
BLADE

NOTE: FOR DADOES, USE RIP FENCE AS STOP

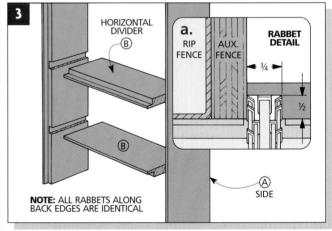

HORIZONTAL
DIVIDER
(B)

a.
RIP
FENCE

AUX.
FENCE

RABBET DETAIL
3/4

1/2

(B)

(A)
SIDE

NOTE: ALL RABBETS ALONG BACK EDGES ARE IDENTICAL

SIDE
(A)

2 1/2" RADIUS

2

3 1/4" RADIUS

3 1/4

3/4

IF YOU PLAN TO ADD THE TOWEL BAR, DRILL 3/4"-DIA. HOLE, 3/8" DEEP

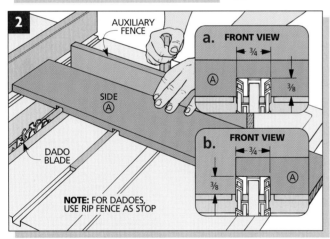

(C)

TOWEL BAR
(3/4"-DIA. DOWEL)

POSITION CLAMPS ACROSS HORIZONTAL DIVIDERS

out for is how you orient the rabbets on the horizontal dividers. They should be positioned to hold the backs. The rabbets on the upper two dividers should face each other. The rabbet on the lower divider should face down *(Fig. 1)*.

UPPER BACK. When the glue is dry, the next step is to add the two backs *(Fig. 6)*. First, the upper back (D) is cut to size from $1/4$"-thick plywood. Then it's simply glued in place.

Because this back is only $1/4$" thick, it's recessed in the back of the case. I utilized this space for hanging the case. Cut two $1/2$"-thick hanging cleats (E) to fit between the sides *(Fig. 6)*. Then glue them to the upper back.

LOWER BACK. I decided against using plywood here because the bottom edge would be seen. Instead, I used $3/4$"-thick oak for the lower back (F) *(Fig. 6)*. You'll need to allow for wood movement with changes in humidity, so don't glue the lower back — just screw it in place.

FILLER STRIPS. The backs only fill the rabbets at the top and bottom of the case. Part of each rabbet is still exposed above the lower shelf. To fill these rabbets, I cut two small filler strips (G) to size and glued them in place *(Fig. 6a)*.

MOLDING. The last step is to add decorative molding to the top of the case *(Fig. 7)*. This molding is built up from two $3/4$"-thick strips.

Begin by cutting two 20"-long blanks for each strip. The molding base (H) is $2^1/2$" wide, while the molding cap (I) is $3^1/4$" wide *(Fig. 7)*.

Next, rout a profile along one edge of each blank *(Fig. 7)*. The base molding has a $1/2$" roundover. The cap has a $1/2$" cove. After the profiles are routed, the blanks can be glued together.

When the glue is dry, the molding can be attached. I started with the front

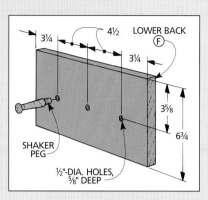

LOWER BACK (F)
$3^1/4$ · $4^1/2$ · $3^1/4$ · $3^5/8$ · $6^3/4$
SHAKER PEG
$1/2$"-DIA. HOLES, $5/8$" DEEP

SHAKER PEGS

■ If you want Shaker pegs instead of a towel bar, first drill holes in the lower back (F) (see drawing).

■ If the pegs fit a bit too snug, sand down the ends slightly, then glue them in place.

molding *(Fig. 8)*. The back edge of this assembly is $1^7/8$" from the front of the case *(Fig. 8a)*.

I mitered the front piece to length and then centered it side-to-side. Then I

clamped the molding, drilled shank and pilot holes, and screwed it in place.

The side pieces are easy to install. Just miter one end, cut them flush with the back, and screw them to the case.

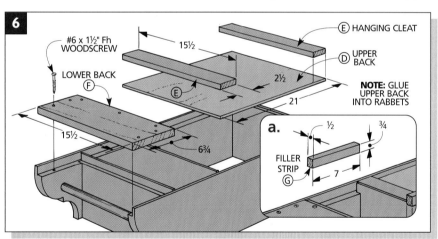

6
#6 x $1^1/2$" Fh WOODSCREW
LOWER BACK (F)
$15^1/2$
$15^1/2$
$6^3/4$
$15^1/2$
(E) HANGING CLEAT
(D) UPPER BACK
$2^1/2$
21
NOTE: GLUE UPPER BACK INTO RABBETS
a. $1/2$ · $3/4$
FILLER STRIP (G) · 7

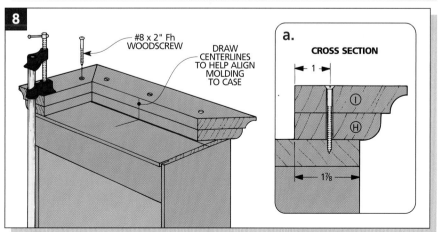

7
MOLDING CAP (I)
$3^1/4$
$3/4$
$1/2$" COVE
MOLDING BASE (H)
$3/4$
$2^1/2$
$1/2$" ROUNDOVER
NOTE: GLUE CAP AND BASE TOGETHER BEFORE MITERING

8
#8 x 2" Fh WOODSCREW
DRAW CENTERLINES TO HELP ALIGN MOLDING TO CASE
a. CROSS SECTION
1
(I)
(H)
$1^7/8$

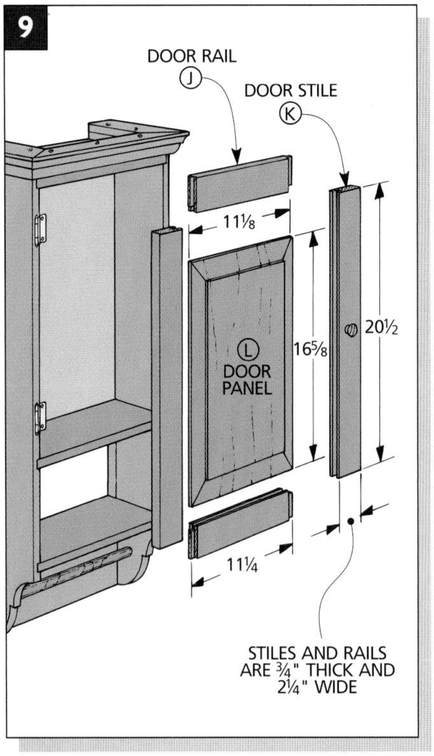

9
DOOR RAIL
J
DOOR STILE
K
11⅛
L
DOOR PANEL
16⅝
20½
11¼
STILES AND RAILS ARE ¾" THICK AND 2¼" WIDE

DOOR & SHELVES

The door on this cabinet is a ½"-thick raised panel in a ¾"-thick frame joined with stub tenons and grooves.

To make the door as easy as possible to install, I built a lipped door. It's ½" larger than the opening, and the lip on the inside face overlaps the case.

RAILS AND STILES. Begin the door by building the frame *(Fig. 9)*. These pieces are all ¾" thick and 2¼" wide. To find the length of the stiles (K), measure the height of the opening and add ½". (Mine were 20½" long.) To find the length of the rails (J), add ½" to the width of the opening, subtract the width of both stiles, and add ¾" for the tenons on the ends. (My rails were 11¼" long.)

After the rails and stiles have been cut to size, the next step is to cut the stub tenons and grooves *(Fig. 10)*. (For more on cutting this joint, see the Joinery article beginning on page 70).

RAISED PANEL. With the rails and stiles complete, work can begin on the door panel (L). First glue up a ½"-thick blank *(Fig. 11)*. To determine the panel's finished size, dry-assemble the door frame and measure the opening (including the depth of the grooves), and subtract ⅛" to allow for wood movement. Then cut the panel to size.

To cut the raised profile on the panel, the first thing I did was establish the square shoulders. This is done by scoring the outside face of the panel with the saw blade *(Fig. 11)*. Simply raise the blade ⅛" above the table and set the rip fence 1½" from the *far* edge of the blade *(Fig. 11a)*. Then make a scoring pass along the sides and ends.

To complete the profile, I used the table saw again, this time standing the panel on edge *(Fig. 12)*. But to do this safely, the panel needs some support. So I built a tall "saddle" jig that slides along the rip fence *(Fig. 12)*.

Next, position the fence so the jig is $\frac{3}{16}$" from the blade *(Fig. 12a)*. Tilt the

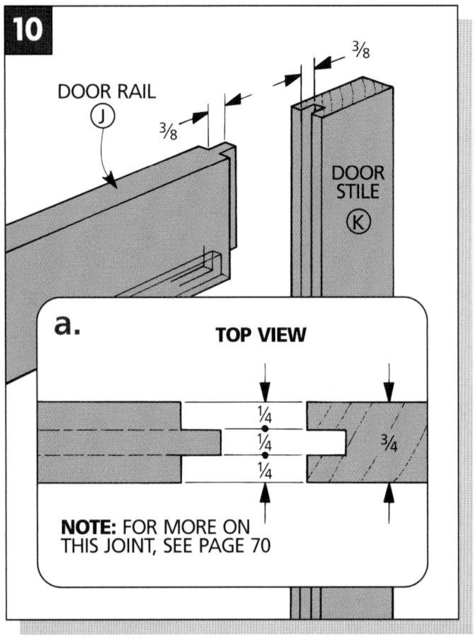

10
DOOR RAIL
J
⅜
⅜
DOOR STILE
K
a.
TOP VIEW
¼
¼
¼
¾
NOTE: FOR MORE ON THIS JOINT, SEE PAGE 70

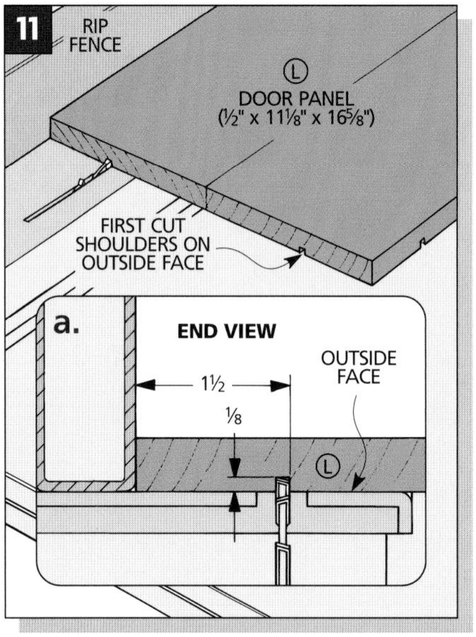

11
RIP FENCE
L
DOOR PANEL
(½" x 11⅛" x 16⅝")
FIRST CUT SHOULDERS ON OUTSIDE FACE
a.
END VIEW
1½
⅛
OUTSIDE FACE
L

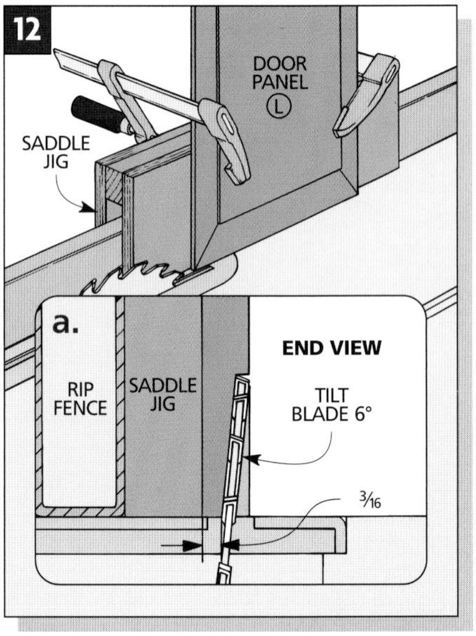

12
DOOR PANEL
L
SADDLE JIG
a.
RIP FENCE
SADDLE JIG
END VIEW
TILT BLADE 6°
3⁄16

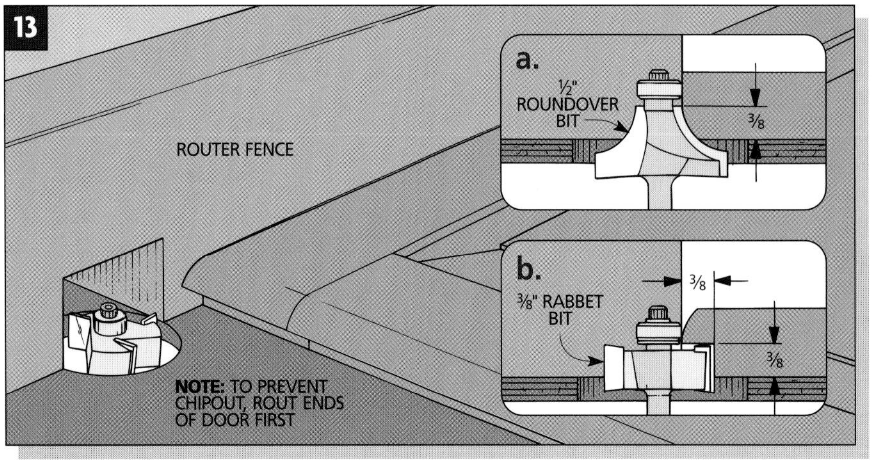

13
ROUTER FENCE
NOTE: TO PREVENT CHIPOUT, ROUT ENDS OF DOOR FIRST
a.
½" ROUNDOVER BIT
⅜
b.
⅜" RABBET BIT
⅜
⅜

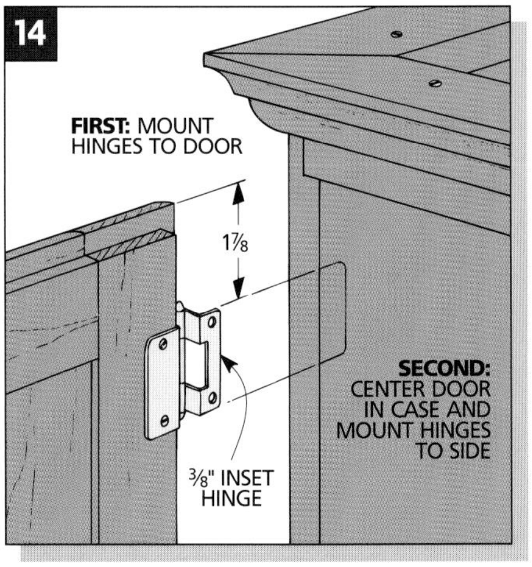

14
FIRST: MOUNT HINGES TO DOOR
1⅞
SECOND: CENTER DOOR IN CASE AND MOUNT HINGES TO SIDE
⅜" INSET HINGE

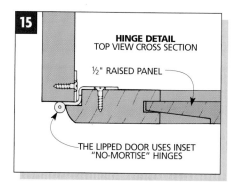

15

HINGE DETAIL
TOP VIEW CROSS SECTION

½" RAISED PANEL

THE LIPPED DOOR USES INSET
"NO-MORTISE" HINGES

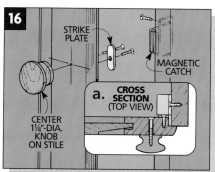

16

STRIKE
PLATE

MAGNETIC
CATCH

a. **CROSS SECTION**
(TOP VIEW)

CENTER
1¼"-DIA.
KNOB
ON STILE

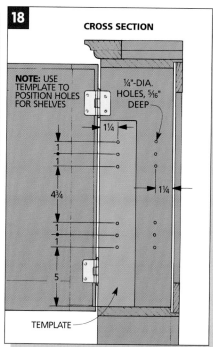

18

CROSS SECTION

NOTE: USE
TEMPLATE TO
POSITION HOLES
FOR SHELVES

¼"-DIA.
HOLES, ⁵⁄₁₆"
DEEP

1¼

1

1

4¾

1

1

1¼

5

TEMPLATE

17

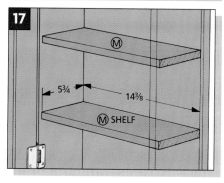

M

5¾

14⅜

M SHELF

blade 6° and raise it to the shoulder on the panel. Then cut the beveled profile on all sides and sand it smooth.

DOOR ASSEMBLY. With the panel complete, the door can be glued and clamped together. But don't glue in the panel. You want it to expand and contract with changes in humidity.

Once the glue dries, round over the outside face of the door *(Fig. 13a)*. Then on the inside face of the door, use a ⅜" rabbet bit to rout the lip *(Fig. 13b)*.

MOUNT DOOR. The next step is to mount the door on the case with ⅜" inset no-mortise hinges *(Fig. 14)*. This type of hinge is quite easy to install. It's simply screwed to the back of the door stile and the inside edge of the case

(Fig. 15). (For sources, see page 126.)

All that's left for the door is to add a knob and a magnetic catch *(Fig. 16)*.

To complete the cabinet, two adjustable shelves are added *(Fig. 17)*. Measure the inside of the case and cut

the shelves (M) ¹⁄₁₆" less than each of these measurements.

Finally, to hold the shelves, I drilled ¼"-dia. holes ⁵⁄₁₆" deep inside the case for shelf supports. A shop-built template helped position them *(Fig. 18)*. ∎

FINISHING TIP.......................... *Antiquing*

Since I built two versions of this cabinet (one with a towel bar and one with pegs), I decided to try a couple of different finishes. On the cabinet with the pegs, I wiped on a few coats of an oil/urethane finish. This highlighted the grain of the oak (see the photo on page 67).

But I was after a different look on the other cabinet. I wanted to give it the look of a painted antique — without

actually distressing it with nicks, dings, and scratches (see photo at right). To do this, I took advantage of oak's open pores.

First, I wiped on three coats of a white pigmented stain. This made the surface of the cabinet white without completely filling in the pores.

The next step was to simulate years of wear on the white finish by "dirtying" it. To do this, I highlighted the pores of the wood by wiping on a coat of a darker stain over the entire surface and then immediately wiping it off again (see photo at left). This leaves the stain just in the pores, so the cabinet instantly looks much older.

JOINERY .... Stub Tenon & Groove

The stub tenon and groove joint is quick and easy to cut. And the entire joint can be made on the table saw.

It's made by first cutting a groove on one edge of each stile (the vertical pieces) and rail (the horizontal pieces). These grooves hold a center panel and short, "stub" tenons cut on the ends of just the rails.

The depth of the groove (and the length of the tenon) can vary depending on the type of panel you plan on using. A ¼"-deep groove works fine with a plywood panel. But if the panel is solid wood, you should use a ⅜"-deep groove. Why the difference?

It has to do with how the frame is assembled. I glue a plywood panel into the groove so it becomes a part of the joint. That way I can get away with a shorter tenon. But a solid panel can't be glued. It has to "float" to allow for wood movement. So deeper grooves (and longer tenons) increase the gluing area.

But there's more to consider than just the depth of the grooves. The grooves and tenons should also be centered on the thickness of the workpieces. And the workpieces should all be the same thickness. This way, there will only be two setups: one for the grooves, and another for the tenons.

GROOVES

The first step is to cut the grooves centered on the frame pieces.

When cutting a groove for a solid panel, I usually make its width ⅓ the thickness of the stock. For example: a ¼"-wide groove in ¾"-thick stock. But for a plywood panel, I cut the groove to match the thickness of the plywood.

Cutting the groove so it's centered on the edge of a frame piece is easy. Simply adjust the rip fence on your table saw so the blade cuts close to the center

(*Fig. 1*). You don't need it to be perfect — here's why.

After making your first pass, just flip the board end-for-end and make a second cut (*Fig. 2*). Now even if your blade isn't centered, the groove will be.

To adjust the width of the groove, nudge the rip fence and make another cut. Remember, you're cutting stock from both sides of the workpiece. So make small adjustments and sneak up on the final width of the groove.

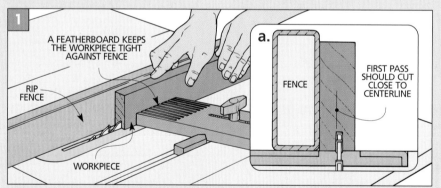

1
- A FEATHERBOARD KEEPS THE WORKPIECE TIGHT AGAINST FENCE
- RIP FENCE
- WORKPIECE
- **a.** FENCE — FIRST PASS SHOULD CUT CLOSE TO CENTERLINE

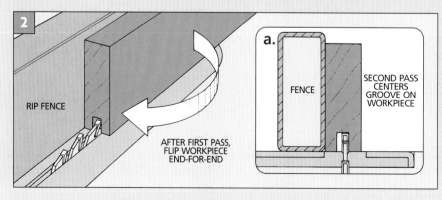

2
- RIP FENCE
- AFTER FIRST PASS, FLIP WORKPIECE END-FOR-END
- **a.** FENCE — SECOND PASS CENTERS GROOVE ON WORKPIECE

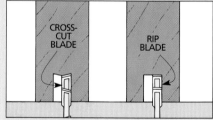

- CROSS-CUT BLADE
- RIP BLADE

Blade Choices. *A rip blade is a good choice for cutting the grooves in the rails and stiles. The flat-topped teeth produce a flat-bottomed groove.*

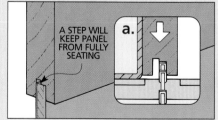

- A STEP WILL KEEP PANEL FROM FULLY SEATING
- **a.**

Downward Pressure. *Hold the workpiece firmly against the table as you make the cut to prevent a "stepped" bottom in the groove.*

STUB TENONS

Once the grooves are complete, the second step is to cut tenons on the ends of the rails. A single blade will work. But it takes several passes to remove the waste. And it leaves small ridges that make fitting the tenon difficult.

That's why I like using a dado blade. It cuts each side of the tenon cleanly and it does it in a single pass.

To use a dado blade, first bury it in an auxiliary fence (*Fig. 3*). Then adjust the fence to set the length of the tenon.

Now set the height of the blade to establish the thickness of the tenon. A quick way to get close is to set the blade flush with the bottom edge of the groove on a stile (*Fig. 4*).

To center the tenon on the work-piece, equal amounts are cut from each side of the rail (*Figs. 5 and 5a*). Make your cuts on a test piece first, then check for a snug fit in the groove.

If needed, adjust the height of the blade a little and make another practice cut. When the tenon fits tight in the groove, you're ready to cut all the tenons on the rail pieces.

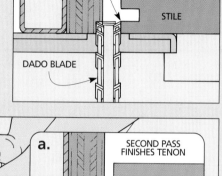

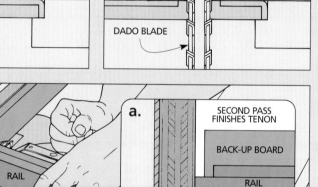

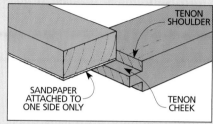

Sand the Cheek. *Sand the tenon cheek to get a snug fit in the groove. Stay clear of the shoulder to keep it sharp.*

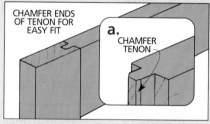

Chamfer Tenon. *Small chamfers on the ends make it easier to fit a tenon into a groove during assembly. It also provides some space for excess glue.*

ASSEMBLY

It's a good idea to dry-assemble the stiles, rails, and center panel to make sure everything fits together tight.

Now is also a good time to sand the face of the center panel and the inside edges of the stiles and rails. These areas can be difficult to sand once the frame has been assembled.

To assemble a frame with a solid panel, apply a thin bead of glue on each tenon cheek only (*Fig. 6*). Then clamp the pieces together (*Fig. 7*). A spacer under the door will keep clamping pressure centered on the frame.

One brad driven in the top rail will keep a solid panel centered. Plywood panels can be glued in place (*Fig. 8*).

Finally, check that the frame is flat and square. If the assembly isn't flat, try loosening the clamps a little. If it isn't square, try repositioning the clamps.

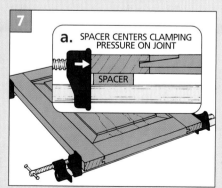

Gluing Up. *A thin bead of glue spread evenly on each cheek of the tenon is all that's needed when gluing up the joint.*

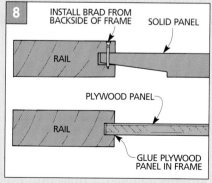

Clamping Pressure. *Putting a spacer under the workpiece aligns the joint with the clamp jaw for even pressure.*

Securing Panel. *A solid panel floats in the frame. Use a brad to keep it centered. A plywood panel can be glued in.*

DESIGNER'S NOTEBOOK

This version of the cabinet is perfect in the kitchen, by the door or wherever clutter tends to collect. It features hooks for hanging your keys, a bin for the mail and a handy cork board on the door.

CONSTRUCTION NOTES:

■ There are only two horizontal dividers on this version of the cabinet, so only cut dadoes for the top and middle horizontal dividers (see drawing below).

■ In each cabinet side (A), drill a $3/16$"-dia. hole with a $3/8$" x $3/8$" counterbore (*Fig. 3* and drawing below). These are used later to screw the bin rail in place.

■ Before gluing up the cabinet pieces, several holes are drilled in the lower back piece (F). First, drill three countersunk $3/16$"-dia. shank holes evenly spaced along the lower back (*Fig. 2*).

■ Next, drill four $1/4$"-dia. holes $1/4$" deep for the Shaker mini-pegs (see drawing). (The pegs are not glued in place until after the mail bin is secured in position.)

■ Now glue up the cabinet sides (A) with the two horizontal dividers (B) and the upper and lower back pieces (D, F).

■ Next, cut the bin rail (N) from $1/2$"-thick stock (*Fig. 1*). Sneak up on its final length until it fits snugly between the cabinet sides.

■ In each end of the bin rail (N), drill a $3/32$" pilot hole $1/2$" deep and centered $1/2$" from the bottom edge (*Fig. 1*).

■ Next, cut the bin base (O) from $3/4$" stock to rough width (5") and to the same length as the bin rail (*Fig. 1*).

■ Rip a 40° bevel on one edge of the bin base so the final width is $4^3/8$" (*Fig. 1*).

■ Using a $1/2$" roundover bit set $3/8$" above the router table, ease just the *bottom* edge of the bin base (*Fig. 1*).

Note: This is the same setup used to rout the profile on the door frame (refer to *Fig. 13a* on page 68).

■ Position the top of the beveled edge of the bin base (O) flush with the top edge of the lower back (F). Drill pilot holes through the shank holes in the lower back and into the bin base (*Fig. 2*).

■ To drill the holes for the spindles (P), first lay out their locations on the bin rail (N) and bin base (O) (*Fig. 1*).

■ When the layout is done, set up a $1/4$" drill bit in the drill press. With the bin

rail (N) on edge under the bit, set the depth stop to drill $3/8$" deep holes.

■ Now secure a fence to the drill press table to help keep the pieces aligned as the holes are drilled.

■ Drill the nine holes in the bin rail (N).

■ To drill the holes in the bin base (O), you'll need to reset the drill press depth stop, since the bin base is only $3/4$" thick.

■ Once the depth stop is properly set, drill the nine holes in the bin base (O).

■ When the holes are finished, rout a bullnose profile on the top edge of the bin rail (N) (*Fig. 1*). To do this, set up a $3/8$" roundover bit in the router table and raise it $3/16$" above the table. Then make a pass on each face.

■ Cut nine $4^1/2$"-long spindles (P) from a length of $1/4$" dowel.

■ When all the pieces for the bin are cut, dry-assemble the bin and check its fit in the cabinet. The pilot holes in the ends of the bin rail (N) should line up with the shank holes in the cabinet sides.

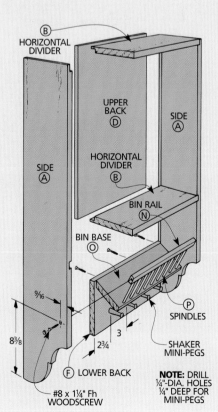

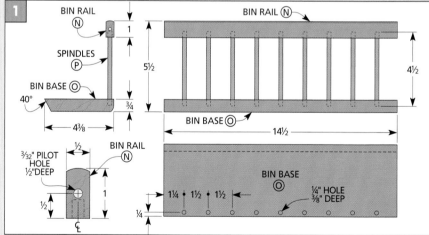

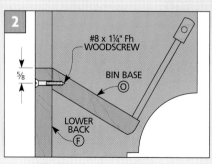

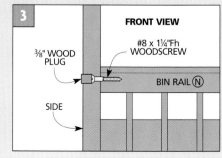

When you're satisfied with the fit, glue the spindles into the bin rail and base.

■ Now you can glue and screw the bin assembly to the lower back and to the cabinet sides *(Figs. 2 and 3)*.

■ Glue a wood plug into each counterbore, then cut and sand them flush.

■ Build the door frame the same as for the regular cabinet, but glue it up *without* the panel in place.

■ The door panel sits in a rabbet in the back of the frame instead of in a groove. To cut this rabbet, use a $\frac{3}{8}$" rabbet bit in the router table to remove the lip from the *inside* edge of the groove, leaving a $\frac{1}{2}$"-deep rabbet *(Figs. 4 and 4a)*. Use a chisel to square up the corners.

Note: To avoid chipout, take several light passes to remove the lip.

■ To make the bulletin board panel, first cut a backing panel (Q) from $\frac{1}{4}$" plywood to fit in the frame *(Fig. 5)*.

■ It's easiest to apply a finish to the cabinet and the good (exposed) side of the backing panel (Q) now before completing the door panel.

■ After the finish has dried, use contact cement to fasten a piece of $\frac{1}{8}$"-thick corrugated cardboard to the unfinished face of the backing panel (Q). Then use contact cement to secure a piece of $\frac{5}{32}$"-thick cork to the cardboard. Finally, trim the cork assembly flush with the edges of the backing panel *(Fig. 5)*.

■ When the bulletin board panel is complete, secure it to the door frame using six turn buttons with screws *(Fig. 5)*.

■ Finally, glue the Shaker mini-pegs into the holes in the lower back.

MESSAGE CENTER

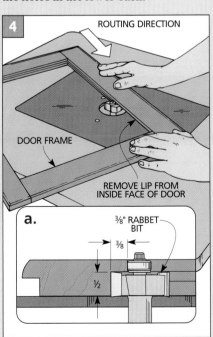

4

ROUTING DIRECTION

DOOR FRAME

REMOVE LIP FROM INSIDE FACE OF DOOR

a.

$\frac{3}{8}$" RABBET BIT

$\frac{3}{8}$

$\frac{1}{2}$

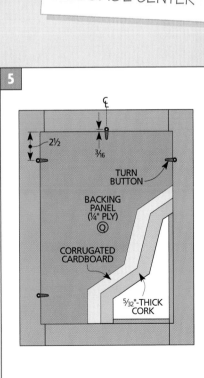

5

$2\frac{1}{2}$

$\frac{3}{16}$

TURN BUTTON

BACKING PANEL ($\frac{1}{4}$" PLY) Q

CORRUGATED CARDBOARD

$\frac{5}{32}$"-THICK CORK

MATERIALS LIST

NEW PARTS
N	Bin Rail (1)	$\frac{1}{2}$ x 1 - 14$\frac{1}{2}$
O	Bin Base (1)	$\frac{3}{4}$ x 4$\frac{3}{8}$ - 14$\frac{1}{2}$
P	Spindles (9)	$\frac{1}{4}$" dowel x 4$\frac{1}{2}$
Q	Backing Panel (1)	$\frac{1}{4}$ ply - 11$\frac{1}{4}$ x 16$\frac{3}{4}$

HARDWARE SUPPLIES
(5) #8 x 1$\frac{1}{4}$" Fh woodscrews
(4) Shaker mini-pegs
(6) Turn buttons w/ screws
(2) $\frac{3}{8}$" wood plugs
(1 pc.) $\frac{5}{32}$"-thick cork 12" x 18" rough
(1 pc.) $\frac{1}{8}$"-thick corrugated cardboard 12" x 18" rough

Note: Do not need parts C or L, only need two of part B.

Scandinavian Cabinet

Despite the scrollwork and the angles, building this cabinet is straightforward. With an optional glass-panel door, it becomes a place to store items while showing them off at the same time.

This corner cabinet is reminiscent of cabinets often found in rural Scandinavian homes. Since these were utilitarian cabinets, they were often made of the least expensive lumber — native pine. The joinery was equally simple and straightforward — butt joints held together with nails.

WOOD. When selecting materials, I followed with tradition and made my cabinet out of pine: clear, quartersawn, 3/4"-thick Ponderosa pine.

JOINERY. However, I couldn't bring myself to use butt joints and nails. Instead, I joined the main pieces of the cabinet with tongue and groove joints. The challenge was cutting the joints accurately and then getting them tight. With all the angles on a project like this, if the joinery doesn't fit tight, the gaps will be noticeable.

FITTING A CORNER. The other challenge was to design the project to hang and fit into a corner — even a corner that's a little out of square. The answer came in lapping the sides over the back so only the edges of the sides come in contact with the wall. In addition, there's a hidden hanging bracket that "bridges" over the corner where the two walls of a room come together.

ADJUSTABLE SHELF. To help make the most of the space inside, you'll find a shelf that matches the shape of the cabinet. It can be adjusted up or down to fit your storage requirements. Or it can be taken out altogether to provide additional space for tall items.

GLASS DOOR. By replacing the plywood door panel with a glass panel, the cabinet doubles as an attractive display case. Details on building this option are in the Designer's Notebook on page 82.

FINISH. I finished the cabinet with an exterior urethane varnish. I chose this finish not because the cabinet would ever hang outside, but because it gives the wood a yellowish tint. This way the pine took on instant age.

EXPLODED VIEW

OVERALL DIMENSIONS:
21³/₄W x 14¹/₄D x 30¹/₄H

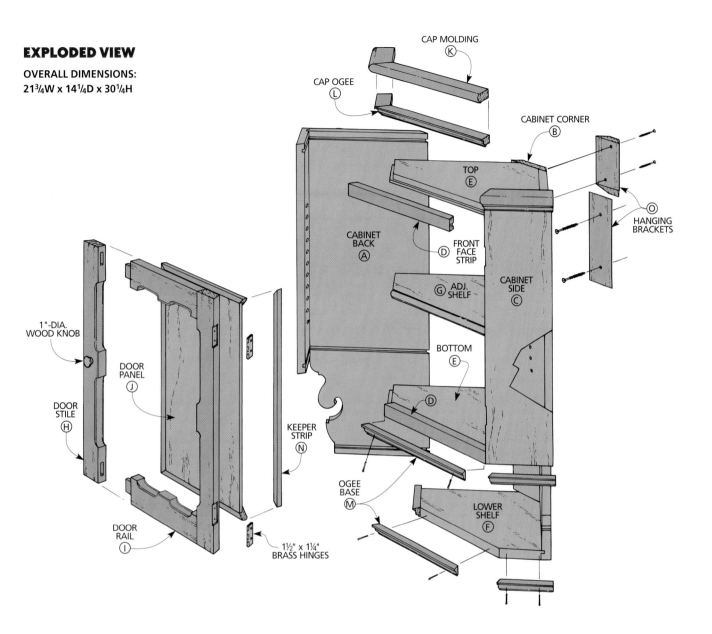

Labels in exploded view:
- CAP MOLDING (K)
- CAP OGEE (L)
- CABINET CORNER (B)
- TOP (E)
- HANGING BRACKETS (O)
- CABINET BACK (A)
- FRONT FACE STRIP (D)
- ADJ. SHELF (G)
- CABINET SIDE (C)
- BOTTOM (E)
- 1"-DIA. WOOD KNOB
- DOOR PANEL (J)
- DOOR STILE (H)
- KEEPER STRIP (N)
- DOOR RAIL (I)
- 1¹/₂" x 1¹/₄" BRASS HINGES
- OGEE BASE (M)
- LOWER SHELF (F)

MATERIALS LIST

WOOD

A	Cabinet Backs (2)	³/₄ x 11¹/₄ - 29
B	Cabinet Corner (1)	³/₄ x 4⁵/₁₆ - 29
C	Cabinet Sides (2)	³/₄ x 5¹/₂ - 20¹/₄
D	Front Face Strips (2)	³/₄ x 1 - cut to fit
E	Top/Bottom (2)	³/₄ x 11¹/₄ - 19
F	Lower Shelf (1)	³/₄ x 11¹/₄ - 19
G	Adjustable Shelf (1)	³/₄ x 10³/₁₆ - 17³/₄
H	Door Stiles (2)	³/₄ x 2 - 18¹/₈
I	Door Rails (2)	³/₄ x 2 - 10³/₈
J	Door Panel (1)	¹/₂ x 9³/₄ - 15³/₄
K	Cap Moldings (3)	³/₄ x 2 - cut to fit
L	Cap Ogees (3)	³/₄ x 1¹/₂ - cut to fit
M	Ogee Bases (6)	³/₄ x 1¹/₂ - cut to fit
N	Keeper Strips (4)	¹/₂ x ⁵/₈ - cut to fit
O	Hanging Bracket (1)	³/₄ x 2³/₄ - 13 rough

HARDWARE SUPPLIES

- (9) No. 8 x 1¹/₂" Fh woodscrews
- (2) No. 8 x 1¹/₄" Fh woodscrews
- (2) 3" drywall screws
- (1 pair) 1¹/₂" x 1¹/₄" brass butt hinges
- (1) 1"-dia. wood knob
- (1) ³/₈"-dia. x 1⁵/₈" dowel
- (3) ¹/₄" spoon-style shelf supports
- (30) 1" brads
- (14) 4d (1¹/₂") finish nails

CUTTING DIAGRAM

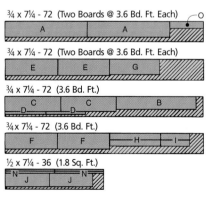

³/₄ x 7¹/₄ - 72 (Two Boards @ 3.6 Bd. Ft. Each) — O

| A | | A | |

³/₄ x 7¹/₄ - 72 (Two Boards @ 3.6 Bd. Ft. Each)

| E | E | G | |

³/₄ x 7¹/₄ - 72 (3.6 Bd. Ft.)

| C | | C | B |
| D | | D | |

³/₄ x 7¹/₄ - 72 (3.6 Bd. Ft.)

| F | F | H | I |

¹/₂ x 7¹/₄ - 36 (1.8 Sq. Ft.)

| N | | N | |
| J | J | | |

NOTE: CUT MOLDING PIECES (K, L, M) FROM WASTE AREAS. CUT LATCH VANE FROM SCRAP.

CABINET BACK PIECES

The unusual shape of this project forced me to come up with names for parts that made sense. The "back" of the cabinet is actually three separate pieces. I call the two wide pieces that fit against the walls the cabinet backs (A). The narrow piece (between the back pieces) is the cabinet corner (B) *(Fig. 1)*.

BACK PIECES. To make the back pieces (A), begin by gluing up two panels about 30" long and 12" wide. When the glue dries, cut the panels to finished length (29").

CORNER PIECE. Next, cut the corner piece (B) to a rough width of 5" and a finished length of 29".

BEVELS & GROOVES

After the three pieces are cut to length, bevels are ripped on the edges.

BEVEL BACKS. The *rear* edge on both back pieces (A) is ripped at 45° to create a finished width of $11\frac{1}{4}$" *(Fig. 1)*. Then both sides of the corner piece (B) are beveled so its width is $4\frac{5}{16}$".

When beveling these edges, it may seem that the bevels are all backwards from the way they should be cut. But note that the cabinet corner piece (B) will be lapped over the beveled edges of the back pieces (A) *(Fig. 1a)*.

BEVEL SIDE PIECES. Next, cut two cabinet sides (C) to a rough width of 6" and final length of $20\frac{1}{4}$" *(Fig. 1)*. The *front* edge of each of these two side pieces is also beveled, but this time at $22\frac{1}{2}°$. Bevel rip each side piece so the finished width is $5\frac{1}{2}$" *(Fig. 1)*.

GROOVES IN SIDES. Each side piece has a vertical groove to accept a tongue cut on the back piece later *(Fig. 2)*. This groove is cut on the inside face and is positioned so when a cabinet side is joined to a back, the edge overlaps (about $\frac{1}{4}$") *(Fig. 3a)*.

This offset allows the edges of the sides to fit tight against the wall, even if the walls aren't perfectly square (refer to *Fig. 14a* on page 79*)*.

FACE STRIPS

Next, I cut the front face strips (D) to size *(Fig. 4)*. (These face strips are attached to the cabinet top and bottom later. They add some "bulk" to the narrow edges of these pieces.)

Then, $\frac{1}{4}$"-wide grooves are cut on

these pieces to join them to the cabinet's top and bottom. To position the fence for this groove, use a piece of the stock that will make up the cabinet top as a gauge. Set the fence so the distance from the *outside* edge of the blade to the fence is equal to the thickness of the stock *(Fig. 4)*.

DADOES & HOLES

The next step is to cut dadoes across the backs (A), corner piece (B), and sides (C) *(Fig. 1)*. The dadoes are used to join these pieces to the cabinet's top, bottom and lower shelf (refer to *Fig. 12* on page 78).

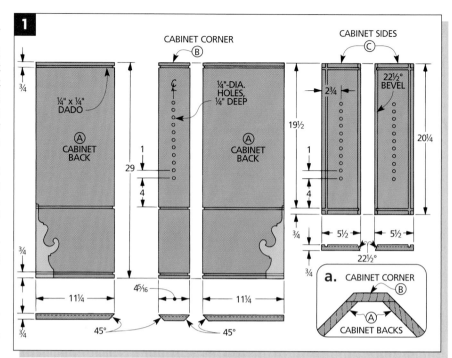

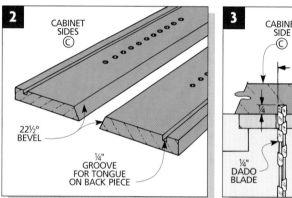

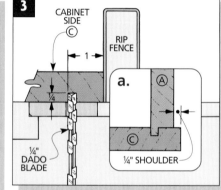

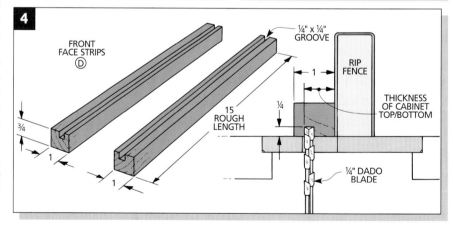

TOP/BOTTOM DADOES. To position the top and bottom dadoes, leave the fence set up in the same position as it was for cutting the grooves in the face strips. Then cut across all five pieces.

MIDDLE DADOES. Another set of dadoes is cut across the backs (A) and corner piece (B) to join to the cabinet's bottom. These dadoes have to be positioned so they align exactly with the bottom dadoes on the cabinet sides (C).

I found the best way to do this was to use a cabinet side (C) as a gauge to position the rip fence. First, butt the top end of the side piece against the fence. Then adjust the fence until the dado blade is aligned precisely with the bottom dado.

SHELF SUPPORT HOLES. Next, holes are drilled in the corner piece (B) and cabinet sides (C) that will be used later for supports for the adjustable shelf *(Fig. 1)*. It's easier to drill these holes now before the case is assembled.

TOP, BOTTOM, & SHELF

After the outside case parts are complete, the cabinet's top, bottom, and shelf can be made. So all the angles would come out the same, I began by making the top and bottom (E) and lower shelf (F) all the same size.

LAYOUT. Begin by gluing up stock to make three blanks 11¼" by 19". Then mark a centerline across each piece *(Fig. 5)*. The centerline is used as the reference point for laying out the shape of each piece.

CUT TO SIZE. Next, the pieces can be cut to size. The first cuts form the angled backs. I used the miter gauge set at 45° with a long auxiliary fence to make these cuts *(Fig. 6)*. Clamp a block to the auxiliary fence to keep the workpiece from shifting.

After making the first cut, flip the blank end for end, keeping the same edge against the auxiliary fence. Now remove the waste on the other back edge. Then repeat the process with the other blanks.

Once the first two angles are cut, the small corners that will fit into the sides can be cut. For this I used the rip fence on my saw as a guide *(Fig. 7)*.

TONGUES

The next step is making the tongues that will fit in the dadoes in the cabinet back and side pieces. These tongues are formed by using a ¼" dado blade to cut rabbets on the cabinet top, bottom, and lower shelf (E, F) *(Fig. 8)*.

FENCE SPACER. To cut the tongues, first I fastened a ¼" hardboard spacer to the rip fence with double-sided carpet tape *(Fig. 8)*. This keeps the dado blade from cutting the fence itself.

TONGUE THICKNESS. The tongues need to be cut to fit the dadoes in the cabinet sides and backs. To set the thickness, raise the dado blade to just under ½" and make a practice cut on a scrap piece of the same thickness. Keep raising the blade a little at a time until the tongue fits snugly into the dado.

FORM TONGUES. I made tongues all the way around all three blanks because they're all identical right now *(Fig. 9)*. (The front and side edges on the lower shelf will be cut away later.)

BACK TONGUES. While the table saw is set up, tongues can be formed on the two cabinet backs (A) to fit the grooves in the cabinet sides (C) *(Fig. 3a)*.

Note: The tongue is formed on the same face as the long point of the bevel (refer to End View Detail in *Fig. 11*).

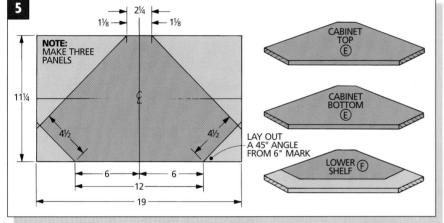

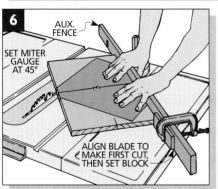

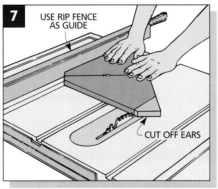

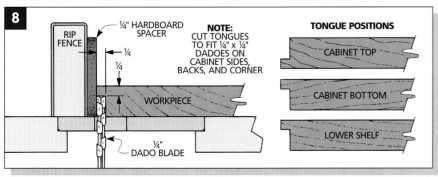

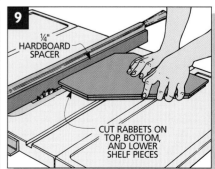

DECORATIVE PROFILE

The next step is laying out and cutting the decorative profile on the lower end of each cabinet back (A). I found it easiest to make a template from ¹⁄₈" hardboard first. Then I traced around the template onto the two cabinet backs. (*Woodsmith Project Supplies* offers a full-size pattern for the profile. See page 126 for more information.)

MAKE TEMPLATE. To make the template, begin by laying out a 1" grid. Then make the profile by drawing circles with a compass and drilling out wherever possible *(Fig. 10)*. Then cut out the remaining areas with a band saw or jig saw and sand the profile smooth.

POSITION PROFILE. To position the profile, align the bottom edge of the template with the bottom edge of the cabinet back (A), and the front edge against the edge with the tongue. Then trace around the template with a pencil. Finally, cut just outside the lines and work up to the lines with a drum sander and a file.

LOWER SHELF

After the profiles are cut out, the lower shelf (F) can be cut to size. Since the front edge of the profile determines the actual size of the shelf, first dry-assemble the cabinet.

SCREW TOGETHER. To temporarily hold the cabinet together, I drilled a pilot hole and shank hole centered on the width of each of the back pieces and the corner piece *(Fig. 12)*. Then I held the cabinet together with No. 8 x 1½" flathead woodscrews. (Don't screw in the lower shelf yet.)

LOWER SHELF. Now the lower shelf can be marked to be cut to its final shape. Begin by pushing it into position and making marks on the front edges of the shelf right at the edges of the profiles *(Fig. 12)*. Next, square out lines from these marks and mark a point 3³⁄₄" from the edge. Then connect these points and cut the shelf to shape.

ASSEMBLY

With all of the main case pieces completed, the case can be assembled.

I started by gluing and screwing the top, bottom and shelf to the cabinet backs (A) *(Fig. 12)*. Then I added the corner piece and cabinet sides (B, C).

ADD FACE STRIPS

After all of the main pieces have been assembled, there are two more pieces to add — the front face strips (D).

CUT TO LENGTH. First, the face strips need to be cut to finished length. To do this, start by cutting a 22½° miter off one end of each piece. Then "sneak up" on the final length by taking small cuts off the other end (also a 22½° miter cut) until the strip fits perfectly between the cabinet sides (C) (Top View in *Fig. 12*).

GLUE IN PLACE. Once the face strips fit, they can be glued into place on the tongues on the front of the cabinet top and bottom (E).

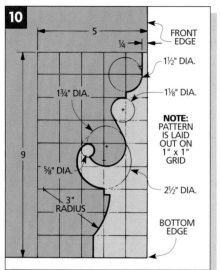

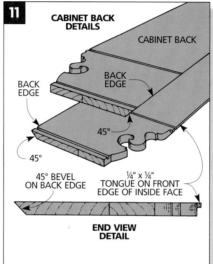

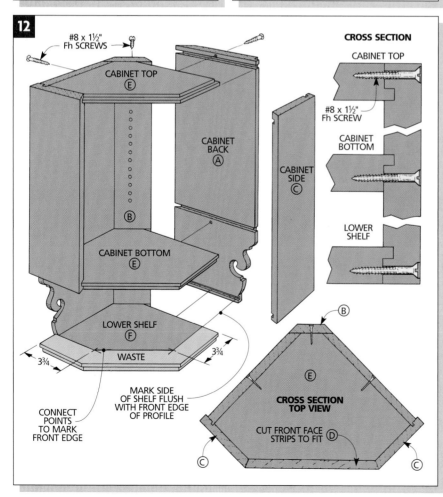

ADJUSTABLE SHELF

With the cabinet done, I then made an adjustable shelf (G) to fit inside the cabinet. This shelf sits on three "spoon-style" shelf supports.

To determine the size of the shelf, measure the inside dimensions of the case. Then, to allow for clearance, subtract $\frac{1}{8}$" from these measurements *(Fig. 13)*. At the front of the shelf, subtract $\frac{5}{8}$" from the depth of the cabinet to allow for the door panel (J) on the back of the door (refer to *Fig. 23* on page 80).

Note: To check my measurements, I quickly cut a "prototype" shelf out of a piece of cardboard to make sure it fit.

Once the measurements are determined, build up a blank and cut it to size using the same technique used for the other shelves (refer to *Figs. 6 and 7*).

PROFILE EDGE. After the adjustable shelf was cut to size, I routed a profile on the front edge using a $\frac{1}{4}$" roundover bit on the router table *(Fig. 13)*.

HANGING BRACKET

The cabinet hangs on the wall with a hidden "hook and bracket" hanger (O).

Begin making the hanger by bevel ripping both edges of a piece of stock so the width between the points of the bevels is the same as the back of the cabinet *(Fig. 14)*.

Next, cut the piece into two sections with the saw set at 45° to form the hook and bracket.

Now glue and screw the upper section (hook) to the cabinet. Finally, screw the lower section (bracket) into the corner studs of the wall with 3"-long drywall screws *(Fig. 14a)*.

DOOR FRAME

With the cabinet case complete, I went about making the door. The door frame consists of two stiles and two rails joined with mortises and tenons.

Begin by ripping all four pieces 2" wide *(Fig. 15)*. Then cut the rails (I) $10\frac{3}{8}$" long. And cut the stiles (H) $\frac{1}{8}$" less than the opening between the top and bottom facing strips (D). (My stiles were $18\frac{1}{8}$" long.)

JOINTS. After cutting the stock to size, cut $\frac{1}{4}$"-wide centered mortises $\frac{1}{2}$" from both ends of the stiles *(Fig. 16)*. Then form matching tenons on the ends of the rails.

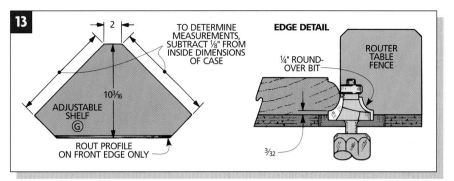

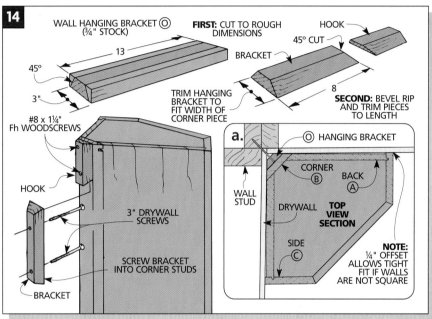

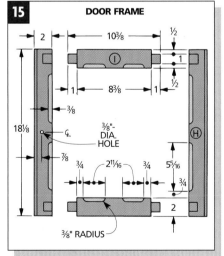

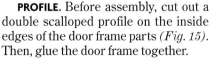

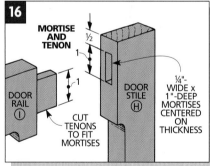

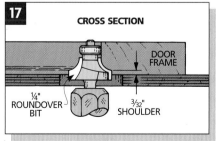

PROFILE. Before assembly, cut out a double scalloped profile on the inside edges of the door frame parts *(Fig. 15)*. Then, glue the door frame together.

ROUT EDGES. To soften the scallops, I routed a profile with a $\frac{1}{4}$" roundover bit on the router table *(Fig. 17)*.

Note: When routing these edges near the corners, be careful not to "slip"

out of the curved end of the scallop. The four inside corners of the door frame should be left with square edges to provide a contrast with the routed edge. Refer to the photo on page 74.

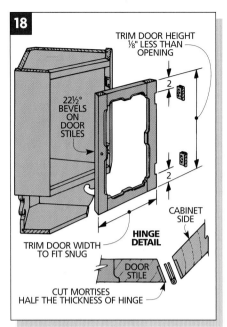

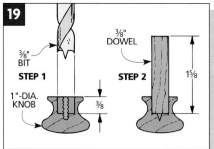

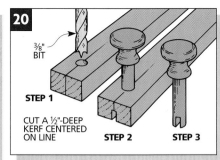

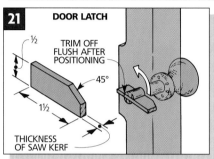

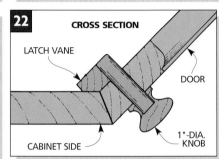

TRIM TO SIZE. To fit the frame to the *height* of the opening in the case, trim the outside edges of the rails until the door fits between the face pieces with $1/16$" to spare on both ends *(Fig. 18)*.

To fit the frame to the *width* of the opening, first rip a $22^1/2°$ bevel off each stile, leaving the door a little oversized. Then, sneak in on the cuts until the face of the door frame fits flush with the beveled edges on the cabinet sides.

HINGES. When the door fits its opening, mortise the door stile and the front edge of the cabinet side to accept two $1^1/2$" x $1^1/4$" hinges *(Fig. 18)*.

DOOR LATCH

Before fitting the panel in the door frame, I fitted the latch.

TINKER TOY. The latch I used looks like a Tinker Toy but works great. The $3/8$" dowel shaft that goes through the door is glued into a wooden knob on one end and has a slot for a flat latch vane on the other *(Fig. 21)*.

KNOB. To make the knob work, I bored a hole in a 1"-dia. wood knob to fit the dowel shaft *(Fig. 19)*.

SLOT JIG. After gluing a short dowel into the knob, I used a simple jig to slot the other end of the shaft *(Fig. 20)*. To make this jig, begin by marking a centerline on a $1^1/2$"-wide piece of scrap. Next, drill a $3/8$" hole through the scrap about 1" from the end on the centerline.

CUT SLOT. To cut the slot, raise the saw blade so it projects just $1/2$" above the table. Next, insert the dowel into the

hole so the end is flush with the bottom of the jig. Then adjust the saw fence so the blade is centered on the centerline, and push the jig through the blade.

LATCH VANE. To make the latch vane, rip a thin scrap of wood to fit the slot (about $1/8$" thick). Next, cut it with a hand saw $1/2$" wide and $1^1/2$" long. Then cut off one corner at 45° *(Fig. 21)*.

FIT LATCH. Now the vane is fitted to hold the door shut. To do this, close the door and slide the vane in the slot until the angled corner of the vane fits in the inside corner of the cabinet *(Fig. 22)*. Then glue in the vane and trim off the excess flush with the dowel.

PANEL

Now the door frame is ready for the panel (J). In keeping with the simplicity

of the cabinet, this panel is mounted to the back of the door frame (rather than set into grooves) *(Fig. 23)*.

CUT TO SIZE. To make the panel, start by gluing up a blank from $1/2$" stock. Then, to determine the final dimensions of the panel, measure the distances between the bottoms of the scallops on the frames and add $1/4$" in each direction *(Fig. 23)*.

RABBET EDGES. The panel is held by rabbeted strips *(Fig. 23)*. Begin by rabbeting the edge of the panel to leave a $1/4$" x $1/4$" tongue around the edge.

KEEPER STRIPS. To make the keeper strips (N), cut $1/4$" x $1/4$" rabbets along both edges of a $1/2$"-thick blank that's 2" wide. Next, rip $5/8$"-wide strips off each edge of the blank. Then rout a roundover on the outside edges with a $1/4$" roundover bit *(Fig. 23a)*.

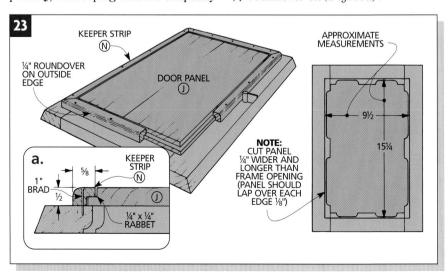

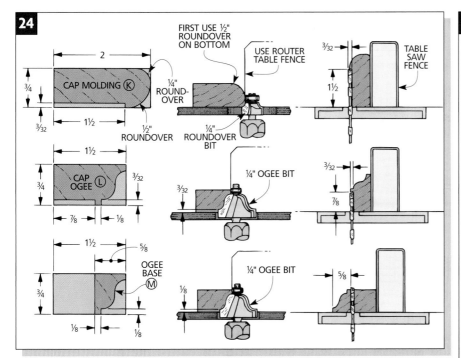

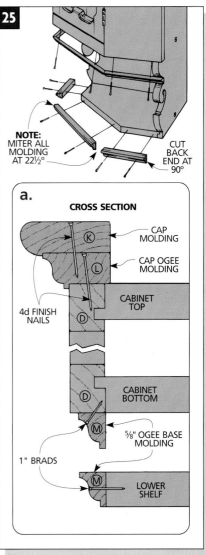

24 (figure with molding profiles)

FIRST USE ½" ROUNDOVER ON BOTTOM
USE ROUTER TABLE FENCE
TABLE SAW FENCE
CAP MOLDING (K)
2
¾
3/32
1½
½" ROUNDOVER
¼" ROUNDOVER
¼" ROUNDOVER BIT
1½
CAP OGEE (L)
¾
3/32
7/8
1/8
¼" OGEE BIT
3/32
7/8
OGEE BASE (M)
1½
5/8
¾
1/8
1/8
¼" OGEE BIT
1/8
5/8

25

NOTE: MITER ALL MOLDING AT 22½°
CUT BACK END AT 90°

a.

CROSS SECTION
CAP MOLDING
CAP OGEE MOLDING
CABINET TOP
4d FINISH NAILS
CABINET BOTTOM
5/8" OGEE BASE MOLDING
1" BRADS
LOWER SHELF

Next, miter the ends of the strips for a tight fit around the panels. Then position the panel and nail through the keeper strips with 1"-long brads to secure the panel in place *(Fig. 23a)*. Finally, mount the door to the cabinet.

TRIM MOLDING

After the door panel was in place, I made trim molding (K, L, M) for the top and bottom of the cabinet and the front of the lower shelf.

SHAPE PROFILES. Begin by using the router table to shape the profiles on blank stock *(Fig. 24)*. Next use the saw to form the shallow rabbets where the molding pieces overlap. Then cut them to final width and miter to length.

ATTACH TRIM. Now the moldings can be glued to the case. I drove two nails through each strip to act as clamps while the glue dried *(Fig. 25)*.

Note: To conceal the nail holes, I "blind nailed" the brads. For more about this, see the Shop Tip below. ■

SHOP TIP .... Blind Nailing

One of the problems of using nails in a project is how to cover the nail holes. I was faced with this when fastening the molding to the top and bottom of the Scandinavian cabinet.

There's a method to hide the nails that's been used by finish carpenters for years – blind nailing. To do this, you lift up a chip, set the nail, then glue the chip back in place. The result is an invisible patch.

If you're careful, you can lift the chip with a small chisel *(Step 1)*.

There's also a special tool available specifically for this task. It's called a blind nailer and looks like a miniature plane that holds a small chisel for a blade. (See page 126 for sources.)

1 With bevel down, wiggle a chisel lightly forward and lift up a chip.

¼" CHISEL

2 Grip brad with pliers and tap it in with a tack hammer and nail set.

NEEDLE-NOSED PLIERS

3 Spread glue under chip with toothpick and press chip down.

ADD GLUE AND ROLL CHIP BACK DOWN

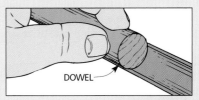

4 Hold chip down with dowel a few minutes until the glue sets.

DOWEL

SCANDINAVIAN CABINET **81**

DESIGNER'S NOTEBOOK

Install a glass panel in the door of the Scandinavian Cabinet to display your treasures. This way, your collectibles are kept safe without hiding them from view.

CONSTRUCTION NOTES:

■ Begin by building the door frame as you would for the regular cabinet. But do not drill the hole for the latch. This hole is drilled later, after glass stops are installed on the back of the door frame.

■ Once the frame is assembled and the scallops are cut, you can measure to determine the length of the long and short muntins (P, Q). Measure the interior dimensions of the door centered on the rails and stiles *(Fig. 1)*.

■ Add $^3/_4$" to each of these measurements to allow for a $^3/_8$" overlap on each end *(Fig. 1)*. Cut the $^1/_2$"-wide muntins to these lengths from $^3/_8$"-thick stock.

■ Cut a $^3/_8$" rabbet $^3/_{16}$" deep across each end of each muntin *(Fig. 1)*.

■ To form a half-lap joint, cut a $^1/_2$" dado $^3/_{16}$" deep and centered on the length of each muntin *(Figs. 1 and 2)*.

Note: All three cuts on the short muntin are on the *same* face *(Fig. 1)*. The dado on the long muntin is on the *opposite* face as the rabbets.

■ Dry-assemble the muntins and center the assembly in the door frame. To locate the positions of the notches in the door frame, trace around the ends of the muntins *(Fig. 3)*.

■ Chisel (or rout) $^3/_{16}$"-deep notches within each set of lines *(Fig. 3)*. When set in the notches, the muntins should be flush with the back of the door frame.

■ Now glue the muntins together at the half-lap joint, and glue the assembly into the door frame.

■ The glass stops (R, S) are first formed on a wide blank, then cut to width. To do this, first cut two 3"-wide blanks. Cut one blank to a rough length of 17" for the long glass stops (R) and the other to a rough length of 11" for the short glass stops (S). You'll end up with two glass stops from each blank.

■ Next, cut a $^5/_8$" rabbet $^1/_8$" deep on each long edge of each blank *(Fig. 4)*. Then rip a 1"-wide stop from each edge.

■ Miter the glass stops to length. The length from short point to short point on each piece should equal the inside dimensions of the door frame (not including the scallops).

■ Drill $^3/_{32}$"-dia. shank holes in the glass stops *(Fig. 4)*. Then temporarily screw the glass stops to the door frame.

■ Next, trim the glass stops to match the profile of the door frame. To do this, first use a $^3/_4$" Forstner bit to remove the waste from the glass stops at each end of each scallop *(Fig. 5)*.

■ To complete the profiles, use a flush trim bit in the router table *(Fig. 6)*. To help reduce chipout, take light passes. If wild grain causes chipout, reverse the feed direction and backrout.

Safety Note: Backrouting can cause the bit to grab the workpiece. Use push blocks to keep your hands safely away from the bit and take *light* cuts.

■ Drill a $^3/_8$"-dia. hole for the latch through the door frame *(Fig. 7)*. This hole will go through the edge of the glass stop. To prevent chipout on the back side, use a cutoff from the glass stops as a backer board *(Fig. 7a)*.

■ Remove one of the long glass stops (R) and slide the glass in place. Then replace the glass stop *(Fig. 8)*. (Do not glue the stops in place. This allows them to be removed if the glass ever needs to be replaced.)

■ Now mount the door to the cabinet and install the door latch the same as for the regular cabinet.

CORNER DISPLAY CABINET

1

NOTE: DOOR FACE DOWN

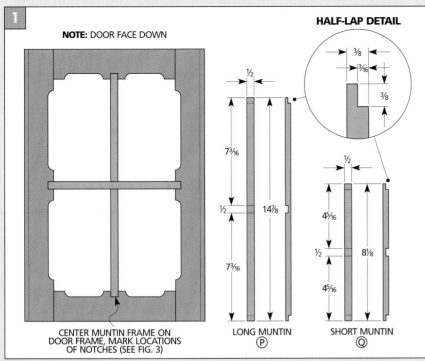

CENTER MUNTIN FRAME ON DOOR FRAME, MARK LOCATIONS OF NOTCHES (SEE FIG. 3)

HALF-LAP DETAIL

$3/8$
$3/16$
$3/8$

$1/2$
$7^3/16$
$1/2$
$14^7/8$
$7^3/16$

LONG MUTIN
Ⓟ

$1/2$
$4^5/16$
$1/2$
$8^1/8$
$4^5/16$

SHORT MUTIN
Ⓠ

2

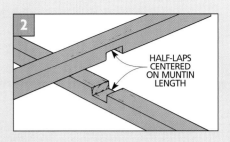

HALF-LAPS CENTERED ON MUNTIN LENGTH

3

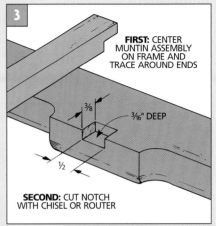

FIRST: CENTER MUNTIN ASSEMBLY ON FRAME AND TRACE AROUND ENDS

$3/8$
$3/16$" DEEP
$1/2$

SECOND: CUT NOTCH WITH CHISEL OR ROUTER

4

NOTE: DOOR FACE DOWN

ATTACH WITH #4 x 3/4" Fh WOODSCREWS

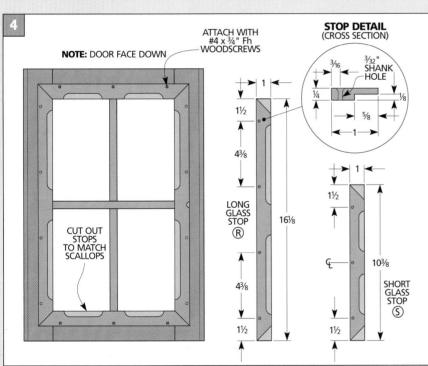

CUT OUT STOPS TO MATCH SCALLOPS

STOP DETAIL
(CROSS SECTION)

$3/16$
$3/32$" SHANK HOLE
$1/4$
$1/8$
$5/8$
1

1
$1^1/2$
$4^3/8$
LONG GLASS STOP Ⓡ
$16^1/8$
$4^3/8$
$1^1/2$

1
$1^1/2$
C_L
$10^3/8$
SHORT GLASS STOP Ⓢ
$1^1/2$

5

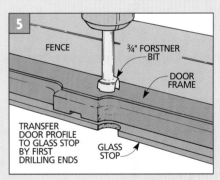

FENCE
$3/4$" FORSTNER BIT
DOOR FRAME
GLASS STOP

TRANSFER DOOR PROFILE TO GLASS STOP BY FIRST DRILLING ENDS

6

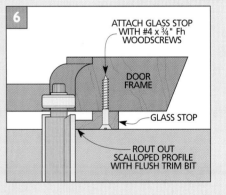

ATTACH GLASS STOP WITH #4 x 3/4" Fh WOODSCREWS
DOOR FRAME
GLASS STOP
ROUT OUT SCALLOPED PROFILE WITH FLUSH TRIM BIT

MATERIALS LIST

NEW PARTS
P Long Muntin (1) $3/8$ x $1/2$ - $14^7/8$
Q Short Muntin (1) $3/8$ x $1/2$ - $8^1/8$
R Long Glass Stops (2) $1/4$ x 1 - 17 rough
S Short Glass Stops (2) $1/4$ x 1 - 11 rough
Note: Do not need parts J or N.

HARDWARE SUPPLIES
(1 pc.) $1/8$"-thick glass, $9^3/4$" x $15^3/4$"
(14) No. 4 x $3/4$" Fh woodscrews

7

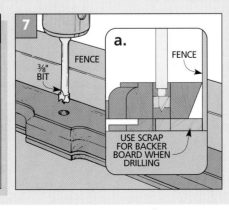

a.

$3/8$" BIT
FENCE
FENCE

USE SCRAP FOR BACKER BOARD WHEN DRILLING

8

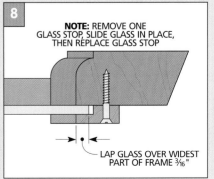

NOTE: REMOVE ONE GLASS STOP, SLIDE GLASS IN PLACE, THEN REPLACE GLASS STOP

LAP GLASS OVER WIDEST PART OF FRAME $3/16$"

HEIRLOOM PIECES

For most woodworkers, an heirloom project is one that the craftsman's family is proud to display, now and for years to come.

The walnut cabinet is a perfect example of a piece of furniture that will serve many generations. Its traditional lines and ogee-profile base will never go out of style. And the optional wine rack makes it as versatile as it is handsome.

The large cherry wardrobe looks impressive, but is less expensive and easier to build than you might think. Designed to be in the classic tradition, it features a roomy dovetailed drawer as well as an optional inner case for increased storage potential.

The tall oak cabinet features a variety of molding treatments and both glass-panel and wood-panel door fronts. Plans for making it into a safe, secure cabinet for firearms or other sporting equipment are also included.

Walnut Cabinet

It's attention to detail that makes for a classic-looking heirloom like this walnut cabinet.
Those details include an ogee profile base, built-in molding, and doors with two good faces.

Attention to details. That's what sets this walnut cabinet apart from your average project, and makes it an heirloom you'll be proud to show. Some of these details are obvious. Others you'd probably miss unless they were pointed out to you.

The cabinet base is a good example. Instead of a plain piece of stock for the cabinet to rest on, there's an ogee profile cut into the front and side pieces. And to strengthen the miter joints used to join these pieces, splines are added at both front corners.

MOLDED STUB TENON. A closer look at the doors reveals the molded stub tenon joint used to hold them together. Typically, molding is added after the door is glued together. But making the molding an integral part of the joint gives you a stronger door. There's more surface area for the glue to hold the door together.

For more on molded stub tenon joints, including plans for making a helpful jig, see pages 94-96.

TWO GOOD FACES. The plywood panel glued in the door frame is also a little out of the ordinary. It's a fact of life that thin hardwood plywood only has one good face. But what do you do when the inside face of a door (like the ones on this cabinet) will be exposed each time it's opened?

The answer is to cover it with veneer. It doesn't add much to the overall thickness of the panel, but it certainly adds to the appearance of the door, and the project as a whole.

When you combine all these details with the natural beauty of walnut, you'll end up with a project that looks good in most any room of your home.

WINE RACK. As an alternative to the single shelf, you can turn the inside of this cabinet into a functional wine rack. For building instructions, see the Designer's Notebook on page 97.

EXPLODED VIEW

OVERALL DIMENSIONS:
$31^3/_4$W x $13^7/_8$D x $36^1/_2$H

CUTTING DIAGRAM

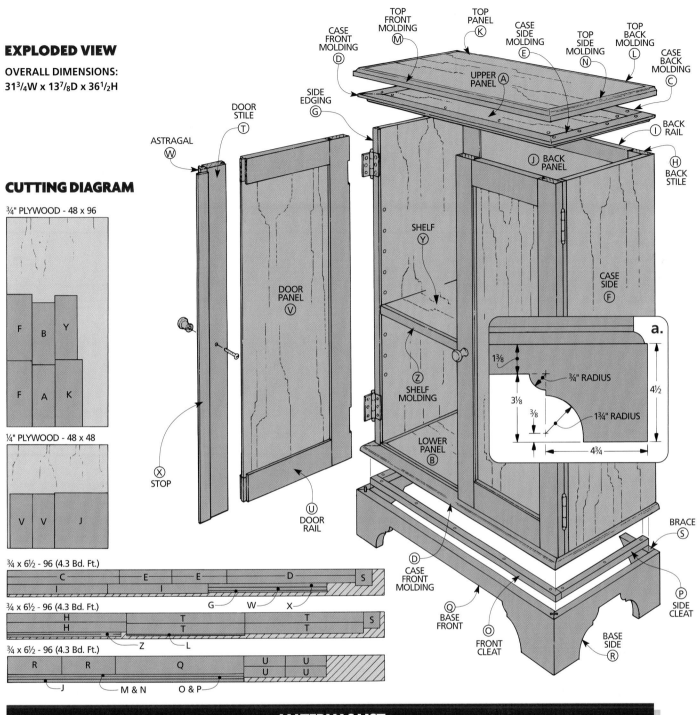

¾" PLYWOOD - 48 x 96

¼" PLYWOOD - 48 x 48

¾ x 6½ - 96 (4.3 Bd. Ft.)

¾ x 6½ - 96 (4.3 Bd. Ft.)

¾ x 6½ - 96 (4.3 Bd. Ft.)

a.
1⅜ · ¾" RADIUS · 4½
3⅛ · ⅜ · 1¾" RADIUS
4¾

MATERIALS LIST

CASE		
A	Upper Panel (1)	¾ ply - 10¾ x 28½
B	Lower Panel (1)	¾ ply - 10¾ x 28½
C	Back Molding (2)	¾ x 1¾ - 28½
D	Front Molding (2)	¾ x 1¾ - 31½
E	Side Molding (4)	¾ x 1¾ - 13¾
F	Case Sides (2)	¾ ply - 12 x 30¼
G	Side Edging (2)	½ x ¾ - 30¼
H	Back Stiles (2)	¾ x 2½ - 30¼
I	Back Rails (2)	¾ x 2½ - 25½
J	Back Panel (1)	¼ ply - 25½ x 25¾
TOP & BASE		
K	Top Panel (1)	¾ ply - 13⅛ x 30¾

L	Back Molding (1)	¼ x ¾ - 30¾
M	Front Molding (1)	½ x ¾ - 31¾
N	Side Molding (2)	½ x ¾ - 13⅞
O	Front Cleat (1)	¾ x ¾ - 30¼
P	Side Cleats (2)	¾ x ¾ - 12⅜
Q	Base Front (1)	¾ x 4½ - 31¾
R	Base Sides (2)	¾ x 4½ - 13⅞
S	Braces (2)	¾ x 4¼ - 4¼
DOORS & SHELF		
T	Door Stiles (4)	¾ x 2¾ - 30⅛
U	Door Rails (4)	¾ x 2¾ - 10½
V	Door Panels (2)	¼ ply - 10½ x 25⅝
W	Astragal (1)	⅜ x ¾ - 30⅛

X	Stop (1)	¼ x ¾ - 29⅝
Y	Shelf (1)	¾ ply - 10½ x 28⅞
Z	Shelf Molding (1)	½ x ¾ - 28⅞

HARDWARE SUPPLIES
(13) No. 8 x 1" Fh woodscrews
(18) No. 8 x 1½" Fh woodscrews
(20) No. 8 x 2" Fh woodscrews
(2) Ball catches
(2 pair) 2½" ball tip hinges
(2) 1" brass knobs
(4) Shelf supports
(2 pcs.) 10½" x 25⅝" flexible back veneer

To build this two-door walnut cabinet, I started with the case. It's basically a large plywood box with an adjustable shelf added in the middle for storage.

UPPER/LOWER PANELS. Two of the main parts of this box are the upper and lower panels. These are $^3/_4$"-thick pieces of walnut plywood surrounded by four wide strips of solid molding.

Since both panels are identical (except for mounting holes drilled in the upper panel later), I made them at the same time. Start by cutting the plywood upper and lower panels (A, B) to a final size of $10^3/_4$" x $28^1/_2$" (Fig. 2).

The next step is to cover the edges of these panels with molding. But sometimes, it can be difficult to get molding aligned perfectly with the edges, especially when you're using wide pieces. (Mine were $1^3/_4$" wide.) To help me do that, I cut a $^1/_4$"-wide tongue on each edge of the plywood panels (Fig. 2a).

The key is to get the tongues centered on the thickness of the plywood. Otherwise the two surfaces won't be flush when the molding is installed. An easy way to do this is to flip the panel over after each pass. That way you're cutting from both sides until the tongue is centered on the panel's edge.

MOLDING. Now you can add the molding. These are $^3/_4$"-thick stock planed to match the plywood thickness. They're cut to final width ($1^3/_4$"), but I left them extra long. This extra stock will come in handy when mitering the molding to fit around the panels. Next,

cut a centered groove on the edge of each piece to accept the tongues on the edges of the panel (Figs. 3 and 3a).

Now the back molding (C) is cut to finished length. It's the same length as the plywood panels ($28^1/_2$"). A stub tenon is cut on each end of this piece to

fit the grooves in the side molding pieces (added next) (Fig. 3b). Glue the back molding to the plywood panel.

The front molding (D) and side molding (E) can be cut next (Fig. 3). This molding is different than the back molding. You don't cut stub tenons.

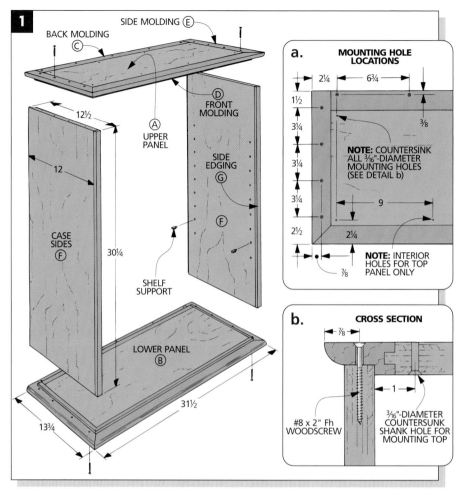

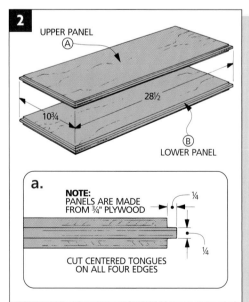

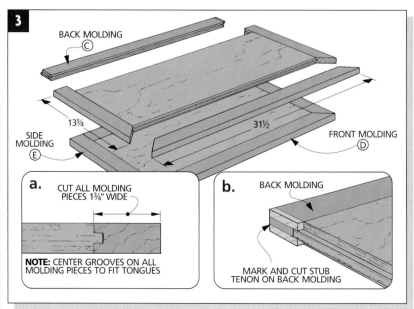

Instead, the front and side pieces are mitered to fit around the center panel.

Miter the front molding to length first and dry-clamp it in place. Next, the side molding pieces are mitered on one end, then trimmed to length flush with the back molding. Glue and clamp the front and side molding pieces to the panel.

RABBETED EDGE. Next, I cut rabbets around the upper and lower panels *(Fig. 4)*. These rabbets are all cut ¼" deep. But the rabbet on the back of the panel is ¾" wide and the rabbets on the front and sides are 1¼" wide *(Figs. 4a and 4b)*. You need the extra width for a decorative profile added next.

EDGE PROFILE. To soften the edges of the upper and lower panels, a profile is cut on the front and sides *(Fig. 5)*. Don't cut a profile in the back edge. Since you don't see it, it's left square.

This decorative profile is created with a ½" roundover bit in the router table *(Fig. 5a)*. But you'll have to use the fence when making the cut, because there's not enough stock on the workpiece for the bearing to ride against.

MOUNTING HOLES. After routing the profile, the last step is drilling mounting holes. Here, the upper and lower panels differ. To hold the cabinet top added later, you'll need eight more holes in the upper panel (A) *(Figs. 1, 1a, and 1b)*.

SIDES. Now you're ready to add the sides. I cut two ¾"-thick plywood sides (F) to a final size of 12" x 30¼" *(Fig. 6)*. But before they can be installed, there are a couple of things to do.

First, on the front edge of each side piece a thin strip of hardwood side edging (G) is attached to cover the plies *(Fig. 6a)*. This is a ½"-thick piece of solid walnut cut to the same length and thickness as the sides and glued flush.

Next, there's a ¾"-wide x ½"-deep rabbet cut on the back edge of each side *(Fig. 6b)*. This rabbet is used to hold the back panel added later.

ASSEMBLY. Now the sides pieces can be used to join the upper and lower panels to form the case. These pieces are simply glued and screwed together.

SHELF HOLES. Before moving on to the back panel, I wanted to drill ¼"-dia. mounting holes in the sides for shelf pins that are installed later *(Fig. 7)*. To help me do that, I used a hardboard template *(Fig. 7a)*. Simply set the template in the case to drill the holes. It helps keep the holes aligned so the shelf doesn't rock.

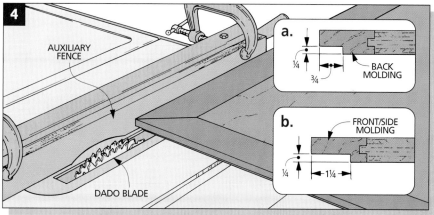

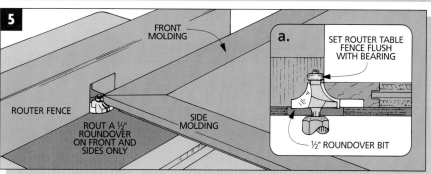

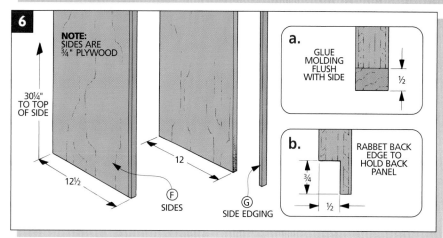

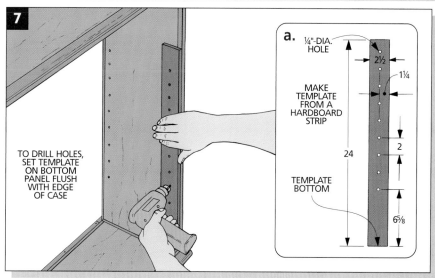

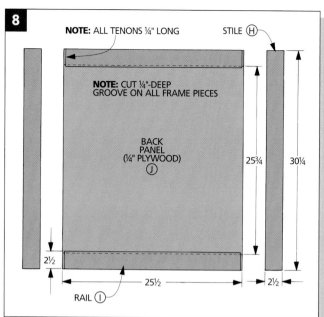

8

NOTE: ALL TENONS ¼" LONG

STILE (H)

NOTE: CUT ¼"-DEEP GROOVE ON ALL FRAME PIECES

BACK PANEL (¼" PLYWOOD) (J)

25¾"

30¼"

2½

25½

2½

RAIL (I)

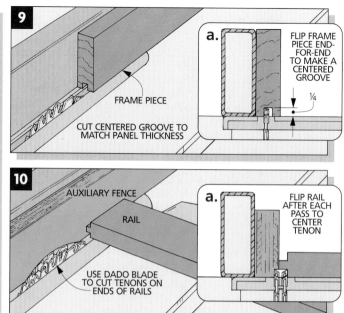

9

FRAME PIECE

CUT CENTERED GROOVE TO MATCH PANEL THICKNESS

a.

FLIP FRAME PIECE END-FOR-END TO MAKE A CENTERED GROOVE

¼

10

AUXILIARY FENCE

RAIL

USE DADO BLADE TO CUT TENONS ON ENDS OF RAILS

a.

FLIP RAIL AFTER EACH PASS TO CENTER TENON

After gluing up the case, the next step is to add the back. It's simply a plywood panel surrounded by a pair of stiles and rails, sized to fit the opening in the back of the case. (My opening was 30" wide x 30¼" high.)

FRAME. I started by cutting the stiles (H) and rails (I) to finished width (2½") (*Fig. 8*). Then cut to finished length (30¼" and 25½" respectively).

Next, a shallow groove, centered on the edge, can be cut on each frame piece. It's cut to match the thickness of the plywood panel that will be added later (*Figs. 9 and 9a*).

Then stub tenons can be cut on the ends of the rails to fit in these grooves. Sneak up on the thickness of the tenon by making several passes and flipping the workpiece between each (*Fig. 10*).

BACK PANEL. With the frame pieces complete, the back panel (J) is cut next. This ¼"-thick piece of plywood is cut to fit in the frame. (My panel was 25½" x 25¾".) After gluing the frame pieces and back panel together, the assembled back can be installed in the case. Just glue and screw it in place (*Fig. 11a*).

CABINET TOP. The cabinet top is added next, once the back is in place. It's made a little larger than the top of the case to overhang the front and side edges (*Fig. 11b*). The top consists of a ¾"-thick plywood top panel (K) (13⅛" x 30¾") surrounded by molding to cover the plies (*Fig. 12*).

MOLDING. What's a little unusual is the molding isn't all the same size. The molding on the front and sides of the

cabinet is ½" wide and the piece on the back is ¼" wide. The extra width is for routing a decorative edge on the front and side pieces.

Since you don't rout the back, I cut the back molding (L) to finished length first (30¾") and then glued it to the top panel (K) (*Figs. 12 and 12a*).

Now the rest of the molding pieces can be added. First, I mitered the front

molding (M) to fit the length of the top panel and glued it in place. Next, miter one end of each side molding (N) with the opposite end trimmed flush with the back edge. Then glue and clamp the side pieces to the panel.

To complete the cabinet top, I used a ¼" roundover bit in the router table to rout the front and side edges (*Figs. 13 and 13a*). But since this cabinet top is a

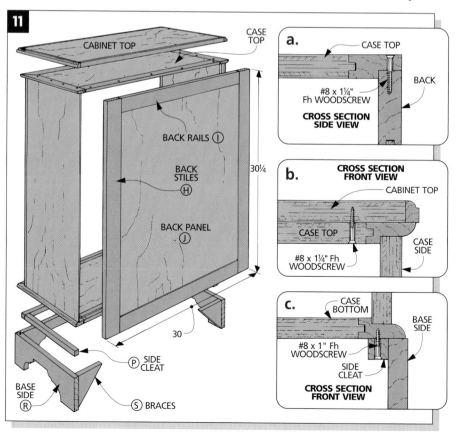

11

CABINET TOP

CASE TOP

BACK RAILS (I)

BACK STILES (H)

BACK PANEL (J)

30¼

30

SIDE CLEAT (P)

BASE SIDE (R)

BRACES (S)

a.

CASE TOP

BACK

#8 x 1¼" Fh WOODSCREW

CROSS SECTION SIDE VIEW

b.

CROSS SECTION FRONT VIEW

CABINET TOP

CASE TOP

CASE SIDE

#8 x 1¼" Fh WOODSCREW

c.

CASE BOTTOM

BASE SIDE

#8 x 1" Fh WOODSCREW

SIDE CLEAT

CROSS SECTION FRONT VIEW

fairly large piece, I clamped a feather-board to my router table to help stabilize the panel.

INSTALLATION. Now you can glue and screw the top to the case *(Fig. 11)*. To do this, center the top from side-to-side, and keep the back edge of the top flush with the back edge of the case.

BASE. Once the top is glued and screwed in place, the case is almost complete. All that's left is adding the base. It's made from three pieces of solid stock mitered at the corners with a decorative profile cut into the face of each piece.

CLEATS. But before you can build the base pieces, three hardwood cleats, a front cleat (O), and two side cleats (P) have to be attached to the bottom panel *(Fig. 14)*. They hold the base to the cabinet. These cleats are $3/4$" x $3/4$" pieces of stock glued and screwed to the bottom *(Figs. 14a and 11c)*.

The interesting thing is where you position the cleats. They're set back $5/8$" from the outside edge. This will give you a $1/8$" reveal when the base pieces are installed.

BASE FRONT AND SIDES. With the cleats in place, the base front and sides can be added next. They're made from $3/4$"-thick pieces of walnut mitered to fit around the bottom of the case *(Fig. 14)*.

Like the front molding (M), the base front (Q) is mitered at both ends. And the base sides (R) are mitered at one

end and cut to length flush with the back edge.

To strengthen the mitered joint, add a $3/4$"-wide, $1/8$"-thick hardboard spline *(Fig. 15)*. But the $3/8$"-deep kerf isn't centered on the miter *(Fig. 15a)*. So the spline is hidden with the base installed.

With the base mitered to fit, you can cut a decorative pattern on the front and side pieces *(Fig. 16)*. (Refer to page 87

for the pattern.) For a tip on cutting the base, refer to the Shop Tip on page 92. Now assemble the base pieces and glue them to the cleats (refer to *Fig. 11c*).

BRACES. Finally, to strengthen the back of the base, I added two triangle-shaped braces (S) *(Figs. 14 and 17)*. These are $3/4$"-thick pieces of stock, glued and screwed to the bottom panel and base sides.

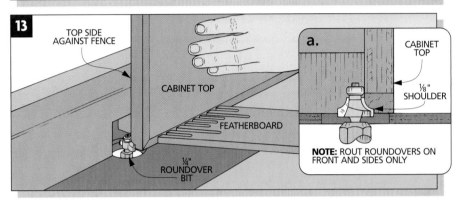

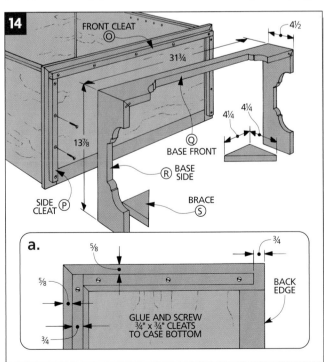

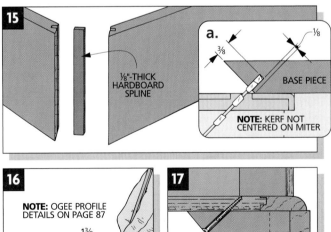

Looking at the base of the walnut cabinet on page 86, you might expect the ogee profiles are the hardest parts to make. But making the straight cut between the two profiles is more of a challenge.

There's nothing tricky about cutting out the profiles. You just follow the layout lines with your band saw (or jig saw) and sand them smooth. But this won't work when cutting along the layout line that separates the profiles.

Here, the goal is to have a line that's perfectly straight. If your blade wanders even a little, it's easy to see. So I don't cut right to the line. Instead, I'll cut on the waste side of the layout line, leaving about 1/16" of stock.

Then I switch to a flush trim bit in my router table to rout to the line. But to get a straight cut, you have to guide the bit. To do this, I use double-sided tape to "clamp" a straightedge flush with the layout line *(Fig. 1)*. Now the bearing on the bit follows the straightedge to rout the line *(Fig. 2)*.

You'll have to stop short of the profile because the diameter of the bit (1/2") won't let you into tight corners. But it's easy to finish the cut. Use a chisel to clean up the corner.

Note: I left the straightedge in place to help guide my chisel.

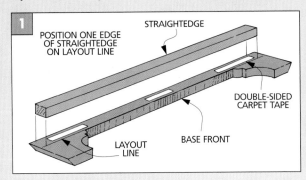

1 POSITION ONE EDGE OF STRAIGHTEDGE ON LAYOUT LINE — STRAIGHTEDGE — DOUBLE-SIDED CARPET TAPE — LAYOUT LINE — BASE FRONT

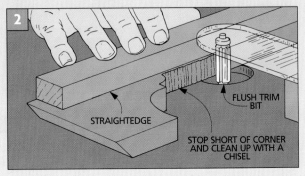

2 STRAIGHTEDGE — FLUSH TRIM BIT — STOP SHORT OF CORNER AND CLEAN UP WITH A CHISEL

DOORS & SHELF

To match the paneled construction used to build the back of the cabinet, a pair of paneled doors are added to the front. But what's a little unusual here is the joinery. It's a molded stub tenon joint that has a decorative roundover on the inside edge.

STILES AND RAILS. To build the doors, I started with the frames (stiles and rails). The width of all these pieces is the same (2$3/4$"), but their lengths vary.

To determine the length of the stiles (T), measure between the upper and lower panels and subtract $1/8$" for clearance *(Fig. 18)*. (My stiles were 30$1/8$".)

But figuring out the length of the rails (U) is a bit more complicated. Here you'll need to take into account the width of the stiles, the stub tenons on the rails, the astragal in the middle, and $1/8$" clearance between the doors *(Figs. 18 and 19)*. (My rails were 10$1/2$" long.)

Once the stiles and rails are cut to finished length, the molded stub tenon joint is cut next. This joint is a little more involved than your typical stub tenon. But I liked the idea of making the roundover an integral part of the frame rather than adding the molding later. For more on cutting this joint, refer to the article on page 94.

PLYWOOD PANEL. The next step is to add a door panel (V). This oversized piece of $1/4$"-thick plywood will be cut to fit between the frame pieces *(Fig. 18)*.

The panel is oversized because before actually doing any cutting, I covered the back side of the plywood with a piece of flexible back veneer. That way, the panel will look good from either side with the doors open. With an oversized panel, I could trim both the veneer and the plywood to final size (10$1/2$" x 25$5/8$") at the same time.

ASSEMBLY. Now you can assemble the doors. For added strength, the plywood panel is glued in the frame. Just apply an even film of glue to the tenons on the rails and also in the grooves.

ASTRAGAL AND STOP. At this point, the astragal and stop can be added. The astragal is a piece of decorative molding attached to the stile on the left-hand door *(Fig. 19)*. It hides the gap normally found between two doors on a cabinet. And the stop, attached to the astragal, holds the left-hand door closed after you've closed the right-hand one.

Because the astragal (W) is a fairly small piece of molding, I found it easier (and safer) to cut it out of an extra wide piece of $3/8$"-thick stock. All it takes are three easy steps once your workpiece is cut to match the length of the door stile. (My astragal was 30$1/8$".)

First, there's a $3/8$"-wide rabbet cut $1/8$" deep on one edge *(Fig. 19a)*. Next, a $1/8$" roundover is routed to create a beaded edge *(Fig. 19b)*. Then rip the astragal to final width ($3/4$") *(Fig. 19c)*. Finally, glue and clamp the astragal to the stile on your left-hand door.

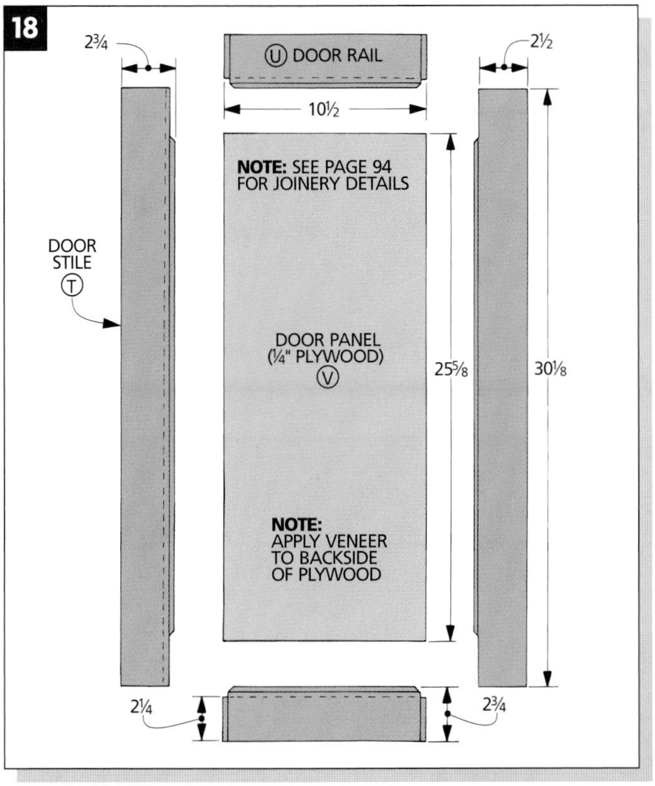
18
2¾
2½
Ⓤ DOOR RAIL
10½
NOTE: SEE PAGE 94 FOR JOINERY DETAILS
DOOR STILE Ⓣ
DOOR PANEL (¼" PLYWOOD) Ⓥ
25⅝
30⅛
NOTE: APPLY VENEER TO BACKSIDE OF PLYWOOD
2¼
2¾

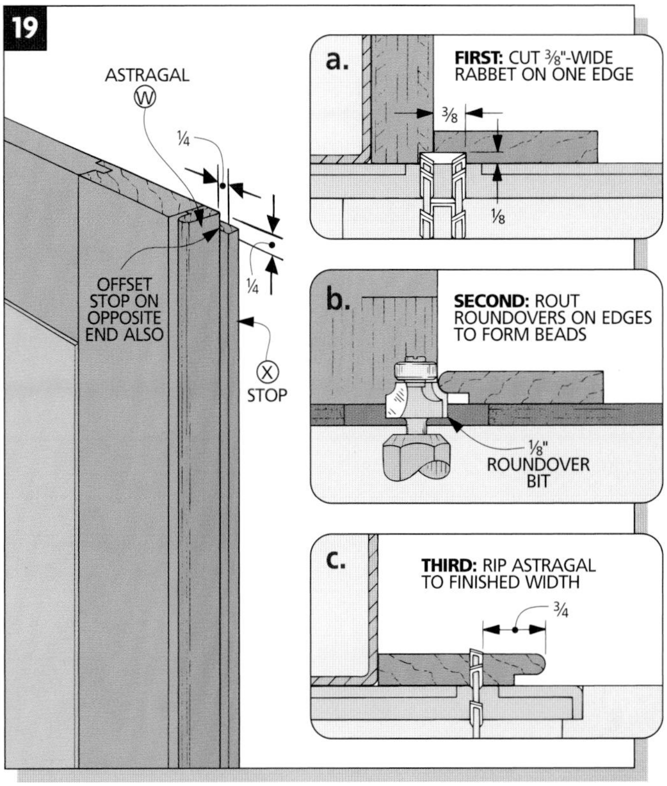
19
ASTRAGAL Ⓦ
¼
OFFSET STOP ON OPPOSITE END ALSO
¼
Ⓧ STOP
a.
FIRST: CUT ⅜"-WIDE RABBET ON ONE EDGE
⅜
⅛
b.
SECOND: ROUT ROUNDOVERS ON EDGES TO FORM BEADS
⅛" ROUNDOVER BIT
c.
THIRD: RIP ASTRAGAL TO FINISHED WIDTH
¾

Making the stop (X) is simple. It's just a $\frac{1}{4}$"-wide strip ripped from the edge of a $\frac{3}{4}$"-thick board.

The stop is cut shorter than the astragal ($29\frac{5}{8}$") for clearance between the upper and lower panels. Then it's simply glued to the back of the astragal with a $\frac{1}{4}$" overhang *(Fig. 19)*.

SHELF. Before hanging the doors, I made a shelf (Y). It's a piece of $\frac{3}{4}$"-thick plywood that's cut to fit inside the case *(Fig. 20)*. Added to the front is a strip of shelf molding (Z) that covers the edge of the plywood *(Fig. 20a)*. To hold the shelf in the cabinet, shelf pins are installed in the holes in the case sides.

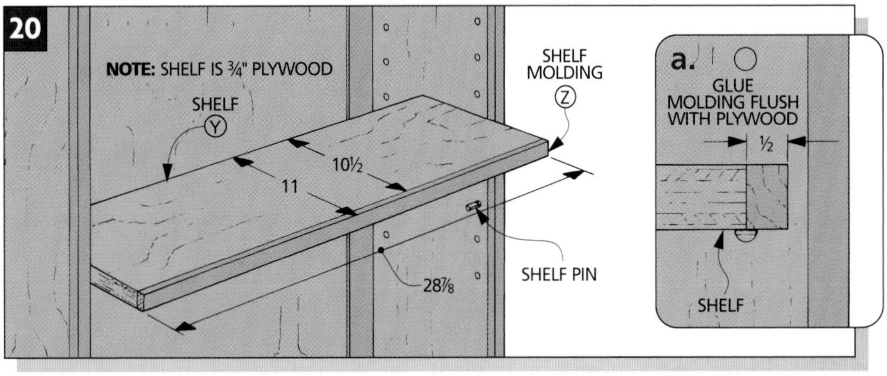
20
NOTE: SHELF IS ¾" PLYWOOD
SHELF Ⓨ
10½
11
28⅞
SHELF MOLDING Ⓩ
SHELF PIN
a.
GLUE MOLDING FLUSH WITH PLYWOOD
½
SHELF

HINGES. After installing the shelf, the doors are hung on the cabinet. There's nothing tricky here, but you want a $\frac{1}{16}$" gap at the top and bottom of the doors.

Note: One way to do this is to set the doors in the cabinet and use a couple of pennies for spacers when marking the hinge location.

Start by cutting a mortise in the door to fit the hinges and screw them in place. Then set the doors in the opening and transfer the hinge location onto the case sides. Now, mortise an opening in the sides and screw the hinges to the case *(Fig. 21)*.

KNOB AND CATCHES. Finally, to complete the cabinet, I added the rest of the hardware: a pair of ball catches and a pair of brass knobs *(Figs. 22 and 23)*.

The knobs are centered on the stiles, and the catches are positioned behind the right-hand door. You don't need any catches for the left-hand door. The stop on the astragal holds it closed. ■

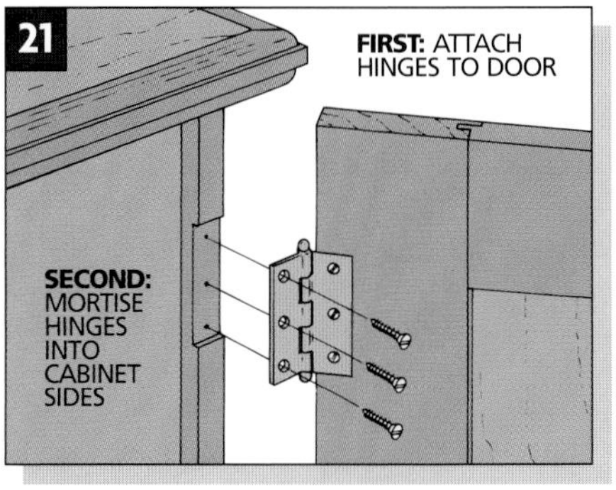
21
FIRST: ATTACH HINGES TO DOOR
SECOND: MORTISE HINGES INTO CABINET SIDES

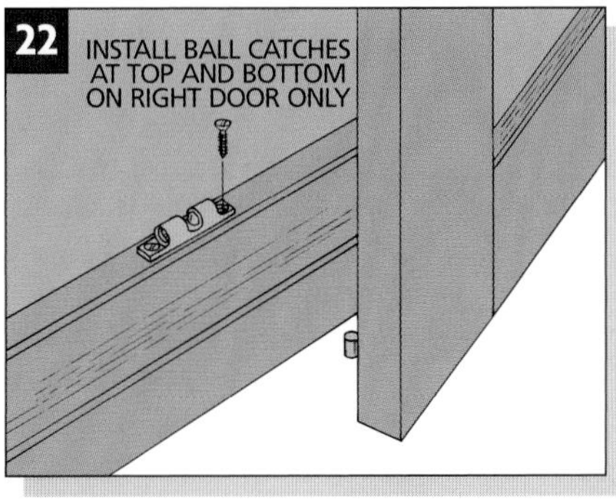
22
INSTALL BALL CATCHES AT TOP AND BOTTOM ON RIGHT DOOR ONLY

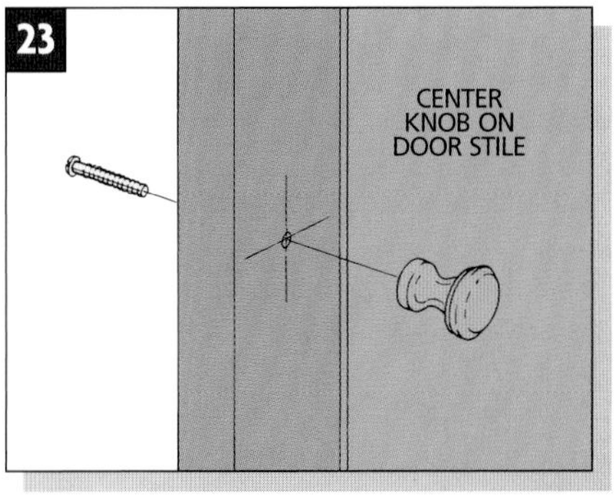
23
CENTER KNOB ON DOOR STILE

TECHNIQUE .... *Molded Stub Tenon*

There are several ways to join frame pieces (stiles and rails) together on a paneled door. But one of my personal favorites is a molded stub tenon joint (like the doors used on the walnut cabinet on page 86). And it's an easy way to add a decorative profile (a quarter-round) to the inside edge on a frame and panel door.

They make special router bits you can use to cut similar joints. But adding profiles to the stiles and rails isn't difficult. It just takes a few more steps and some careful planning to get the same results without spending a lot of money. To do this, I use my table saw, router, chisel, and a shop-made jig (see the section below).

SIZING. The first step to making a "perfect joint" is to make sure your stiles and rails are all cut to finished size. This not only means length and width, but also consistent thickness. If the thickness varies between your frame pieces, they won't fit together flush during assembly.

GROOVES. Once I cut the stiles and rails to finished size, the next step is to

cut a groove on one edge of each of the frame pieces. The width of the groove should match the thickness of the ply-wood panel *(Fig. 1)*.

But to allow for the built-in molding on the edges of the door frame, I cut these grooves a little bit deeper ($1/2$") than the grooves for a typical stub tenon joint would be. This added depth is necessary to help strengthen the door frame once the plywood door panel has

been glued in place.

Note: I like to use a rip blade when cutting the grooves on the frame pieces. The teeth are ground flat on top, so it cuts a flat-bottomed groove.

The only thing a little unusual about the groove is its location. It's not centered on the thickness like a typical stub tenon and groove joint. Instead, it's offset to provide room for the roundover *(Figs. 1a and 1b)*.

MOLDED EDGE. After cutting the grooves in all of the frame pieces, the molded edges can be routed *(Fig. 2)*. To do this, all I used was a $1/4$" roundover bit in the router table.

The only problem I found when using a roundover bit is the bearing on the end. If it falls into the grooves cut on the edges of the frame pieces, it can gouge your workpiece. So instead of relying on the bearing to guide my workpiece, I decided to use the router table fence.

I start by setting the router bit to the correct height. Simply adjust the fence to make a light cut. Then check the size

SHOP-MADE MITER JIG

The secret to fitting a molded stub tenon joint is to use a simple, shop-made miter jig. It fits over the frame pieces and can be used two ways. First, it guides your chisel when cutting the miters on the molded edge (see photo below right). And second, by flipping the jig over, it can also help when removing the waste from the molded edge on the stiles.

The miter jig is easy to make, con-sisting of only three parts. Just glue a spacer between two guide rails and cut a miter on one end (see drawing below). This forms a pocket for the frame pieces to fit into. The depth of this pocket is equal to the distance from the edge of your stile or rail to the shoulder of the molded edge. (This measure-ment was $2^1/2$" in my case.)

To use the jig to miter the molded edge, simply set it over your frame piece and clamp it in place. The angle will then help guide your chisel to cut 45° miters.

By turning the jig over, it can be used to clean up the molded edge on your stiles (refer to *Figs. 6 and 7* on page 96). The jig guides your chisel and keeps it square to the workpiece.

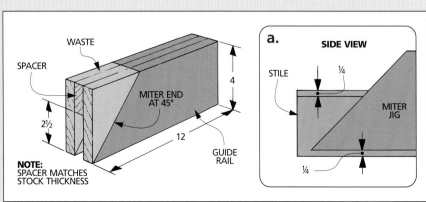

WASTE
SPACER
MITER END AT 45°
$2^1/2$
12
GUIDE RAIL
4
NOTE: SPACER MATCHES STOCK THICKNESS

a. SIDE VIEW
STILE
$1/4$
MITER JIG
$1/4$

of the shoulder *(Fig. 2a)*. Once it's set to rout a $\frac{1}{8}$"-deep shoulder, I move the router fence until the bearing on the bit is perfectly flush with the edge of the fence *(Fig. 2b)*. Now rout the molded edge on all the frame pieces.

TENONS. After you have completed the roundovers, stub tenons can be cut on the ends of the rails. I like to use a dado blade to cut these tenons. This way, each face can be cut to finished size (length and depth) with a single pass *(Fig. 3)*.

But there are a couple of things that are different about cutting the tenons for this type of joint. First, the tenons aren't centered on the thickness of the rails. Instead, they're offset to match the location of the groove already cut in each frame piece.

Something else that's a little different with this type of joint is the *length* of the tenon. The front cheek is shorter

($\frac{1}{4}$" long) than the back cheek ($\frac{1}{2}$" long) (see photo at right). Here's the reason why.

The back cheek is cut $\frac{1}{2}$" long to match the full depth of the groove that's already been cut in the stiles *(Fig. 3a)*. This way, once the frame pieces are assembled, the end of the tenon will fit flush with the bottom of the groove. The $\frac{1}{2}$" length also lets the back shoulder of the tenon fit flush with the inside edge of the stile.

Once you have the tenon length set, adjusting the depth is easy. Simply raise the blade until the cut is flush with the *back* shoulder of the groove *(Fig. 3a)*.

The front cheek is shorter for a different reason. It has to match the height of the molded edge *(Fig. 3b)*. This way, just like the back shoulder, the front shoulder will fit flush with the inside edge of the stile.

Here again, the depth is set just like

Molded edge. *After cutting a groove on the inside edge of the door frame, a molded edge is routed on all the pieces. Then offset tenons are cut on the rails.*

the back cheek. But this time, it's cut flush with the *front* shoulder of the groove *(Fig. 3b)*.

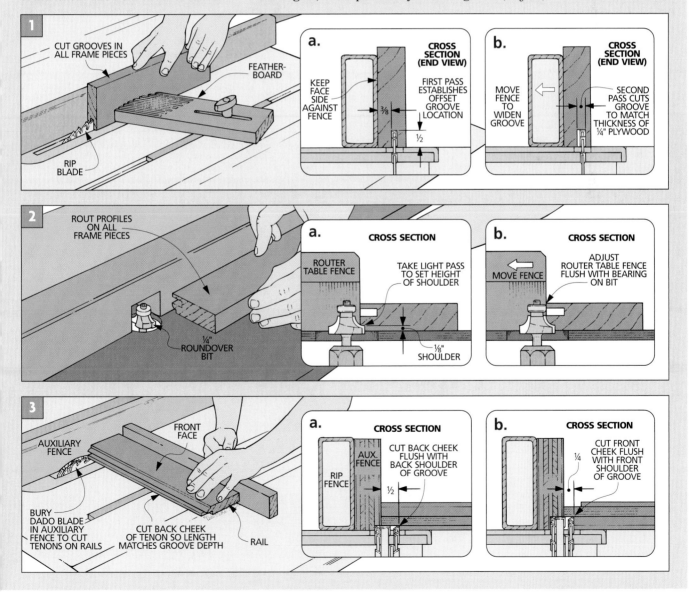

1
CUT GROOVES IN ALL FRAME PIECES
FEATHER-BOARD
RIP BLADE

a. KEEP FACE SIDE AGAINST FENCE — FIRST PASS ESTABLISHES OFFSET GROOVE LOCATION — CROSS SECTION (END VIEW) — $\frac{3}{8}$ — $\frac{1}{2}$

b. MOVE FENCE TO WIDEN GROOVE — SECOND PASS CUTS GROOVE TO MATCH THICKNESS OF $\frac{1}{4}$" PLYWOOD — CROSS SECTION (END VIEW)

2
ROUT PROFILES ON ALL FRAME PIECES
$\frac{1}{4}$" ROUNDOVER BIT

a. ROUTER TABLE FENCE — TAKE LIGHT PASS TO SET HEIGHT OF SHOULDER — $\frac{1}{8}$" SHOULDER — CROSS SECTION

b. MOVE FENCE — ADJUST ROUTER TABLE FENCE FLUSH WITH BEARING ON BIT — CROSS SECTION

3
AUXILIARY FENCE
FRONT FACE
BURY DADO BLADE IN AUXILIARY FENCE TO CUT TENONS ON RAILS
CUT BACK CHEEK OF TENON SO LENGTH MATCHES GROOVE DEPTH
RAIL

a. RIP FENCE — AUX. FENCE — CUT BACK CHEEK FLUSH WITH BACK SHOULDER OF GROOVE — $\frac{1}{2}$ — CROSS SECTION

b. CUT FRONT CHEEK FLUSH WITH FRONT SHOULDER OF GROOVE — $\frac{1}{4}$ — CROSS SECTION

After the tenons and grooves are cut and the profile's been routed, you might think this joint is ready to fit together. But before you can do that, there's still a little work to do to the molded edge.

MITER RAILS. The first step is to miter the molded edge at the ends of the rails. To do this, clamp the miter jig over the rail so the 45° angle on the jig is aligned with the corner of the molded edge (*Figs. 4 and 4a* and the bottom of page 94). Then use a sharp chisel to remove most of the waste. But on the final pass, I made a light cut and let the jig guide the chisel to cut the angle.

MARK STILES. Once you have the miters cut on the rails, the next step is to work on the molded edges on the stiles. Here, before the frame pieces will fit together, part of the molded edge is removed, and a mating miter is cut.

The most accurate way to mark the locations for the miters is to use the rails as a guide. Insert the rail in the stile and align a try square with the

rail's shoulder *(Fig. 5)*. Then make a mark on the shoulder of the stile to indicate where the angle starts *(Fig. 5a)*.

REMOVE WASTE FROM STILE. Now you can remove the waste from the molded edge. Here again, I used the miter jig. Only now, I set the jig on its back and used the opposite end *(Figs. 6 and 6a)*.

The goal is to remove most of the waste with light cuts. Stop short of the layout line that marks the start of the miter *(Fig. 6a)*. Then, once most of the waste is removed, rest the chisel on the edge of the jig to make your final cut *(Figs. 7 and 7a)*. But be careful. You don't want to damage the 1/8" shoulder previously cut by the roundover bit.

MITER STILE. Once the waste has been removed, the final step to completing this joint is mitering the molded edge of the stile *(Fig. 8)*. Just like the rails, I used the angled end of the jig to cut the miter. Simply align the jig with the layout mark on the stile before you start to cut *(Fig. 8a)*.

It's a good idea to test the fit of the joint as you trim away the waste. To do

Remove waste. *The secret to making a tight-fitting molded stub tenon joint is carefully paring away the waste from both the shoulder and the molded edge.*

this, I made a cut and slid the rail up to the miter to check the fit *(Fig. 9)*. The part of the rail that extends past the end of the stile is an indicator of how much stock still has to be removed *(Fig. 9a)*. Then once all the corners are complete, you're ready to glue the door together.

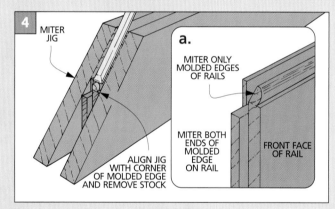

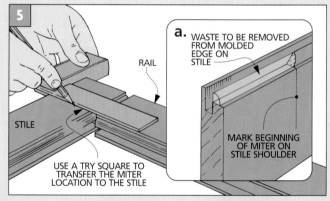

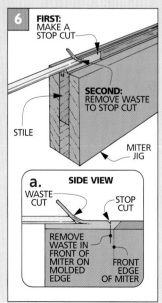

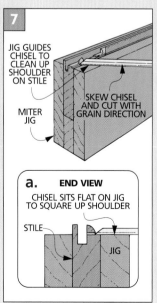

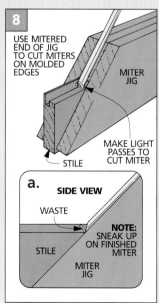

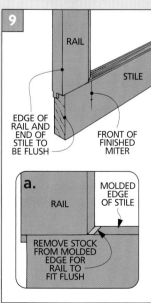

DESIGNER'S NOTEBOOK

Adding extra shelves to the inside of the walnut cabinet to suit your needs is quite simple. It doesn't take much work to turn those shelves into a functional wine rack.

CONSTRUCTION NOTES:

■ If you plan to include a wine rack, you'll need to add space inside the cabinet. To do this, just add 2" to each part that affects the *depth* of the cabinet (the upper, lower, and top panels, side moldings, case sides, and base sides). See the Materials List below for parts and new measurements.

■ Once you're finished building the cabinet, cut *two* $^3/_4$"-plywood shelves, 2" wider than the shelf for the regular cabinet. Racks will then be added to these to hold wine bottles horizontally (see drawing at right).

■ Now you can cut blanks for the front racks (AA) and back racks (BB) from $^3/_4$"-thick hardwood (see drawing below). To make the two wine racks (one for each shelf), start with each blank $5^1/_8$" wide. (These blanks are then ripped in half after the holes are drilled.)

Note: For *one* rack, cut each piece to rough width (3") and finished length.

■ Use a $1^1/_2$"-dia. Forstner bit to drill out the recesses in the front racks (AA).

■ For the recesses in the back racks (BB), use a compass to lay out the cut lines. Then make the cuts with a band saw or jig saw. (To drill holes in a $5^1/_8$"-wide blank, use a fly cutter.)

■ Rip the front and back racks to finished width ($2^1/_2$").

■ Now position the racks on each of the shelves and secure each piece with three woodscrews (see drawing).

WINE RACK

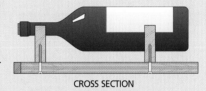

CROSS SECTION

MATERIALS LIST

CHANGED PARTS

A	Upper Panel (1)	$^3/_4$ ply - $12^3/_4$ x $28^1/_2$
B	Lower Panel (1)	$^3/_4$ ply - $12^3/_4$ x $28^1/_2$
E	Case Side Mldg. (4)	$^3/_4$ x $1^3/_4$ - $15^3/_4$
F	Case Sides (2)	$^3/_4$ ply - 14 x $30^1/_4$
K	Top Panel (1)	$^3/_4$ ply - $15^1/_8$ x $30^3/_4$
N	Top Side Mldg. (2)	$^1/_2$ x $^3/_4$ - $15^7/_8$
P	Side Cleats (2)	$^3/_4$ x $^3/_4$ - $14^3/_8$
R	Base Sides (2)	$^3/_4$ x $4^1/_2$ - $15^7/_8$
Y	Shelves (2)	$^3/_4$ ply - $12^1/_2$ x $28^7/_8$

NEW PARTS

AA	Front Rack (2)	$^3/_4$ x $2^1/_2$ - $28^7/_8$
BB	Back Rack (2)	$^3/_4$ x $2^1/_2$ - $28^7/_8$

Note: Need two shelf moldings (part Z).

HARDWARE SUPPLIES

Need 12 additional No. 8 x 2" Fh woodscrews and 4 additional shelf supports.

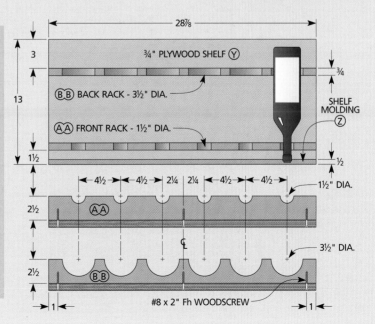

Cherry Wardrobe

Just because a project is big doesn't mean it has to be complicated to build. When planning this wardrobe, I kept the design and joinery simple and the materials relatively inexpensive.

One problem with large furniture projects is that they can seem much more intimidating than they really are.

Take this cherry wardrobe, for instance. You might think at first glance that a project this size would be really complex to design and build. But the joinery isn't complicated at all. The case is assembled with simple mortise and tenon joints, rabbets, and stub tenon and groove joints.

Even the curved upper rails on the doors are easier than they look. Rather than buy a special router bit, I cut the groove to hold the door panels before the curve is cut. It's deeper than usual, but it can be done on the table saw, and it also lets me avoid cutting curves on the panels that fit into the rail (see page 106 for more on this).

INNER CASE. Adding the optional four-drawer inner case might also seem like a formidable challenge, but it just slides inside the wardrobe.

Complete instructions for building this case are in the Designer's Notebook on pages 108-109.

MATERIALS. Another question that often comes up with large projects is cost. After all, hardwoods can be expensive. But take a closer look. Much of what you see is plywood, not hardwood.

Both the door and side panels are made up of two layers of $1/4$" cherry plywood placed back-to-back. Two layers are used because $1/4$" plywood has only one good face, and I wanted the doors to look as good when they were opened as when they were closed.

Of course, other combinations of hardwood and plywood will also work, depending on how you want the final project to look.

FINISH. Finishing a project this size is a big job, so I used a wipe-on varnish. To apply the finish to the large areas quickly, I found that a common paint pad works well.

EXPLODED VIEW

OVERALL DIMENSIONS:
46W x 22D x 72H

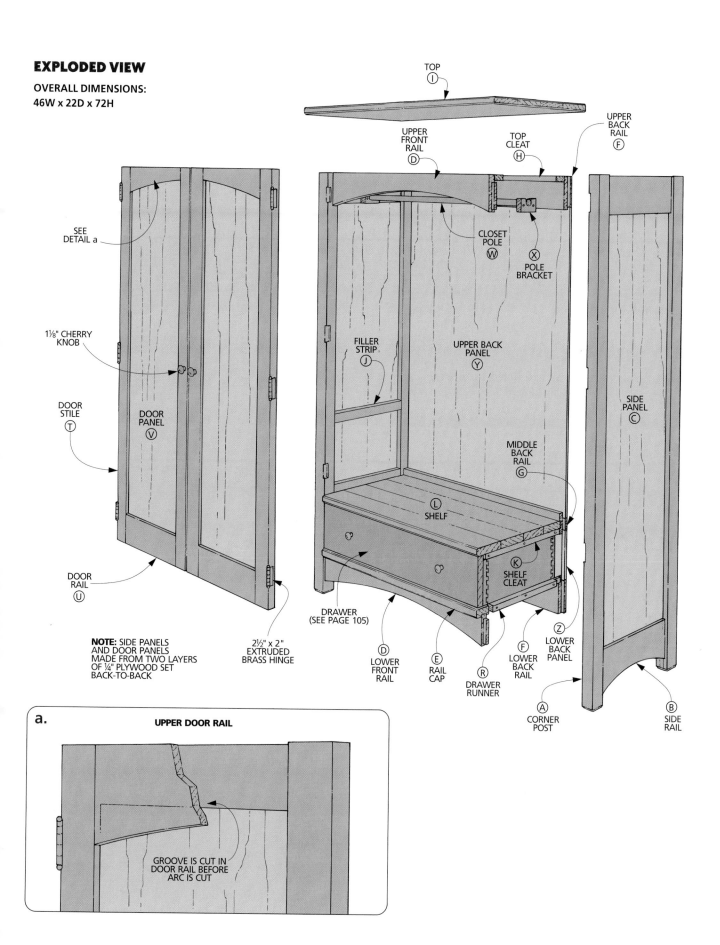

TOP
Ⓘ

UPPER
FRONT
RAIL
Ⓓ

TOP
CLEAT
Ⓗ

UPPER
BACK
RAIL
Ⓕ

SEE
DETAIL a

CLOSET
POLE
Ⓦ

POLE
BRACKET
Ⓧ

1⅛" CHERRY
KNOB

FILLER
STRIP
Ⓙ

UPPER BACK
PANEL
Ⓨ

DOOR
STILE
Ⓣ

DOOR
PANEL
Ⓥ

SIDE
PANEL
Ⓒ

MIDDLE
BACK
RAIL
Ⓖ

SHELF
Ⓛ

DOOR
RAIL
Ⓤ

SHELF
CLEAT
Ⓚ

NOTE: SIDE PANELS
AND DOOR PANELS
MADE FROM TWO LAYERS
OF ¼" PLYWOOD SET
BACK-TO-BACK

2½" x 2"
EXTRUDED
BRASS HINGE

DRAWER
(SEE PAGE 105)

LOWER
FRONT
RAIL
Ⓓ

RAIL
CAP
Ⓔ

DRAWER
RUNNER
Ⓡ

LOWER
BACK
RAIL
Ⓕ

LOWER
BACK
PANEL
Ⓩ

CORNER
POST
Ⓐ

SIDE
RAIL
Ⓑ

a.

UPPER DOOR RAIL

GROOVE IS CUT IN
DOOR RAIL BEFORE
ARC IS CUT

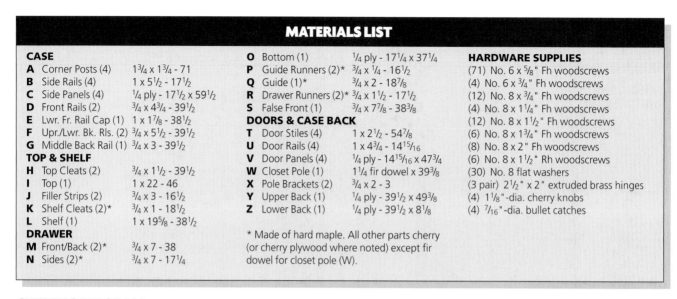

CASE

A	Corner Posts (4)	$1\frac{3}{4}$ x $1\frac{3}{4}$ - 71
B	Side Rails (4)	1 x $5\frac{1}{2}$ - $17\frac{1}{2}$
C	Side Panels (4)	$\frac{1}{4}$ ply - $17\frac{1}{2}$ x $59\frac{1}{2}$
D	Front Rails (2)	$\frac{3}{4}$ x $4\frac{3}{4}$ - $39\frac{1}{2}$
E	Lwr. Fr. Rail Cap (1)	1 x $1\frac{7}{8}$ - $38\frac{1}{2}$
F	Upr./Lwr. Bk. Rls. (2)	$\frac{3}{4}$ x $5\frac{1}{2}$ - $39\frac{1}{2}$
G	Middle Back Rail (1)	$\frac{3}{4}$ x 3 - $39\frac{1}{2}$

TOP & SHELF

H	Top Cleats (2)	$\frac{3}{4}$ x $1\frac{1}{2}$ - $39\frac{1}{2}$
I	Top (1)	1 x 22 - 46
J	Filler Strips (2)	$\frac{3}{4}$ x 3 - $16\frac{1}{2}$
K	Shelf Cleats (2)*	$\frac{3}{4}$ x 1 - $18\frac{1}{2}$
L	Shelf (1)	1 x $19\frac{5}{8}$ - $38\frac{1}{2}$

DRAWER

M	Front/Back (2)*	$\frac{3}{4}$ x 7 - 38
N	Sides (2)*	$\frac{3}{4}$ x 7 - $17\frac{1}{4}$

O	Bottom (1)	$\frac{1}{4}$ ply - $17\frac{1}{4}$ x $37\frac{1}{4}$
P	Guide Runners (2)*	$\frac{3}{4}$ x $\frac{1}{4}$ - $16\frac{1}{2}$
Q	Guide (1)*	$\frac{3}{4}$ x 2 - $18\frac{7}{8}$
R	Drawer Runners (2)*	$\frac{3}{4}$ x $1\frac{1}{2}$ - $17\frac{1}{2}$
S	False Front (1)	$\frac{3}{4}$ x $7\frac{7}{8}$ - $38\frac{3}{8}$

DOORS & CASE BACK

T	Door Stiles (4)	1 x $2\frac{1}{2}$ - $54\frac{7}{8}$
U	Door Rails (4)	1 x $4\frac{3}{4}$ - $14\frac{15}{16}$
V	Door Panels (4)	$\frac{1}{4}$ ply - $14\frac{15}{16}$ x $47\frac{3}{4}$
W	Closet Pole (1)	$1\frac{1}{4}$ fir dowel x $39\frac{3}{8}$
X	Pole Brackets (2)	$\frac{3}{4}$ x 2 - 3
Y	Upper Back (1)	$\frac{1}{4}$ ply - $39\frac{1}{2}$ x $49\frac{3}{8}$
Z	Lower Back (1)	$\frac{1}{4}$ ply - $39\frac{1}{2}$ x $8\frac{1}{8}$

* Made of hard maple. All other parts cherry (or cherry plywood where noted) except fir dowel for closet pole (W).

HARDWARE SUPPLIES

- (71) No. 6 x $\frac{5}{8}$" Fh woodscrews
- (4) No. 6 x $\frac{3}{4}$" Fh woodscrews
- (12) No. 8 x $\frac{3}{4}$" Fh woodscrews
- (4) No. 8 x $1\frac{1}{4}$" Fh woodscrews
- (12) No. 8 x $1\frac{1}{2}$" Fh woodscrews
- (6) No. 8 x $1\frac{3}{4}$" Fh woodscrews
- (8) No. 8 x 2" Fh woodscrews
- (6) No. 8 x $1\frac{1}{2}$" Rh woodscrews
- (30) No. 8 flat washers
- (3 pair) $2\frac{1}{2}$" x 2" extruded brass hinges
- (4) $1\frac{1}{8}$"-dia. cherry knobs
- (4) $\frac{7}{16}$"-dia. bullet catches

CUTTING DIAGRAM

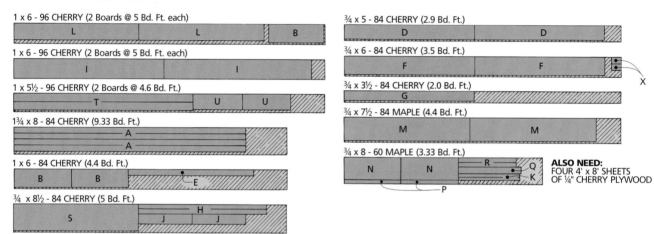

1 x 6 - 96 CHERRY (2 Boards @ 5 Bd. Ft. each) — L L B
1 x 6 - 96 CHERRY (2 Boards @ 5 Bd. Ft. each) — I I
1 x $5\frac{1}{2}$ - 96 CHERRY (2 Boards @ 4.6 Bd. Ft.) — T U U
$1\frac{3}{4}$ x 8 - 84 CHERRY (9.33 Bd. Ft.) — A A
1 x 6 - 84 CHERRY (4.4 Bd. Ft.) — B B E
$\frac{3}{4}$ x $8\frac{1}{2}$ - 84 CHERRY (5 Bd. Ft.) — S H J J

$\frac{3}{4}$ x 5 - 84 CHERRY (2.9 Bd. Ft.) — D D
$\frac{3}{4}$ x 6 - 84 CHERRY (3.5 Bd. Ft.) — F F X
$\frac{3}{4}$ x $3\frac{1}{2}$ - 84 CHERRY (2.0 Bd. Ft.) — G
$\frac{3}{4}$ x $7\frac{1}{2}$ - 84 MAPLE (4.4 Bd. Ft.) — M M
$\frac{3}{4}$ x 8 - 60 MAPLE (3.33 Bd. Ft.) — N N R Q K P

ALSO NEED:
FOUR 4' x 8' SHEETS
OF $\frac{1}{4}$" CHERRY PLYWOOD

CASE SIDES

The easiest way to build the case of this wardrobe is to do it in sections. I started with the sides of the wardrobe. Then I connected these side assemblies with rails at the front and back.

CORNER POSTS. The first step is to make the corner posts (A). This is like building a fence. You set the corner posts and work your way in. With these corner posts, there are several things to cut: grooves for the sides, mortises for the front, and rabbets for the back.

The trick is getting the grooves, mortises, and rabbets positioned correctly on each post *(Fig. 1)*. So after I cut the corner posts to size from 8/4 stock, I took the time to carefully lay out the cuts on each post *(Figs. 1 and 2)*.

When all the grooves, mortises, and rabbets have been laid out, the first step is to cut a groove $\frac{3}{4}$" from the inside

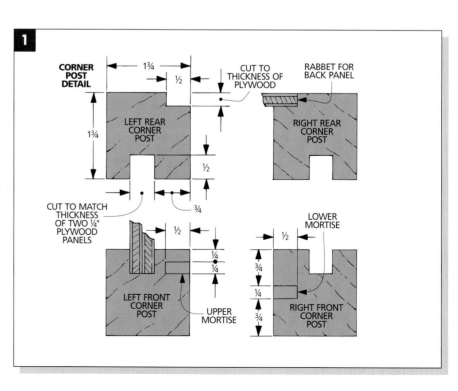

1

CORNER POST DETAIL

$1\frac{3}{4}$ • $\frac{1}{2}$ • CUT TO THICKNESS OF PLYWOOD • RABBET FOR BACK PANEL

LEFT REAR CORNER POST • $1\frac{3}{4}$ • $\frac{1}{2}$

RIGHT REAR CORNER POST

CUT TO MATCH THICKNESS OF TWO $\frac{1}{4}$" PLYWOOD PANELS • $\frac{3}{4}$

LEFT FRONT CORNER POST • $\frac{1}{2}$ • $\frac{1}{4}$ $\frac{1}{4}$ • UPPER MORTISE

LOWER MORTISE • $\frac{1}{2}$ • $\frac{3}{4}$ $\frac{1}{4}$ $\frac{3}{4}$ • RIGHT FRONT CORNER POST

face of each post. This groove will hold a couple of side rails and *two* $\frac{1}{4}$"-thick plywood side panels.

The reason for using two panels is simple. Finding $\frac{1}{2}$" cherry plywood is difficult, and $\frac{1}{4}$" plywood has only one good face. So to get two good faces, I used two sheets and set them back-to-back (see photo at right). This determines the width of each groove.

Since these grooves run the length of the posts, there will be gaps at the bottoms after the sides are assembled. To remedy this, I cut some $1\frac{3}{4}$"-long plugs and glued them in the grooves flush with the bottom of each post *(Fig. 2b)*. This will fill the gap and create a shoulder for the bottom rail to sit on later.

After putting plugs in all four grooves, I decided to cut the mortises and rabbets on the posts for the front and back rails before assembling the sides.

First, I worked on the front posts. Each post requires two mortises: one for the upper rail and another for the

lower rail *(Fig. 2a)*. These mortises are the same size, but they don't line up with each other. The lower mortise is centered, while the upper rail mortise is offset towards the inside of the case to allow room for the doors.

When the mortises on the front posts are complete, it's time to set them aside and work on the back corner posts. Both back posts need a $\frac{1}{2}$"-wide rabbet on their back, inside edges that's deep enough to hold the $\frac{1}{4}$" plywood backs (there are two — an upper back and a lower one) added later *(Fig. 1)*.

Finally, I chamfered the bottom edges of all four corner posts *(Fig. 3)*.

RAILS. Next, a pair of rails can be added. These rails connect the corner posts to create a frame. The 1"-thick side rails (B) are the same size ($5\frac{1}{2}$" x $17\frac{1}{2}$"). And they also have grooves cut on their inside edges that match the grooves on the corner posts.

The lower rail still requires a little more work. First, a shoulder needs to be

Panel Construction.

The groove on this side rail has been sized to hold two $\frac{1}{4}$"-thick plywood panels, instead of just one $\frac{1}{2}$" panel. These panels are set back-to-back, so there's a good face both inside and out.

cut on the bottom edge of the stub tenon *(Fig. 4)*. (The shoulder on top is created by the groove.) Second, there's an arc cut along the bottom edge (see the Shop Jig on page 107 to lay out the arcs).

SIDE PANELS. Now the posts and rails can be dry-assembled to measure the opening for the side panels. Cut the two $\frac{1}{4}$" plywood side panels (C) for each assembly to fit the grooves. Then glue the posts, rails, and panels together.

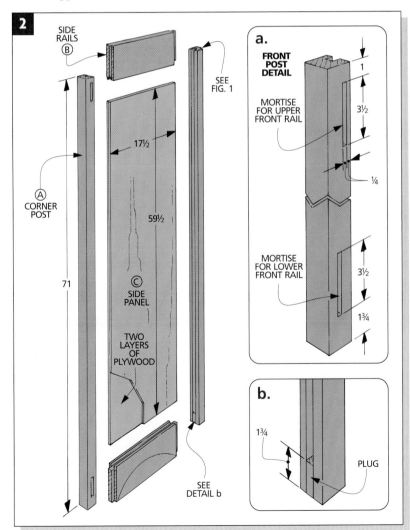

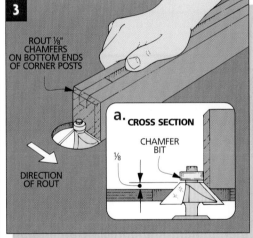

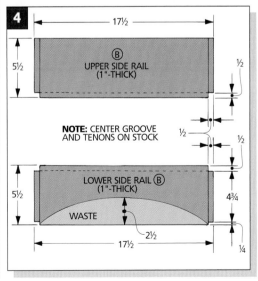

The side assemblies can now be joined with a pair of rails at the front of the case.

FRONT RAILS. The front rails (D) are identical. First, cut $3/4$"-thick blanks to finished length and width *(Fig. 5d)*. (Mine were $4^3/4$" x $39^1/2$".) Then cut tenons on both ends of each blank. These tenons are sized to fit the mortises in the corner posts (refer to *Fig. 2a*).

Note: The top front rail fits flush with the top of the side rails. But the lower rail sits $3/4$" below the bottom side rails to leave room for a cap added later *(Fig. 5c)*.

Now the only thing left is to cut a gentle arc at the bottom of each piece (see the Shop Jig on page 107.)

Once the front rails are complete, glue them between the two sides. Since the case is only being held together at the front, make sure it's square.

RAIL CAP. Before moving to the back of the case, a "cap" is added to the lower rail to create a lip below the drawer that will be added later *(Fig. 5c)*.

This rail cap (E) is cut from 1"-thick stock to fit between the posts. I wanted this cap flush with the back edges of the posts, but the cap should stick out $1/8$" in front to create a lip below the drawer.

To hold the cap in position, a groove is cut on its bottom face *(Fig. 5c)*. But the groove won't be centered on the width of the cap. Also keep in mind that the depth of this groove should put the top of the rail cap flush with the top of the lower rails on the sides. (The depth of my groove was $1/4$".)

To complete the rail cap, create $1/8$" chamfers on all four edges of the front face *(Fig. 5c)*. Then glue the rail cap to the lower front rail.

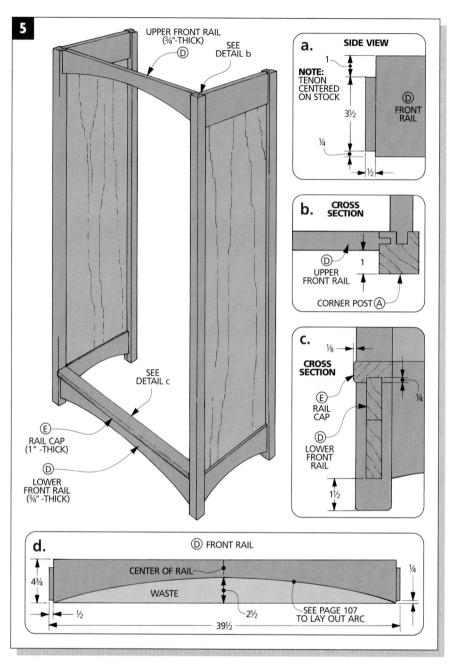

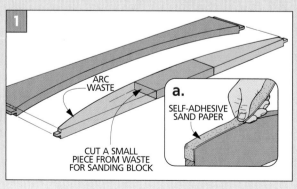

After adding the front rails, I started work on the back side. There are three rails that connect the corner posts in back *(Fig. 6)*. They also hold the two ¼"-thick plywood back panels (added later), and the middle back rail will hold a shelf (refer to *Fig. 13* on page 104).

RACK RAILS. All three back rails are ¾" thick and are cut to the same length *(Fig. 6)*. They have to be long enough to hold the case square, so measure the opening at the front of the case and add 1" for the tongues on the ends of the rails. (Mine were 39½" long.) Both the upper and lower back rails (F) are 5½" wide, while the middle rail (G) is 3" wide.

The rabbets that hold the rails have already been cut on the back posts. So the next step is to cut a tongue on each end *(Figs. 6a and 6b)*. The length and depth of these tongues should match the rabbets on the posts.

Next, I cut rabbets on the rails that hold the back panels *(Fig. 6b)*. These rabbets are identical to the ones on the back corner posts — ½" wide and deep enough to match the thickness of ¼" plywood. Cut the rabbets on the back inside edge of the upper and lower rails, but on *both* back edges of the middle rail.

SHELF POCKET. The middle rail still needs work. There's a 1"-thick shelf that will be added to the inside of the case, so I created a "pocket" in the middle rail to support it. This pocket is a ⅜"-deep groove that's cut on the front face of the rail, ⅞" from the bottom *(Fig. 6b)*.

INSTALLATION. Now the back rails are glued and screwed in place. First, the upper rail is installed flush with the top of the case *(Fig. 7)*. But the lower rail should end up level with the rail cap in front *(Fig. 8)*. To do this accurately, I set a framing square on the cap, held it against the front corner post, and

marked the position of the rail.

The position of the middle rail is important. It determines the position of the shelf (added later), which in turn determines the height of the lower drawer underneath the shelf. I glued and screwed the middle rail 7⅛" up

from the top of the lower rail *(Fig. 9)*.

Note: At this point, you could cut the upper and lower back panels to size from ¼"-thick plywood and screw them in place. But I decided not to add them yet. It's easier to install the shelf and lower drawer while the backs are off.

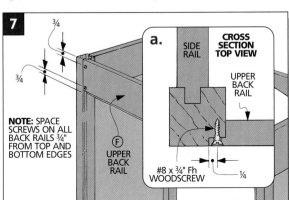

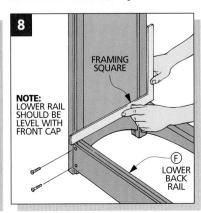

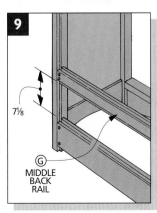

Now it's time to add a top and a shelf. Since these are both solid 1"-thick wood panels, they must be able to expand and contract with changes in humidity. The solution for both the top and the shelf was to use cleats, but they're not used the same way.

TOP. I started at the top, cutting two ³/₄"-thick top cleats (H) to fit between the side rails *(Fig. 10)*. The front cleat will work without any problem, but the back corner posts get in the way. So I notched the corners of the back cleat *(Fig. 10a)*.

To solve the expansion/contraction problem, I drilled oversize mounting holes *(Figs. 10a and 11a)*. These holes are counterbored to hide the round-head screws used to attach the top.

Now the cleats can be glued flush with the top of the case *(Fig. 10)*.

To add the top (I), start with a 1"-thick oversize panel. Cut it to size (mine was 22" x 46") and chamfer the top and bottom edges *(Fig. 11)*. When securing the top, center it side-to-side with a ¹/₈" overhang in back *(Fig. 11a)*.

SHELF. Before adding the shelf, I made some filler strips (J) to fill the gap that will be formed between the shelf and side panels *(Fig. 12)*. These strips are ripped 3" wide and are cut to fit between the corner posts.

After gluing the filler strips in place, cut two hard maple cleats (K) for the ends of the shelf to rest on *(Fig. 12)*. These are 1"-wide strips, screwed to the inside of the case.

But positioning these cleats is a little more work than with the top cleats. They have to set back at least ⁷/₈" from the front of the case *(Fig. 12a)*. And at the back, they must line up with the bottom of the groove on the middle back rail *(Fig. 12)*.

Once the cleats are in place, the shelf (L) is glued up and cut to size *(Fig. 13)*. The shelf should be deep (wide) enough so that when it sticks out ¹/₈" in front, there's still ¹/₄" that fits inside the pocket in the middle back rail *(Fig. 13b)*. And like the rail cap that sits below the shelf, all four front edges are chamfered.

When installing the shelf, I wanted to direct the expansion of the shelf panel into the pocket on the back rail. To do this, I attached the shelf with glue and screws in the front only. The pocket holds the shelf at the back and gives it room to expand.

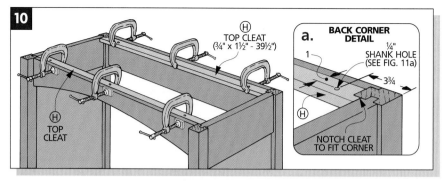

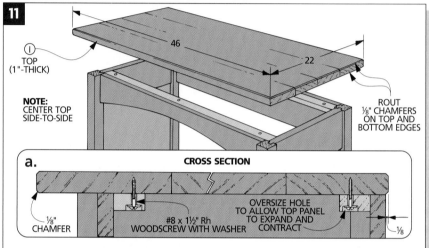

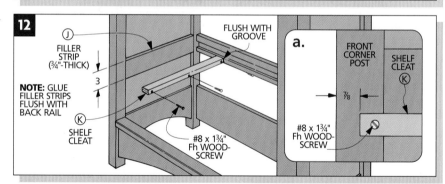

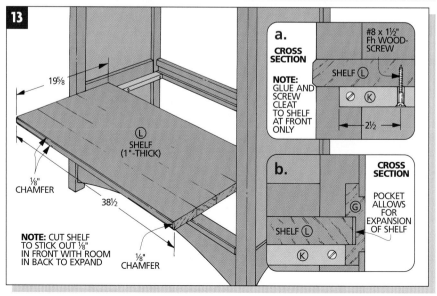

Now you can build the drawer under the shelf. I made the drawer from hard maple using a dovetail jig and a $\frac{1}{2}$" bit *(Fig. 14)*. The height of the drawer is based on the dovetails (I wanted a half pin at the top and bottom). Size the drawer so it sets back $\frac{3}{4}$" from the front of the posts to allow for a false front (S) and has room in the back for a stop *(Figs. 17 and 18)*.

The $\frac{1}{4}$" plywood bottom (O) is located $\frac{5}{16}$" up to allow for a guide *(Fig. 14a)*.

GUIDE. After the drawer is glued up, I began on the guide system. The drawer follows a centered guide (Q) that rides in a channel under the drawer. (For more on this, see Shop Info on page 110.)

To create the channel, cut a centered notch on the drawer front and back *(Fig. 14b)*. This notch determines the width of the channel. Then add two guide runners (P) to the drawer bottom.

Next, cut the drawer guide to fit the channel and install it *(Fig. 15)*. Rabbet its ends so it can be screwed to the front rail cap and back rail *(Figs. 15a and 15b)*.

RUNNERS. The weight of the drawer shouldn't rest on the guide. So cut two drawer runners (R) to size and notch the back corners so they fit around the

posts in back *(Fig. 16)*. These runners are installed $\frac{1}{16}$" above the rail cap in front *(Fig. 16a)* to create the gap needed between the rail cap and drawer.

FALSE FRONT. Now add the false front (S) to the drawer front *(Fig. 17)*. This false front is cut to fit the opening minus

$\frac{1}{16}$" on each side for clearance. Screw the false front to the drawer, centered side-to-side with the bottom edges flush *(Fig. 17a)*. Then add two cherry knobs.

DRAWER STOPS. Finally, to stop the drawer at the back, glue two stop blocks to the back corner posts *(Fig. 18)*.

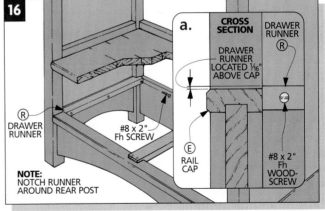

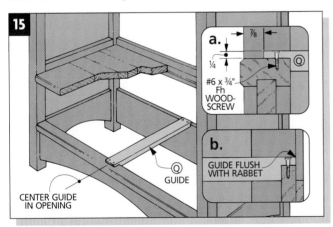

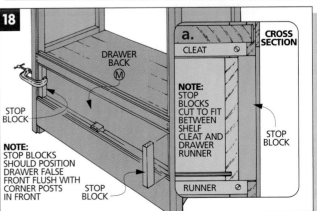

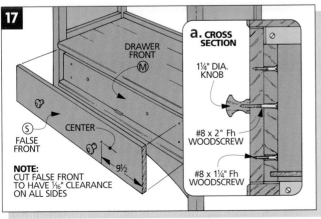

Next, I started on the doors. But before beginning to build them, you need to figure out their overall size.

The doors are inset in the case, so I made mine $1/8$" shorter than the opening to allow a $1/16$" gap at the top and bottom (*Fig. 22a*). Then I did the same with the side-to-side measurement. This way I can trim the inside edges of the doors until there's a perfect $1/16$" gap between them to match the gap at the top, bottom, and sides (*Fig. 22b*).

I started the doors by cutting both the 1"-thick stiles (T) and rails (U) to size (*Fig. 19*). The next step is to cut the stub tenon and groove joints that connect the frame. These are the same joints that were used on the side panels earlier, but there is one difference. The upper rails have arcs cut along the bottom edges to match the arc cut on the lower front rail (refer to *Fig. 22*).

UPPER RAIL GROOVE. Cutting the arc isn't a problem, but the groove in the arc is another matter. You could use a slot cutter bit and a router, but instead of cutting the groove after the arc, I cut the groove *first* on the table saw. I made this groove deeper and then left the panels square (*Fig. 19*).

To do this, raise the blade to 2" and make a second pass on the upper rails only (*Fig. 20*). Then dry-assemble the

door frame and cut the panels (V) to fit in the grooves.

ARCS. Now the arcs are laid out on the upper rails. To do this, first dry-assemble the doors and set them side by side (*Fig. 21*). Then use the template you used earlier on the front rails and draw the arcs.

Note: The upper rail groove is $3/8$" deep at its narrowest part.

After the arcs are cut, the doors are glued up. Trim them so they fit the case opening with a $1/16$" gap all the way around and between the doors (*Fig. 19*).

MOUNT DOORS. To hang the doors, cut three mortises for the hinges. (They should match the thickness of the hinge leaf.) When the hinges are screwed to the doors, set the doors in the case on spacers (I used pennies) to create a $1/16$" gap at the bottom.

Mark the hinge positions on the corner posts, and cut the mortises to leave a $1/16$" gap. Mount the doors to the case.

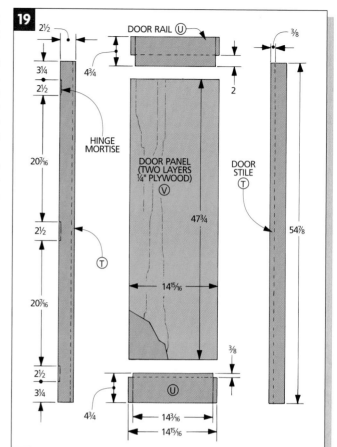

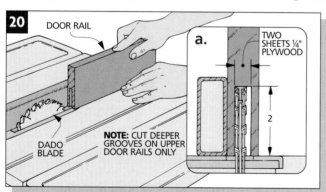

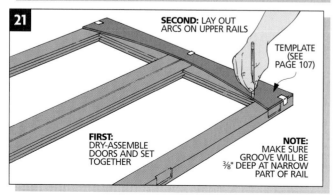

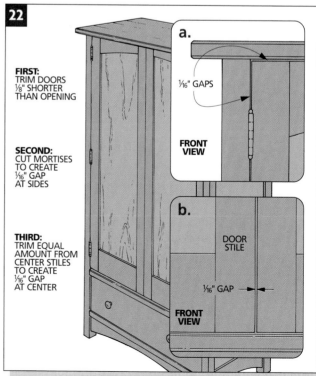

FINAL ASSEMBLY

Now the wardrobe is almost complete. All that's left are some odds and ends.

KNOBS AND CATCHES. The first thing I did was to attach the cherry knobs to the doors *(Fig. 23a)*. Since these doors are fairly large, I also installed bullet catches at the top and bottom of the doors *(Fig. 23b)*. These catches aren't difficult to install, but they must be set at exactly the right depth.

CLOSET POLE. Next, I hung the closet pole (W) inside the wardrobe. This pole is a 1¼"-dia. fir dowel. To hold it in place, I made a couple "U"-shaped pole brackets (X) with chamfered edges *(Fig. 23c)*. They're simply screwed to the insides of the case, and the pole rests inside them.

CASE BACKS. The last step is to add the upper and lower backs (Y, Z). These are ¼"-thick cherry plywood panels, cut to fit the rabbets in the back posts and screwed in place *(Fig. 23d)*.

FINISH. Finally, I finished the project with a wipe-on varnish. ∎

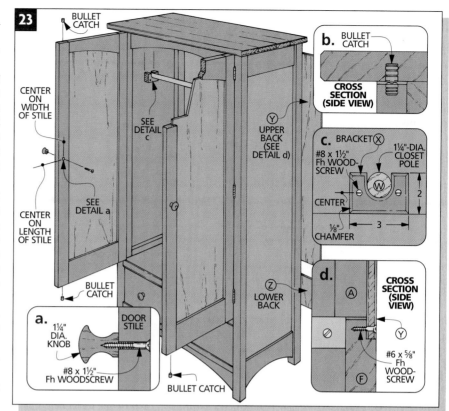

SHOP JIG . . . . *Arc Drawing Jig*

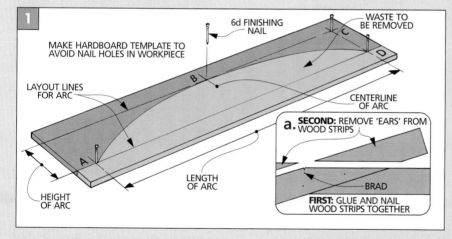

MAKE HARDBOARD TEMPLATE TO AVOID NAIL HOLES IN WORKPIECE

a. SECOND: REMOVE 'EARS' FROM WOOD STRIPS
FIRST: GLUE AND NAIL WOOD STRIPS TOGETHER

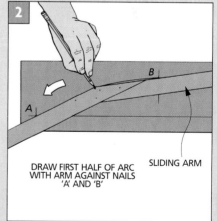

DRAW FIRST HALF OF ARC WITH ARM AGAINST NAILS 'A' AND 'B'

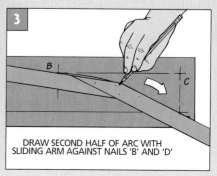

DRAW SECOND HALF OF ARC WITH SLIDING ARM AGAINST NAILS 'B' AND 'D'

This simple jig (two strips of wood and some finishing nails) lets you draw perfect arcs. First mark layout lines for the length, height, and center of the arc *(Fig. 1)*. I drew these on hardboard to be used as a template.

Now four nails are driven in at points 'A', 'B', 'C', and 'D' *(Fig. 1)*. These nails help construct a sliding arm (the two strips of wood) and guide the arm when drawing the arc.

To make the sliding arm, lay the strips against nails 'A', 'B', and 'C' and join them with glue and brads. Cut off the overlapping "ears" and make a notch (for your pencil) at the corner where the pieces intersect *(Fig. 1a)*.

To use the jig, remove nail 'C' and slide the arm along nails 'A' and 'B' *(Fig. 2)*. When half the arc is complete, move the sliding arm against nails 'B' and 'D' and finish the arc *(Fig. 3)*.

DESIGNER'S NOTEBOOK

To help organize and create extra storage space, you can build this four-drawer inner case. Built almost entirely from ³⁄₄"-thick glued-up panels, it's designed to simply slide into the Cherry Wardrobe.

INNER CASE

CONSTRUCTION NOTES:

■ Begin by gluing up panels for the top and bottom (AA), sides (BB), and center divider (CC) *(Fig. 1)*. Then cut all the panels to size except the divider. It is cut later to fit inside the case.

Note: The case height is determined by the dovetailed drawers. If you use different joinery, you can make the drawers whatever height you want.

■ Next, cut ¹⁄₄"-deep rabbets on the ends of the sides to hold the top and bottom panels *(Fig. 1b)*.

■ Cut dadoes on the top and bottom for the center divider *(Fig. 1a)*. And to hold

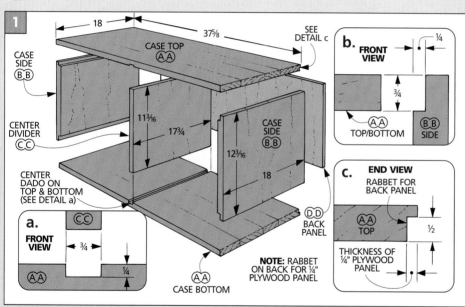

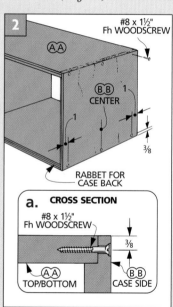

MATERIALS LIST

WOOD
AA	Top/Bottom (2)	³⁄₄ x 18 - 37⁵⁄₈
BB	Sides (2)	³⁄₄ x 18 - 12³⁄₁₆
CC	Center Divider (1)	³⁄₄ x 17³⁄₄ - 11³⁄₁₆
DD	Back (1)	¹⁄₄ ply - 37⁵⁄₈ x 11⁷⁄₁₆
EE	Drawer Fronts (4)	³⁄₄ x 5¹⁄₄ - 17¹⁵⁄₁₆
FF	Drawer Backs (4)*	³⁄₄ x 5¹⁄₄ - 17¹⁵⁄₁₆
GG	Drawer Sides (8)*	³⁄₄ x 5¹⁄₄ - 16³⁄₄
HH	Drawer Bottoms (4) ¹⁄₄ ply - 16³⁄₄ x 17³⁄₁₆	
II	Drawer Runners (8)*	³⁄₄ x ⁷⁄₁₆ - 17
JJ	Side Filler Strips (2) ³⁄₄ x 3 - 16¹⁄₂	
KK	Back Filler Strip (1)	¹⁄₂ x 3 - 38³⁄₈

* Hard maple. All other parts cherry.
Note: Need (12) additional No. 8 x 1¹⁄₂" Fh screws, and (24) No. 8 x ⁵⁄₈" Ph screws.

CUTTING DIAGRAM

³⁄₄ x 5 - 96 CHERRY (4 boards @ 3.3 Bd. Ft. ea.)

AA	AA		CC

³⁄₄ x 5 - 96 CHERRY (3.3 Bd. Ft. ea.)

BB	BB	BB	BB	BB	BB	BB	

³⁄₄ x 5¹⁄₂ - 96 CHERRY (3.7 Bd. Ft.)

EE	EE	EE	EE		BB

³⁄₄ x 5¹⁄₂ - 96 MAPLE (2 boards @ 3.7 Bd. Ft. ea.)

GG	GG	GG	GG	

³⁄₄ x 5¹⁄₂ - 96 MAPLE (3.7 Bd. Ft.)

FF	FF	FF	FF	II	

³⁄₄ x 3¹⁄₂ - 72 CHERRY (1.8 Bd. Ft.)

JJ	JJ	KK

a $\frac{1}{4}$" plywood back, cut $\frac{1}{2}$"-wide rabbets on the top, bottom, and sides *(Fig. 1c)*.

■ Dry-assemble the case and cut the divider (CC) to fit between the grooves in the top and bottom *(Fig. 1)*. Then rip it to width so it's flush with the front of the case and stops at the shoulder of the rabbet for the case back.

■ Next, glue and screw the inner case together *(Fig. 2)*. The center divider is glued in place because I didn't want screws visible from the top. When the glue's dry, cut a back (DD) to fit the rabbets and screw it in place *(Fig. 1)*.

■ Now, to determine the height of the drawers, measure the opening and subtract $\frac{3}{16}$" for the gaps at the top, bottom, and between the drawers. Divide this number by two. (Mine were $5\frac{1}{4}$" tall.)

■ With the pieces cut and the dovetails routed, cut the openings for the handles on the drawer fronts *(Figs. 3 and 3c)*.

Note: After the handle was cut out of one drawer front, I used it as a template for marking the other fronts.

■ Assemble the drawers. Then rout a stopped groove along each side *(Figs. 3a and 3b)*. This groove is centered on the side pieces and is part of the drawer runner system (see page 110).

■ To install the drawers in the case, cut a drawer runner (II) that attaches to the inner case and fits into the grooves on

the sides of the drawer *(Fig. 4)*. I used spacers to ensure they would all be parallel, level, and located $\frac{3}{4}$" from the case front. And to allow for expansion and contraction, I used slotted screw holes *(Fig. 5 and page 110)*.

■ Add two side filler strips (JJ) to fill the gaps in the case. These are identical to the ones used in the wardrobe *(Fig. 6)*.

■ Then add a back filler strip (KK). This is thinner than the side strips (mine was $\frac{1}{2}$") *(Fig. 7)*. Instead of gluing it to the back of the wardrobe, screw it to the inner case, making sure it's flush with the tops of the side filler strips.

■ Finish the case just like the wardrobe. When it's dry, slide it inside *(Fig. 7)*. It's heavy, so you won't need to secure it.

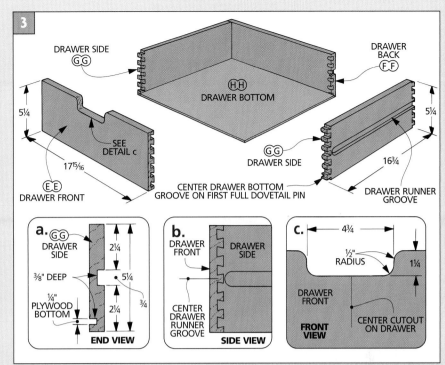

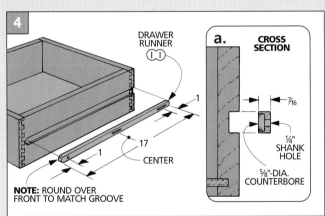

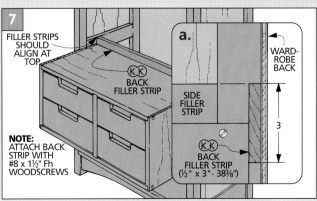

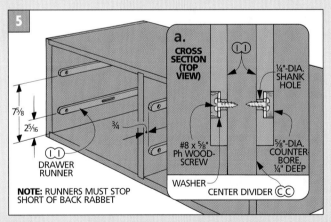

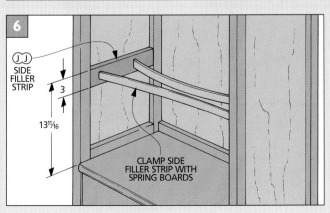

There are a lot of things to consider when adding a drawer to a project. Of course, the first thing you think of is sizing the drawer to fit into its opening.

But the drawer also has to slide in and out smoothly. So the drawer has to fit loose enough to slide easily, but not so loose that it racks when pulled out. To help with this, runners and guides are usually added. Of course, the types of runners and guides you use will depend on the project and how it's put together.

In the wardrobe on page 98, there are two types of drawers: a large drawer in the wardrobe case and four smaller drawers in the inner case. Because they're different, the wood guides I used were different too. One is mounted at the sides, the other is guided at the bottom.

I thought you might like to know some how's and why's of adding drawer guides. They may be very useful on your next project.

GLOSSARY

Before going on, it's worth it to take a few moments to explain the way I use some key words here.

RUNNERS. Runners are strips of wood that support a drawer as it's opened and closed. These can be located below the drawer, above it, or at its sides, and they may also serve as guides for the drawer.

GUIDES. Guides prevent a drawer from moving side-to-side. Often these are thin wood strips applied to the sides of the carcase. But for wider drawers, the guide can be located at the center, below the drawer.

SLIDES. Slides are metal runners or guides attached to the sides or below a drawer. This hardware creates a gap that must be covered by a rabbeted front or a false front.

GLIDES. Glides are added to reduce the friction between a drawer and a runner. Usually made of nylon, glides can be either buttons or strips of tape.

STOPS AND CATCHES. Stops keep a drawer from being pushed too far in. Catches prevent a drawer from being pulled completely out.

KICKERS. Kickers are strips of wood attached above a drawer to prevent the drawer from dropping as it's opened.

SIDE-MOUNTED DRAWERS

Side-mounted runners are one of the most common ways to support and guide a drawer. The inner case of the wardrobe is a good example *(Fig. 1)*. There's nothing between the top and bottom drawers, so the best solution was to mount them at the sides.

Side-mounted drawers are a two-part system. There are wooden runners screwed to the sides of the case. And stopped grooves routed in the drawer sides that fit over these runners. The location of the grooves isn't critical, but I find it's easiest to center them on the drawer sides.

These runners may sound like a lot of work, but they do a lot of work. They support the weight of the drawer and guide it as it's opened. They even provide a built-in stop as the door is closed. The only thing you may want to add is a catch so the drawer can't be pulled out completely (see the next page).

INSTALLATION. When installing runners, you need to watch for three things. They must line up with the grooves in the drawers. They must be level. And they must set back the right distance from the front of the case. But this isn't as hard as it sounds. To line up the runners and get them level, use a simple spacer. Its height should match the location of the groove plus an extra $1/16$" for the gap below the drawer. Then when

attaching the runners, all you have to worry about is getting them set back from the front the correct distance.

EXPANSION. Because these runners are screwed to solid wood, they have to allow the panels to expand and contract with changes in humidity. Otherwise, the sides of the carcase could split. The solution is to use a slotted shank hole at the back of the runner so the panel can move *(Fig. 1a)*.

You'll find that once the drawers are in place, they won't necessarily slide smoothly. All that's required is a little sandpaper. But remember, with side-mounted drawers, you should sand the *bottoms* of the runners only. Sanding the top will change the position of the drawer slightly.

BOTTOM-SUPPORTED DRAWERS

Like the side-mounted drawers in the inner case, the drawer at the bottom of the wardrobe doesn't have a frame under it either. But I didn't mount this drawer on the sides. Instead, it's supported from the bottom.

The reason is simple. This drawer is large and wide. A large drawer is harder to build exactly square and exactly the right size, so it's harder to build it to fit exactly in an opening. And because it's wide, the drawer will rack much easier as it's pulled out.

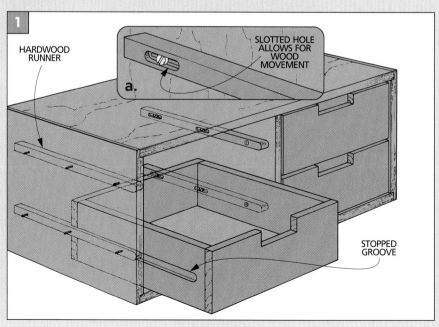

1

HARDWOOD RUNNER

a.

SLOTTED HOLE ALLOWS FOR WOOD MOVEMENT

STOPPED GROOVE

There are two solutions to getting a large, wide drawer to slide in and out smoothly. One is to support the weight of the drawer by adding runners at each side of the case. And the other is to guide the drawer with a center guide system.

RUNNERS. To support the weight of the drawer, I added runners to the sides of the wardrobe case *(Fig. 2)*. These runners were made of hard maple, because it's both smooth and durable.

I installed the runners $1/16$" above the rail cap at the front of the case. This automatically sets the gap between the drawer and the cap, which ensures the drawer won't rub against the cap.

KICKERS. Runners will support a drawer from below, but drawers need support from above too. Otherwise, the front of the drawer will drop as it's pulled out. With the wardrobe, the shelf cleat above the drawer prevents this from happening. But if the cleat weren't there, you would have to add kickers.

GUIDE SYSTEM. Now that the drawer has some support, the next step is to work on getting the drawer to slide in and out smoothly. On a narrow drawer, you could add thin strips at the sides of the case to guide it. But with a wide drawer, the best solution is to guide it at the center — below the drawer.

With a wide drawer, a single drawer guide works best. This is simply a single strip of wood that the drawer rides over. To get the drawer to ride

over the guide, I create a custom-fitted groove on the bottom of the drawer. But this groove isn't cut out of the bottom (which is only $1/4$"-thick plywood). Instead, it's "built up" on the bottom.

To do this, cut a notch on both the front and back of the drawer and glue narrow guide runners on either side. This creates a "channel" for the guide to run in *(Fig. 3)*.

There are two things to keep in mind about this system. You don't want the weight of the drawer to rest on the guide. The drawer should rest on the runners at the sides. So when building the drawer, make sure the drawer bottom is high enough to pass over the guide.

Also, you'll need to add a false front to cover the notches in the drawer. But don't be tempted to use this false front

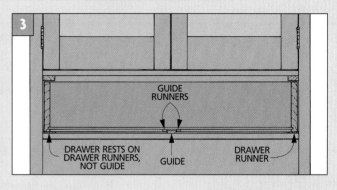

as a stop. On the other hand, you don't want to stop the drawer against the thin back of the case. Either of these "solutions" can create problems for you later. Instead, your last step will be to add a couple stops and catches (see below).

DRAWER STOPS & CATCHES

There are a couple questions that often get overlooked when designing a project: "How do the drawers stop when you're pushing them closed?" And "What catches them from being pulled all the way out (and spilling their con-

tents on the floor)?" The answers to both questions are fairly simple.

The best way I've found to stop a drawer when closing it is to add a stop block (or a pair of blocks) at the back of the case *(Fig. 4)*.

When pulling a drawer open, the answer will depend on the carcase. If there's a solid panel above the drawer, you'll need to use a small block and cut a notch in the drawer. Otherwise, you can use a turnbutton *(Figs. 5 and 6)*.

Stop In. *A drawer shouldn't stop against the case back. A simple block does the trick.*

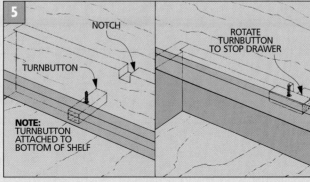

Panel Catch. *To keep a drawer from coming all the way out, add a turnbutton. When there's a solid panel above the drawer, you'll need to cut a notch in the back of the drawer.*

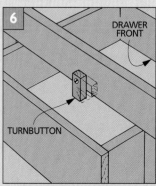

Frame Catch. *When there's a case frame, a simple turnbutton is all you need.*

Tall Oak Cabinet

Much of the beauty of this project is in its traditional appearance. What doesn't immediately meet the eye is the clever technique used to build the glass-paned doors.

The most prominent feature of this cabinet is its large glass doors. Each door has eight glass "lights" or panes, and each pane is framed by a molded edge. Instead of making these moldings with traditional coped miters, I employed a technique using a router and a few commonly used bits. It's explained on pages 122-123, and you should read these pages before beginning the cabinet.

TOP MOLDING. The door is not the only part that has interesting details. The built-up molding at the top of the cabinet finishes up with dentil molding, which must fit the width of the cabinet precisely to end up with equally spaced blocks and a full block at each end. Not one but two methods for cutting this classic molding are shown on page 119.

WOOD. I built this cabinet from red oak. The doors, facings, molding, and shelves are made of solid stock, but the large panels are made from oak-faced plywood so they remain flat and stable even with seasonal changes in temperature and humidity.

HARDWARE. A modern touch is the use of threaded inserts to join the upper case to the lower, and they make it easy to disassemble if necessary. To complete the classic effect, the decorative hardware is of solid, long-lasting brass.

FINISH. Every heirloom project deserves a first-class finish. To deepen the color, the red oak was stained with a special blend made by mixing eight teaspoons of burnt umber artist's oil into one quart of linseed oil. After 48 hours drying time, I applied three coats of a satin finish.

DESIGN OPTIONS. A cabinet of this type lends itself to all kinds of uses. An option to customize the cabinet for the safe, secure storage of firearms, fishing gear, or other sports equipment will appeal to any outdoorsman. Complete instructions for this are shown in the Designer's Notebook on pages 124-125.

EXPLODED VIEW

OVERALL DIMENSIONS:
42¼"W x 16D x 77⅞"H

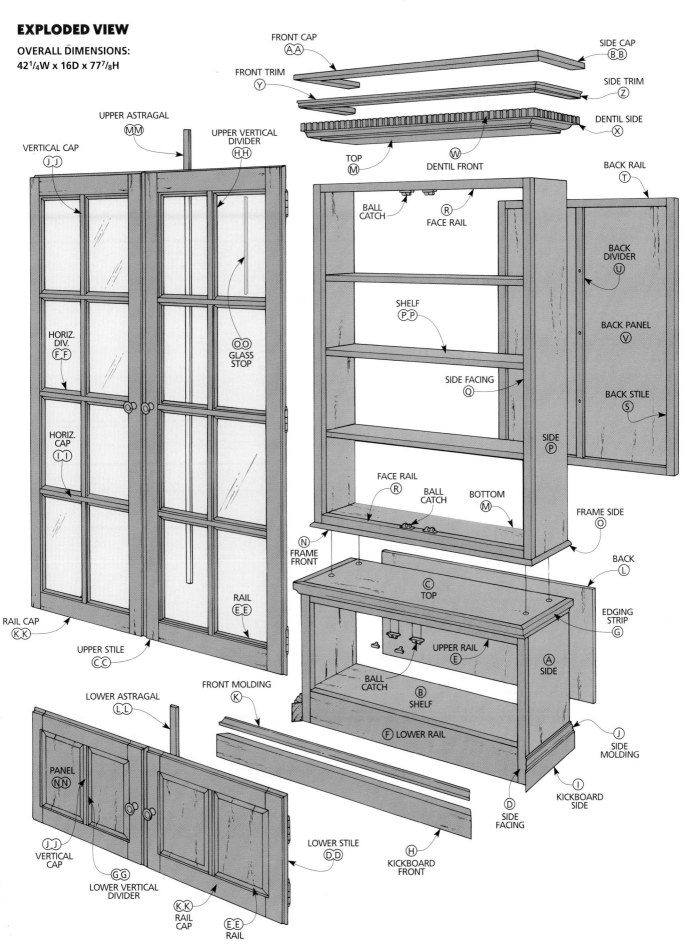

FRONT CAP
(AA)

SIDE CAP
(BB)

FRONT TRIM
(Y)

SIDE TRIM
(Z)

DENTIL SIDE
(X)

TOP
(M)

DENTIL FRONT

W

UPPER ASTRAGAL
(MM)

UPPER VERTICAL
DIVIDER
(HH)

BACK RAIL
(T)

VERTICAL CAP
(JJ)

BALL
CATCH

R

FACE RAIL

BACK
DIVIDER
(U)

HORIZ.
DIV.
(FF)

BACK PANEL
(V)

(OO)
GLASS
STOP

SHELF
(PP)

SIDE FACING
(Q)

BACK STILE
(S)

HORIZ.
CAP
(II)

FACE RAIL

R

BALL
CATCH

BOTTOM
(M)

SIDE
(P)

FRAME SIDE
(O)

RAIL
(EE)

N
FRAME
FRONT

C
TOP

BACK
(L)

RAIL CAP
(KK)

EDGING
STRIP
(G)

UPPER STILE
(CC)

BALL
CATCH

UPPER RAIL
(E)

A
SIDE

FRONT MOLDING
(K)

B
SHELF

J
SIDE
MOLDING

LOWER ASTRAGAL
(LL)

F LOWER RAIL

I
KICKBOARD
SIDE

PANEL
(NN)

LOWER STILE
(DD)

D
SIDE
FACING

(JJ)
VERTICAL
CAP

H
KICKBOARD
FRONT

(GG)
LOWER VERTICAL
DIVIDER

(KK)
RAIL
CAP

(EE)
RAIL

MATERIALS LIST

LOWER CASE

A	Sides (2)	$3/4$ ply - $14^3/4$ x $21^5/8$
B	Shelf (1)	$3/4$ ply - $14^1/4$ x $38^1/4$
C	Top (1)	$3/4$ ply - $15^5/8$ x 40
D	Side Facings (2)	$3/4$ x 1 - $21^5/8$
E	Upper Rail (1)	$3/4$ x $1^3/4$ - $37^1/4$
F	Lower Rail (1)	$3/4$ x $4^3/4$ - $37^1/4$
G	Edging Strip (1)	$3/8$ x $3/4$ - 75 rough
H	Kickboard Front (1)	$3/4$ x 3 - $40^3/4$
I	Kickboard Sides (2)	$3/4$ x 3 - 16
J	Side Moldings (4)	$3/4$ x $1/2$ - 16 rough
K	Front Moldings (2)	$3/4$ x $1/2$ - 41 rough
L	Back (1)	$1/4$ ply - $38^3/4$ x $22^1/8$

UPPER CASE

M	Top/Bottom (2)	$3/4$ ply - $11^1/4$ x $37^3/4$
N	Frame Fronts (2)	$1/2$ x $1^1/2$ - $40^1/4$
O	Frame Sides (4)	$1/2$ x $1^1/2$ - $12^1/2$
P	Sides (2)	$3/4$ ply - $11^1/2$ x 52
Q	Side Facings (2)	$3/4$ x 1 - 52

R	Face Rails (2)	$3/4$ x 1 - $37^1/4$
S	Back Stiles (2)	$3/4$ x $1^1/2$ - 52
T	Back Rails (2)	$3/4$ x $1^1/4$ - $36^1/4$
U	Back Divider (1)	$3/4$ x 1 - 50
V	Back Panels (2)	$1/4$ ply - $17^7/8$ x 50
W	Dentil Front (1)	$1^1/2$ x 1 - $40^3/4$
X	Dentil Sides (2)	$1^1/2$ x 1 - $12^3/4$
Y	Front Trim (1)	$3/4$ x $1^1/4$ - $41^3/4$
Z	Side Trim (2)	$3/4$ x $1^1/4$ - $13^1/2$
AA	Front Cap (1)	$3/4$ x $1^1/2$ - $42^1/4$
BB	Side Caps (2)	$3/4$ x $1^1/2$ - $13^1/2$

DOORS

CC	Upper Stiles (4)	$3/4$ x $2^1/2$ - $50^1/2$
DD	Lower Stiles (4)	$3/4$ x $2^1/2$ - $15^5/8$
EE	Rails (8)	$3/8$ x $2^1/4$ - $14^1/2$
FF	Horiz. Dividers (6)	$3/8$ x $1/2$ - $14^1/2$
GG	Lwr. Vrt. Dividers (2)	$3/8$ x $1/2$ - $15^5/8$
HH	Upr. Vrt. Dividers (2)	$3/8$ x $1/2$ - $50^1/2$
II	Horizontal Caps (6)	$3/8$ x 1 - $14^1/4$

JJ	Vertical Caps (10)	$3/8$ x 1 - $11^1/8$
KK	Rail Caps (8)	$3/8$ x $2^1/2$ - $14^1/4$
LL	Lower Astragal (1)	$3/8$ x $3/4$ - $14^7/8$
MM	Upper Astragal (1)	$3/8$ x $3/4$ - $49^3/4$
NN	Panels (4)	$5/8$ x $6^7/8$ - $11^1/8$
OO	Glass Stops (80)	$1/4$ x $1/4$ - 70 lin. ft.
PP	Shelves (3)	$3/4$ x $10^1/4$ - $37^3/4$

HARDWARE SUPPLIES

- (25) No. 6 x $3/4$" Fh woodscrews
- (67) No. 8 x $1^1/4$" Fh woodscrews
- (4) No. 8 x $1^1/2$" Fh woodscrews
- (14) No. 8 x 2" Fh woodscrews
- (5 pairs) Inset brass hinges w/ screws
- (4) $1/4$" threaded inserts
- (4) $1/4$" x $1^1/4$" Rh machine screws
- (4) Brass knobs
- (6) Double ball catches
- (15) $1/4$" shelf supports
- (16) $1/8$" glass panes, $6^7/8$" x $11^1/8$"

CUTTING DIAGRAM

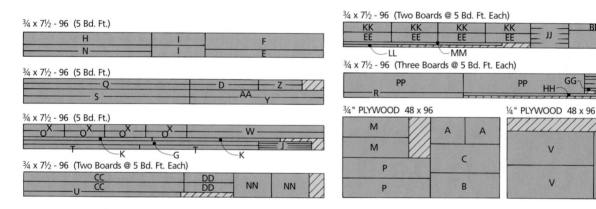

$3/4$ x $7^1/2$ - 96 (5 Bd. Ft.)

$3/4$ x $7^1/2$ - 96 (5 Bd. Ft.)

$3/4$ x $7^1/2$ - 96 (5 Bd. Ft.)

$3/4$ x $7^1/2$ - 96 (Two Boards @ 5 Bd. Ft. Each)

$3/4$ x $7^1/2$ - 96 (Two Boards @ 5 Bd. Ft. Each)

$3/4$ x $7^1/2$ - 96 (Three Boards @ 5 Bd. Ft. Each)

$3/4$" PLYWOOD 48 x 96

$1/4$" PLYWOOD 48 x 96

LOWER CASE

The cabinet is constructed by stacking a tall case on top of a short case. I began work by building the lower case.

The lower case starts with two sides that are mirror images of each other. They are joined by a shelf to form an "H" shape, and then a top is added to help hold the assembly together *(Fig. 1)*.

SIDES AND SHELF. Start by cutting two sides (A) and a shelf (B) from $3/4$"-thick plywood *(Fig. 1)*. (The grain looks best if it runs vertically on the sides and along the length of the shelf.)

DADO FOR SHELF. After the sides and shelf have been cut to finished size, cut a $1/4$"-wide dado across the inside face of each side piece. These dadoes will receive tongues cut on the ends of the shelf *(Fig. 1)*. (See the Shop Tip on the opposite page to see why I chose to cut tongues on the shelf.)

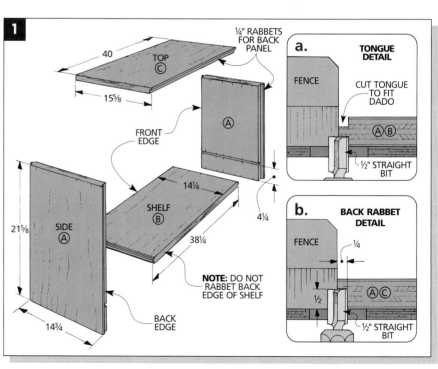

To cut the dadoes, you can use either a table saw with a dado blade or a $1/4$" straight bit on the router table. To allow the shelf to pull up tight to the side during assembly, cut the dadoes slightly deeper than $1/4$" (lower photo at right).

TONGUES. Next, cut the tongues on the shelf (B) to fit the dadoes. The tongues are formed by cutting two rabbets on each end *(Fig. 1a)*.

To do this, I mounted a $1/2$" straight bit in the router table. Then I cut the tongue in a couple of passes, sneaking up on the final depth until the tongue just fit the dado in the side panel.

After the tongues have been routed on the shelves, rout a tongue the same size on the front edge of each side (A) *(Fig. 1)*. These tongues will hold facing pieces added later (refer to *Fig. 3*).

CASE TOP. Once you have routed the tongues on the sides, the next step is to cut the top (C) to finished size *(Fig. 1)*. (Again, note the grain direction.)

RABBETS FOR BACK. Now $1/4$" rabbets are cut along the back edges of the sides (A) and top (C) to accept a back panel. Cut the rabbets on the inside faces of the sides and the bottom of the top panel *(Figs. 1 and 1b)*.

Note: Don't rabbet the back edge of the shelf — the back extends to the floor.

HOLES IN TOP. Now two sets of holes are drilled in the top (C). First, drill and countersink $3/16$" shank holes near each end for screws that hold the top to the sides *(Figs. 2 and 2a)*. Then drill four $5/16$" holes for bolts that will hold the top case to the bottom case *(Fig. 2)*.

ASSEMBLY. To assemble the lower case, first glue and clamp the shelf in the side dadoes to form an "H" shape *(Fig. 2)*. Then check the case for square.

Next, position the top (C) on the sides (A) so that it overhangs each side equally and is flush along the back. Then glue and screw the top down through the pre-drilled holes *(Fig. 2a)*.

FACING & RAILS

The next step is to add the facing pieces to the side panels and add the rails between each facing.

SIDE FACING. First rip two side facing (D) pieces to final width (1") *(Fig. 3a)*. Then cut the pieces to the same length as the sides *(Fig. 3)*.

Next, cut grooves on the back side of each facing to fit the tongues on the plywood *(Fig. 3a)*. (To make sure they fit, I

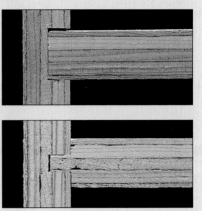

There are several ways to join a shelf to the side of a cabinet. A full-width dado (see upper photo at right) normally works fine, but if the shelf doesn't fit the dado exactly, there will be a visible gap.

The tongue and dado joint (lower photo) looks better because it hides any gap above the tongue of the shelf. Another benefit is that it also covers up any splintering along the edges of the dado.

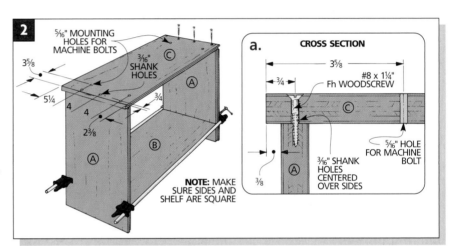

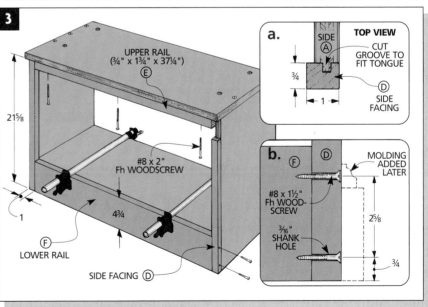

used the same dado setup I used for the shelf dado.) Glue the facings in place.

UPPER AND LOWER RAIL. Cut an upper rail (E) and a lower rail (F) to fit between the facings *(Fig. 3)*. Glue and screw the upper rail under the top (C). Then glue the lower rail to the shelf, and screw it to the facing *(Fig. 3b)*.

After adding the facing and rails, the next step is to add edging strips, a kickboard, and molding to the lower case. All these pieces are mitered at the front corners and cut flush with the back.

EDGING STRIP. To hide the edges of the plywood top, I cut $3/8$"-thick edging strips (G) and glued them to the front and sides *(Fig. 4)*. Start by ripping a blank to match the thickness of the top. Then rough cut the strip into three separate pieces.

Next, miter both ends of the front strip to length to fit across the front edge of the plywood *(Fig. 4)*. Then glue it in place.

Now you can miter the front ends of the side strips, and cut the back ends flush with the back. Then glue these strips in place.

KICKBOARD. To make the kickboard, start by ripping three pieces of $3/4$"-thick stock to width and rough length *(Fig. 4)*. Next, miter both ends of the kickboard front (H) and the front ends of the kickboard sides (I). To complete the kickboard, cut the back edges flush with the back. Then glue and clamp all the pieces to the lower case.

ROMAN OGEE. I added strips of Roman ogee molding to the top edge of the kickboard and under the top of the lower case *(Figs. 4 and 5)*.

The safest way to make this ogee molding is to start with wider pieces *(Fig. 5a)*. (I used $1^1/4$"-wide blanks.) Rip enough stock to make four side molding strips (J) and two front molding strips (K).

Next, rout a Roman ogee profile on the outside edge of each strip. Then rip each piece of molding to a width of $1/2$" *(Fig. 5a)*. Cut the molding strips to length as you did for the edging strips and kickboard. Then glue and clamp them in place *(Fig. 5)*.

Note: There are actually two different ogee styles you could use for the molding on the lower case (see the Shop Tip box below).

BACK. Once you're finished with the molding, a back panel (L) is all that's needed to finish the lower case. To find the dimensions for the back panel, measure between the rabbets on the sides, and between the rabbet on the top and the floor. Cut the back to size, then screw it in place *(Fig. 4)*.

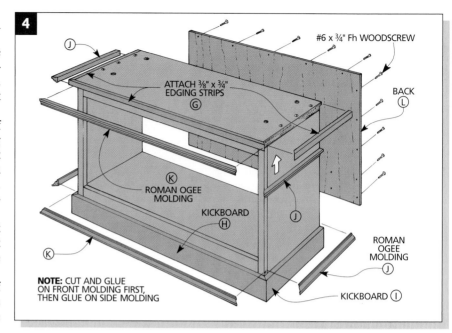

4

#6 x ¾" Fh WOODSCREW

ATTACH ⅜" x ¾" EDGING STRIPS ⓖ

BACK ⓛ

ROMAN OGEE MOLDING ⓚ

KICKBOARD ⓗ

ⓙ

ROMAN OGEE MOLDING ⓙ

KICKBOARD ⓘ

NOTE: CUT AND GLUE ON FRONT MOLDING FIRST, THEN GLUE ON SIDE MOLDING

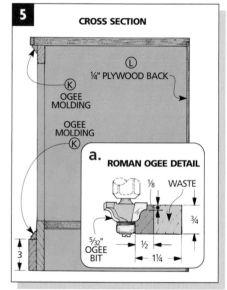

5

CROSS SECTION

ⓛ

¼" PLYWOOD BACK

ⓚ OGEE MOLDING

OGEE MOLDING ⓚ

3

a. **ROMAN OGEE DETAIL**

⅛ WASTE

¾

$5/32$" OGEE BIT

½

$1^1/4$

SHOP TIP . . . . *Ogee Bits*

An ogee router bit is simply one that has two radii (one concave and one convex) that are the same size, which create a distinct profile.

When it came time to rout profiles on the molding pieces for the Tall Oak Cabinet, I decided to use a Roman ogee bit (see top bit in drawing at right). But this isn't your only option.

An alternative would be to use a standard ogee bit. This is similar to a Roman ogee, but the locations of the concave and convex curves are reversed (see bottom bit in drawing). (If an extra shoulder is added to the ogee bit it is called an ogee with a fillet.)

This is a convenient substitution because it doesn't affect the *size* of the profile, only the style.

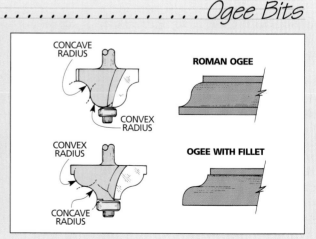

CONCAVE RADIUS

CONVEX RADIUS

CONVEX RADIUS

CONCAVE RADIUS

ROMAN OGEE

OGEE WITH FILLET

The upper case is built like the lower, but the shelves aren't fixed to the sides.

TOP/BOTTOM. The top and bottom (M) are identical. Each one is a $3/4$" plywood panel framed on three sides. Start by cutting the panels to size *(Fig. 6)*.

Next, to accept the frame pieces, cut grooves centered on the front and side edges of the plywood *(Fig. 6a)*. Then cut a $3/4$"-wide rabbet on the back edge of each panel for the back *(Fig. 6b)*.

TOP/BOTTOM FRAME. Now the frame pieces are added. The frame fronts (N) and sides (O) are only $1/2$" thick. Since the plywood is $3/4$" thick, a rabbet is formed when the frame pieces are glued to the panels *(Fig. 6)*. This rabbet accepts the sides and front faces of the case.

After cutting the frame pieces to width, rout a $1/2$" roundover on one edge of each piece *(Fig. 6a)*. Then cut a rabbet on the opposite edge to create a tongue that fits the groove in the top/bottom (M).

The next step is to miter the frame pieces to fit the panels *(Fig. 6)*. Then cut the ends of the frame sides (O) flush with the back edges of the panels.

THREADED INSERTS. After gluing the frame in place, install threaded inserts in the bottom panel to connect the cases *(Fig. 8a)*. To locate the inserts, center the bottom panel on top of the lower case, making sure the back edges are flush. Then mark through the holes drilled in the top (C) of the lower case.

SIDES. Now you can start on the two sides (P). First, cut two pieces of $3/4$" plywood to final dimensions *(Fig. 7)*. Cut tongues for the facing (Q) on the front edge of each panel, and a rabbet for the back frame on the inside back edge of each panel *(Figs. 7a and 7b)*.

ASSEMBLY. To assemble the case, drill holes through the top/bottom assemblies *(Fig. 8)*. Then glue and screw them to the sides (P) *(Fig. 8a)*.

SIDE FACING. To hide the edges of the side panels, glue a 1"-wide face frame to the upper case. To do this, first cut two side facings (Q) to length to fit between the top/bottom (M) panels *(Fig. 8)*.

Next, cut grooves on the back face of each side facing (Q) to fit the tongues on the front edges of the sides (P). Then glue the facing to the sides *(Fig. 8)*.

FACE RAILS. Now cut two 1"-wide face rails (R) to fit between the side facings *(Fig. 8)*. Then glue and screw them to the frame front pieces (N).

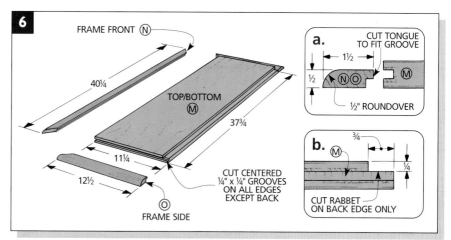

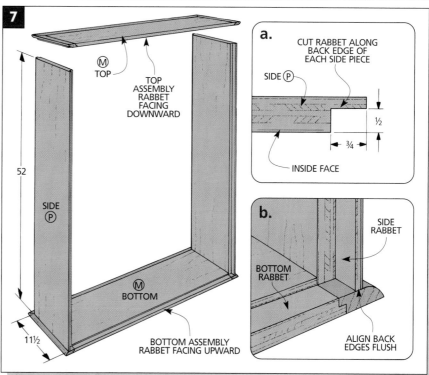

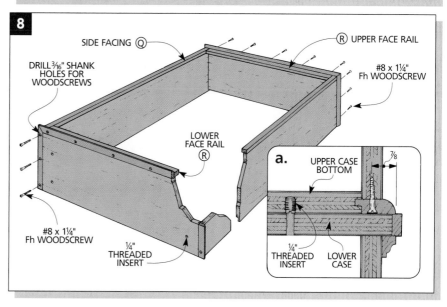

Building the back is the next step in completing the upper case. It consists of two ¼" plywood panels in a frame joined with stub tenons and grooves.

FRAME. To build the frame, first rip the stiles (S), rails (T), and divider (U) to final widths *(Fig. 9)*. (Notice they're all different widths.)

To find the rough length of these pieces, measure the opening in back of the cabinet (from rabbet to rabbet) and add 1". Cut the pieces to this length.

Next, cut a groove centered on the inside edge of each piece to accept the plywood back panels (V) *(Fig. 9a)*.

Note: Cut grooves on *both* edges of the center divider (U).

Now the pieces are cut to length. First, cut the stiles to fit the height of the opening (52") and dry-clamp them in place. To find the length of the rails (T), take the distance between the stiles (S) plus the depth of both grooves *(Fig. 9)*.

After the rails are cut to length, dry-clamp them in place. Find the length of the vertical divider (U) by using the same procedure as for the rails.

STUB TENONS. Now cut stub tenons on the ends of the rails (T) and divider (U) to fit the grooves *(Fig. 9a)*.

PANELS. Next, dry-clamp the frame in the cabinet to find the final sizes of the back panels (V) *(Fig. 9)*. Cut the panels from ¼" plywood, and glue the frames and panels together. Then glue and screw the back frame in place *(Fig. 9b)*.

MOLDING

To finish the upper case, I added molding to the top of the cabinet. The molding is built up out of three strips: a dentil molding, a Roman ogee molding, and a square edge cap *(Fig. 11)*.

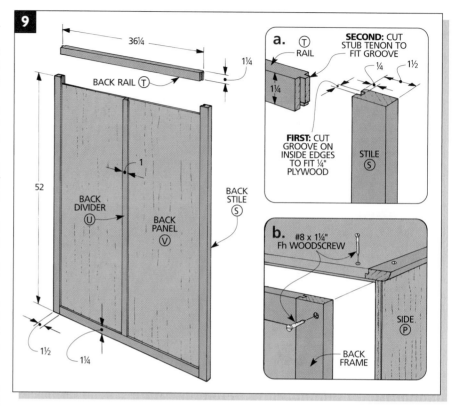

DENTIL MOLDING. I wanted the blocks in the dentil to be equal in width and evenly spaced apart. I also wanted full blocks on both ends *(Fig. 10)*. (Refer to the Technique article on the opposite page for a couple of ways to make dentil molding.)

I made blanks for the dentil front (W) and side (X) pieces from two pieces of ¾"-thick stock glued together *(Fig. 11a)*. (Or you could use a single piece of 1½"-thick stock.)

After you're finished cutting dadoes for the dentils, miter the dentil pieces to fit around the front and sides of the cabinet *(Fig. 10)*. Then glue and screw them down securely to the case *(Fig. 11a)*.

TOP MOLDING. It's easier to make the ¾"-thick Roman ogee molding pieces

and glue them to the front and side caps before cutting them to final length. To make the front (Y) and side (Z) Roman ogee moldings, rout a Roman ogee profile into the edge of 1¼"-wide stock *(Fig. 11a)*. (Also refer back to *Fig. 5a*.)

Now you can cut the pieces for the front (AA) and side (BB) caps 1½" wide. Then glue and clamp the caps to the ogee trim pieces with the back edges flush *(Fig. 11a)*. After the glued-up pieces are dry, miter them to fit on top of the dentil molding.

CABINET ASSEMBLY. After the top molding is glued and screwed in place, set the upper case on top of the lower case. Then fasten the two cases together using ¼" machine screws to fit the threaded inserts.

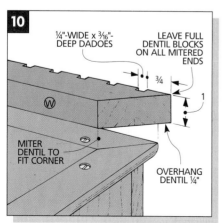

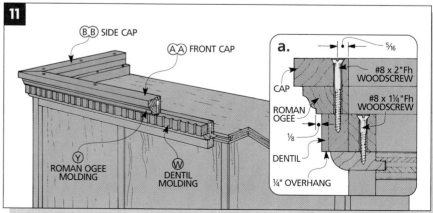

TECHNIQUE .... *Making Dentil Molding*

There are two projects in this book that use the same type of dentil molding: the Curio Cabinet (page 38) and the Tall Oak Cabinet (page 112). But there are two ways of making this molding.

CUTTING JIG

For the Curio Cabinet, I built the cabinet around the dentil to ensure a full-width block at each corner. So I used an indexing jig, similar to a box joint jig.

To make the dentil, first rip the stock to width — slightly wider than needed so any chipout on the kerfs can be removed when it's trimmed to final width.

JIG. Then the cutting jig is made to space the kerfs consistently along the dentil. To make the jig, cut a $3/4$" plywood fence 3" high and 24" long.

Cut a notch near the center of the fence for an indexing pin. The width of this notch must equal the width of the dentil kerfs. (I wanted $1/4$"-wide kerfs, so I used a dado set to cut a $1/4$"-wide notch.)

The height of the notch should be a tad under the depth of cut you want for the kerfs. (I wanted $1/8$"-deep kerfs, so I set the depth of cut to about $3/32$".)

Note: The reason for the lower depth

of cut is to reduce the size of the indexing pin. This lets the dentil rest flat on the table saw, not on the top of the pin.

PIN. Now cut a $1^1/2$"-long indexing pin to the same width and height as the notch, and glue it into the notch.

POSITION THE FENCE. Next, clamp the fence to the miter gauge so the distance between the pin and the blade equals the width of the blocks you want *(Fig. 1)*. (I wanted $1/2$"-wide blocks, so I set the pin $1/2$" from the blade.)

Check this measurement by nicking the edge of the fence with the blade. If the distance between the nick and the pin is correct, drill pilot holes in the fence and attach it to the miter gauge. Then double check the fence position.

CUT KERFS. To cut the kerfs in the dentil, raise the dado blade to a $1/8$" depth of cut. Butt the end of the stock against the indexing pin, and make a pass over the dado blade *(Fig. 2)*.

For the remaining cuts, place the new kerf over the pin and make another pass.

CLEANUP. The kerf bottoms may be rough. I used a chisel to "plane" them.

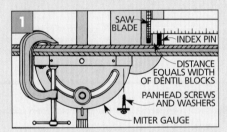

1
SAW BLADE
INDEX PIN
DISTANCE EQUALS WIDTH OF DENTIL BLOCKS
PANHEAD SCREWS AND WASHERS
MITER GAUGE

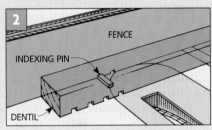

2
FENCE
INDEXING PIN
DENTIL

LAYING OUT BY HAND

If you use an indexing jig like the one above, there could be a problem. If the jig isn't set up right, there can be a slight gain (or loss) with each cut that can add up. By the time you get to the end of a long workpiece, the last dentil block won't be the same size as the rest, and you'll see the difference *(Fig. 1)*.

MEASURE AND MARK. Another way to get dentil blocks that all look the same is to lay out the positions of the dadoes with a pencil instead of using a jig. (I used this technique on the Tall Oak Cabinet, with $1/4$" dadoes that are $3/4$" apart.)

If you're cutting to a mark, it's important that the dado marks are laid out accurately. So use a tape measure that's as least as long as the workpiece, and don't move the tape as you're marking. Otherwise, you'll have the "gain" problem again.

COMPENSATING. What if you cut a molding strip that fits your cabinet, but it's not the same length as called for in the plans? Won't each of the blocks be different than specified in the plans? Yes, but there's a trick you can use to get all the dentil blocks to *appear* very close to the same size.

After you've measured and marked, you'll know whether the last cut is going to produce a dentil block the same size as the first. If it doesn't work out exactly,

you can "cheat" slightly on the layout to compensate for the difference.

Say your dentil molding strip has to be cut $1/8$" longer to fit the cabinet. It's not practical to divide the extra $1/8$" among all the blocks to get them the exact same size.

Instead, start cheating by $1/64$" on just the last eight marks *(Fig. 2)*. This way, each of the last eight blocks will be $1/64$" too large, but this shouldn't be noticeable on the finished molding.

1
LAST DENTIL BLOCK IS SAME SIZE AS OTHERS
LAY OUT STRIP FIRST, THEN CUT DADOES TO MARKS
LAST DENTIL BLOCK IS NARROWER THAN OTHERS
POSITIONS OF DADOES CUT WITH INDEXING JIG CAN GAIN AFTER MANY CUTS

2
TO "CHEAT," LAY OUT DADO MARKS SLIGHTLY OUTSIDE DESIRED LOCATIONS
2 38 3 39 4 40

I think the doors are the biggest challenge on this project. (See pages 122-123 for more on joining the door parts.)

DOOR STILES. To find the lengths of the stiles (CC, DD), first measure the height of the door openings. Then add $1/2$" since the doors are lipped with a $1/4$" overlap *(Fig. 12)*.

Next, cut a groove and round over the inside edge of each stile *(Fig. 12a)*.

DOOR WIDTH. To find the length of the rest of the door pieces, first measure the width of the opening and divide this measurement in half for the two doors (in my case, $18^5/8$").

Now subtract half the gap you want between the two doors ($1/16$"), and add the overhang for the inset hinges ($3/16$"). This made each door $18^3/4$" wide.

RAILS AND DIVIDERS. To determine the length of the rails (EE) and horizontal dividers (FF), lay out two stiles like a finished door (routed edges facing *in* with $18^3/4$" outside-to-outside distance) *(Fig. 12)*. Measure between the grooves.

After cutting the rails and horizontal dividers to this length, cut the tongues and dadoes on each (see page 123).

VERTICAL DIVIDERS. Find the length of the vertical dividers (GG, HH) by dry-assembling the stiles and rails. Cut the dividers to length, cut the tongues and half-lap joints (see page 123), and glue and clamp the rails and dividers together.

CAPS. The rails and dividers have molded caps (II, JJ, KK) glued on top. The caps are rounded over on top and coved on the ends to match the molded edges of the stiles and rails *(Figs. 13 and 13a)*. To determine the length of all the caps, measure your assembled door (once again, refer to page 123).

OVERHANG AND ROUNDOVERS. Once the door is assembled, rout $3/8$" rabbets around the back edges *(Fig. 14)*. This forms a lip and provides clearance between the door and the cabinet opening. Next, rout $1/4$" roundovers on the front edges of the doors *(Fig. 14a)*.

ASTRAGALS. The next step is to add an astragal (LL, MM). That's the strip that hides the gap when the doors are closed. Glue one into the rabbet in each left door *(Figs. 14 and 14a)*.

HANG DOORS. Before installing the glass and panels in the doors, I positioned the hinges and drilled the screw holes (see the Shop Tip box on the opposite page.) Then I removed the hinges to mount the glass and panels.

PANELS, STOPS, HARDWARE. On the bottom doors, I made $5/8$"-thick raised panels (NN). They're "raised" on both faces with a $1/2$" core box bit *(Fig. 15a)*. Install the panels and glass with quarter-round glass stops (OO) *(Fig. 15b)*. After the doors are rehung, install the knobs and door catches.

SHELVES. Finally, glue up and cut stock for three shelves (PP).

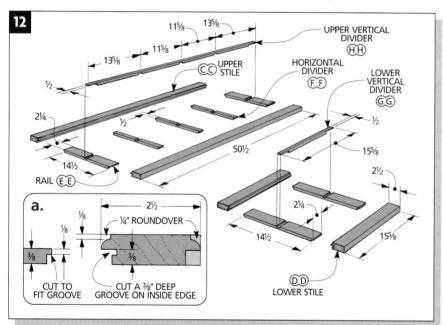

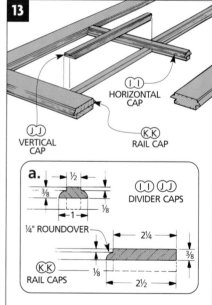

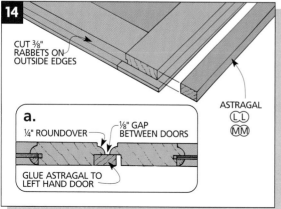

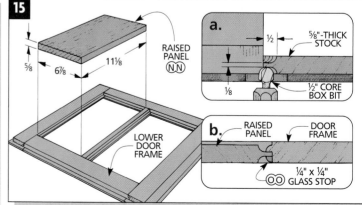

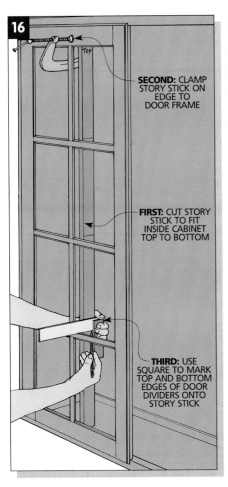

16

SECOND: CLAMP STORY STICK ON EDGE TO DOOR FRAME

FIRST: CUT STORY STICK TO FIT INSIDE CABINET TOP TO BOTTOM

THIRD: USE SQUARE TO MARK TOP AND BOTTOM EDGES OF DOOR DIVIDERS ONTO STORY STICK

SHELF POSITIONS

When there are shelves behind a glass door, I think it looks best if the shelves line up with the window dividers.

STORY STICK. To position the shelves, I used a story stick. This is just a stick with holes drilled in it to mark the locations for the shelf support holes.

To make a story stick, first rip a piece of scrap wood to a width of 2″. Then cut this stick to length so it fits tightly up and down inside the cabinet. To keep everything straight, I labeled one end "Top."

To mark the holes on the story stick, clamp the stick to the door (*Fig. 16*). Make sure it's straight up and down, and turn it so a narrow edge faces the front.

MARK DIVIDER EDGES. Use a try square to make pencil marks on the stick that correspond to the bottom and top edge of each window divider (*Fig. 16*).

MARK SHELF EDGES. Now, lay out the shelf positions on the stick (*Fig. 17*).

MARK PIN LOCATIONS. Finally, lay out the locations of the holes for the shelf support pins on the story stick. I used spoon-shaped pins (*Fig. 17a*). (For different pins, adjust the positions of the holes accordingly.)

By centering the hole on the width of the story stick, the hole will be the same distance from the edge when marking the front and back of the cabinet.

USING THE STICK. After holes are drilled through the stick for all the shelves, the stick can be used as a guide for drilling holes for the shelf supports.

The only secret to using the story stick is to keep the front edge of the stick flush to the inside edge of the cabinet when drilling the holes for the front pins. Then butt the back edge of the stick to the back of the cabinet when you drill the rear pin holes.

Note: To keep the shelves from sagging, I also put shelf pins in the vertical divider (U) in the back (see the Exploded View on page 113). ■

17

MARK EDGES OF DIVIDERS ONTO STORY STICK

a.

SHELF SUPPORT PIN

ALIGN CENTER OF PIN HOLE WITH BOTTOM OF SHELF LINE

LAY OUT SHELF THICKNESS CENTERED BETWEEN MARKS

SHOP TIP . . . . *Installing Inset Hinges*

Inset hinges, like the ones used on this tall oak cabinet, can be more frustrating to install than ordinary butt hinges. When the door is closed, both leaves of the hinge are inside the cabinet. This makes the screw holes in the hinge almost impossible to reach.

To solve this problem, I installed the hinges *before* the glass panes were in place. And I used clamps to hold the hinges to the doors.

To do this, first screw all the hinges to the cabinet frame (*Fig. 1*).

Now lay the cabinet on its back, and put the doors in the opening centered up and down and also left to right.

Then, to hold the doors in this position, I clamped the free leaf of each hinge to the door stile through the opening where the glass will be (*Fig. 2*).

With a clamp on each hinge, open the door and

drill pilot holes for the screws (*Fig. 3*). (I used a self-centering drill bit. See page 126 for sources.) Then, screw in the screws and remove the clamps to check the fit.

Now, the screws should be removed and then reinstalled later, after the glass is in place.

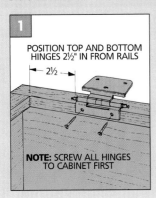

1

POSITION TOP AND BOTTOM HINGES 2½″ IN FROM RAILS

← 2½ →

NOTE: SCREW ALL HINGES TO CABINET FIRST

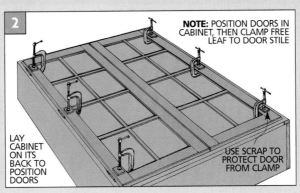

2

NOTE: POSITION DOORS IN CABINET, THEN CLAMP FREE LEAF TO DOOR STILE

LAY CABINET ON ITS BACK TO POSITION DOORS

USE SCRAP TO PROTECT DOOR FROM CLAMP

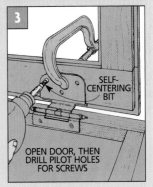

3

SELF-CENTERING BIT

OPEN DOOR, THEN DRILL PILOT HOLES FOR SCREWS

JOINERY .... Cutting Matched Moldings

When I see a well-built cabinet door with glass panes and wood dividers, I'll usually spend just as much time looking at the coped and mitered joints as I spend looking at what's on display behind the door.

To build a door like this, normally you might feel limited to either cutting the coped miters by hand or using an expensive set of router bits. Instead, I use another technique for making matched molding joints. At first, it may look complicated, but it's not difficult.

The key to this technique is in the rails and dividers. Each consists of two separate pieces of wood (a $3/8$"-thick bottom divider or rail and a cap) glued together to look like one (see photo).

The advantage of this technique is that you can break down the operations into simple steps. First, kerfs and roundover profiles are cut on the stiles (*Steps 1, 2, and 3*). Then tongues and half laps are cut on the bottom rails and dividers (see next page). Finally, the ends of the caps are "coped" with a core box bit to match the roundover profile.

When all these pieces are glued up, the parts should mate perfectly. The tongue on the divider or rail fits into a groove cut in the stile. And the decorative roundover on the stile fits into the coped end of the cap like a nut in a shell.

Using this technique to build a divided door requires a few more pieces (and steps) than a typical door frame. To keep them all organized, I just take it one step at a time, starting with the stiles. When they're finished, I move on to the dividers and then finally the caps.

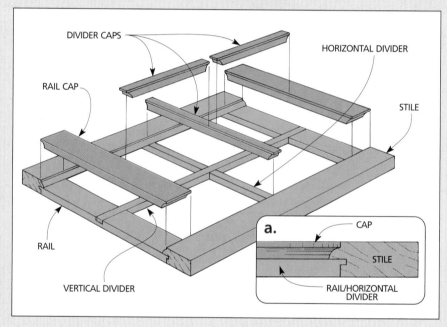

STILES

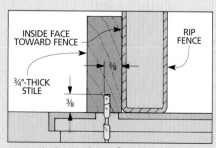

1 Lock the rip fence $3/8$" from outside of the saw blade. Then, with the inside face of the stile against fence, cut a $3/8$"-deep kerf on the inside edge of the stile.

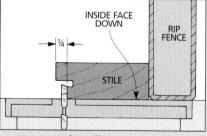

2 Next, trim $1/4$" off the back inside edge of each stile. Set height of blade to just cut into kerf. Position fence to let trimmed pieces fall to waste side.

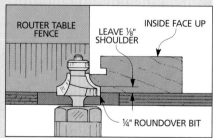

3 Use a $1/4$" roundover bit, and adjust height to leave a $1/8$" shoulder. Then rout the inside edge of each stile. (Save this setup for routing the cap pieces.)

The dividers and rails separate the glass panes and hold the frame together. First, cut tongues on the ends of each horizontal piece (Step 4). After the half-lap joints are cut (Steps 5 and 6), the pieces are assembled and glued to the stiles (Step 8).

To find the length of the horizontal rails and dividers, begin with the final outside measurements of your door. Subtract the width of the *inside* faces of the stiles, and add ³/₄". The vertical divider is the same length as the stiles.

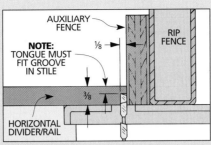

4 To cut the tongues, first clamp an auxiliary fence to the rip fence. Set the fence ¹/₈" away from the outside of the blade, and make the cut.

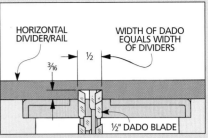

5 Center a half-lap on the length of each horizontal divider/rail. Set height of ¹/₂" dado (or width of your dividers) to half the thickness of stock.

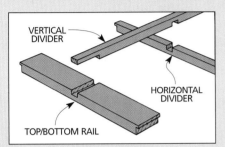

6 Cut matching half-laps on vertical divider with same dado setup. End half-laps at top and bottom are longer to fit wider top and bottom rails.

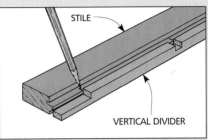

7 To help position horizontal dividers for assembly, use the vertical divider as a "story stick." Mark location of each half-lap on back inside edge of the stile.

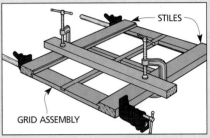

8 First, glue up the dividers and rails into a grid. Then glue the stiles to the grid. To keep the corners flat, clamp a flat piece of wood across the stiles.

CAPS

Once the frame is assembled, the last steps are to add the caps and insert the glass panes or wood panels. The caps help to stiffen the frame and match the molding to the roundovers on the stiles.

To determine the thickness of the caps, measure from the front face of the stile down to the grid (³/₈" in my case).

In a divided door, the horizontal and vertical caps can't both run uncut. For a rigid door, I always span the shortest distance with the uncut cap. Then piece in the caps running in the other direction.

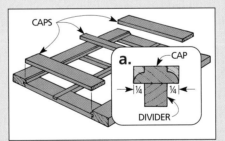

9 Rip caps to width allowing ¹/₄" overhang on each edge (inside edge only for rail caps). The overhang forms a rabbet that holds glass or wood panel.

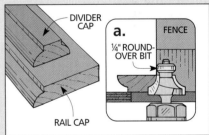

10 With height of router bit set the same as when routing the stiles, rout the profile on both edges of divider caps and the inside edge of each rail cap.

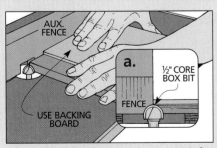

11 Cut ends of all cap pieces with ¹/₂" core box bit to match roundovers on mating pieces. Make trial cuts to determine height of bit and depth of cut.

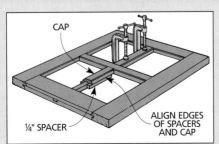

12 Position cap pieces on bottom grid, using a ¹/₄" spacer as a gauge. Align edge of spacer with edge of cap. Then glue and clamp in place.

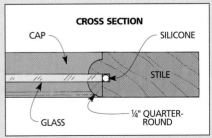

13 Apply a few spots of silicone in the grooves. The silicone will keep glass from moving sideways. Insert glass and secure with ¹/₄" quarter-round.

DESIGNER'S NOTEBOOK

Just a few modifications to the doors and the addition of sturdy locks are needed to turn the tall oak cabinet into a safe, secure case for showing off firearms or other sporting goods.

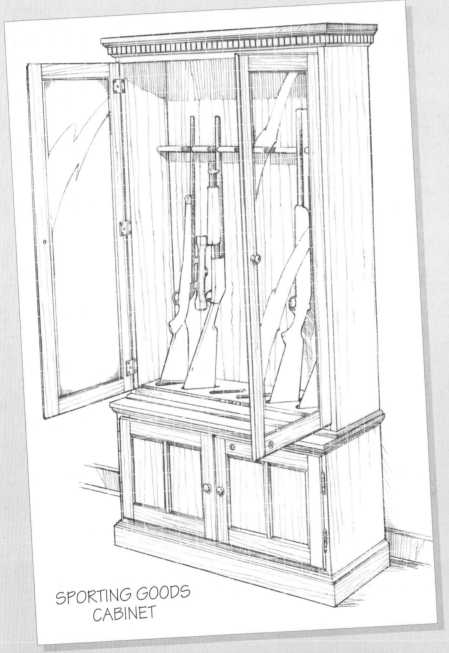

SPORTING GOODS
CABINET

CONSTRUCTION NOTES:

■ With a few changes, the tall oak cabinet plans on pages 112-123 can be modified to securely display a collection of rifles and ammunition, other types of hunting, fishing or sporting goods, or any other large items that you want to have in full view.

You can follow all of the instructions for building the tall oak cabinet exactly until you come to the procedure for making the dividers for the upper doors on page 120.

■ For safety, I used a sheet of clear polycarbonate plastic in each door, instead of small glass panes. (Another option would be a single sheet of glass.) The stiles and rails remain the same, but you don't need any of the dividers (see the Materials List below left).

This also means you won't have to cut the half laps in the rails.

■ Once the door frames are built, you can have the plastic (or glass) cut to fit between the grooves in the doors (mine were each $14^1/_2$" x $46^1/_4$").

Note: Remember, don't install the panes until *after* you have installed the inset hinges (refer to the Shop Tip box on page 121). And again, apply a few spots of silicone in the grooves to keep the plastic (or glass) from moving (refer to *Step 13* on page 123).

■ The major change on the inside of this cabinet is the addition of a two-part rack to support guns (see drawing at right). Of course, the style of these pieces can be modified to fit other types of fishing or sporting equipment, or the racks can be left out altogether so you can display large items in an open case.

Note: If you decide to build the rack, or if you want an open case, you won't have to build the shelves, part PP on the tall oak cabinet (refer to the Materials List below left).

■ I based the dimensions for my rack on standard rifle barrels and butts. If you have a gun that's a little different from the measurements shown here or if you're going to display different sporting goods, then you may have to modify your rack.

MATERIALS LIST

NEW PARTS
QQ Barrel Rail (1)* $3/_4$ x $3^1/_4$ - $37^3/_4$
RR Rifle Base (1)* $3/_4$ x $10^1/_2$ - $37^3/_4$
* Cut from one board, $3/_4$ x $7^1/_2$ - 96 (5 Bd. Ft.).

Note: Do not need parts FF, HH, II, PP. Only need 2 of part JJ & 40 lin. ft. of glass stop (OO).

HARDWARE SUPPLIES★★
(73) No. 8 x $1^1/_4$" Fh woodscrews
(7) No. 8 x $1^1/_2$" Fh woodscrews
(2) Cam locks with keys and strike plates
(2) $1/_8$" glass or plastic, $14^1/_2$" x $46^1/_4$"
★★ All other hardware is identical to Tall Oak Cabinet (see page 114).

■ The rack I designed consists of two parts, a barrel rail and a base. I started by working on the rail.

To build the barrel rail (QQ), first cut a piece of $3/4$"-thick stock to width. Mine was $3^{1}/4$" (see drawing below). Then, to determine the correct length, measure the distance between the sides in the upper case of the cabinet.

■ After cutting the rail to length (mine measured $37^{3}/4$"), cut three notches along the back edge of the barrel rail to fit around the stiles (S) and divider (U) in the back frame (see drawing below).

■ The barrels rest in notches cut in the front of the rail. To make these notches, first drill 1"-diameter holes as shown in the drawing below. Now cut up to the holes to complete the notches.

■ Once the notches are cut, round over the top and bottom edges of each notch and the front edges of the barrel rail with a $1/4$" roundover bit.

■ I used No. 8 x $1^{1}/2$" woodscrews to screw the barrel rail in place through the back frame about two-thirds of the way up on the upper case (see detail 'a' in drawing below).

Note: You may need to change the location of your rail on the upper case, based on the length of your rifles or other sports equipment.

■ With the barrel rail in place, I started on the rifle base (RR). Begin by edge-gluing three pieces of $3/4$"-thick stock so the base is wider than the inside depth of the cabinet (see drawing below).

■ Cut the base to width and length to fit inside the upper case. Mine was $10^{1}/2$" x $37^{3}/4$" (see detail 'b' in drawing below).

■ After the base is cut to size, lay out the slots for the rifle butts (see drawing below). (Again, you can customize the base to fit your equipment.)

■ I cut each slot by drilling two $1^{3}/4$"-diameter holes as shown, then cutting between them with a jig saw to remove the waste. Then sand each slot smooth.

■ Round over the top edges of each slot and the front edge of the base piece with a $1/4$" roundover bit.

■ Finally, screw (don't glue) the base in place from the bottom of the upper case with No. 8 x $1^{1}/4$" woodscrews (see detail 'b' in drawing below).

Safety Note: If you build this cabinet for guns and ammunition, you should add secure locks on both the upper and lower doors (see the Shop Tip box below).

Keep both doors locked at all times and the keys safely away from anyone who should not be in the cabinet.

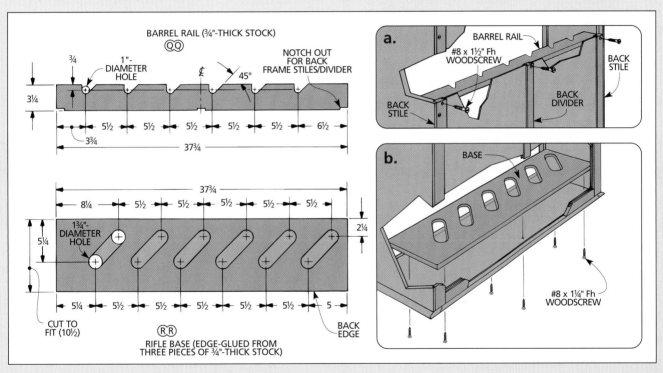

BARREL RAIL (¾"-THICK STOCK)
QQ

RIFLE BASE (EDGE-GLUED FROM THREE PIECES OF ¾"-THICK STOCK)
RR

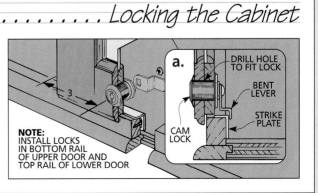

One of the first things we take into consideration when designing projects at *Woodsmith* is whether the hardware is commonly available. Most of the hardware and supplies for the projects in this book can be found at local hardware stores or home centers. Sometimes, though, you may have to order the hardware through the mail. If that's the case, we've tried to find reputable national mail order sources with toll-free phone numbers (see box at right).

In addition, *Woodsmith Project Supplies* offers hardware for some of the projects in this book (see below).

WOODSMITH PROJECT SUPPLIES

At the time of printing, the following project supply kits were available from *Woodsmith Project Supplies*. The kits include the items listed, but you must supply any lumber, plywood, or finish. For current prices and availability, call toll free:

1-800-444-7527

Scandinavian Cabinet
(pages 74-83) ....No. 8005017
This is a full-size pattern for the design on the cabinet sides.

Walnut Cabinet
(pages 86-97)
Hardware Kit ....No. 7101-100
Includes woodscrews, ball-tipped hinges, ball catches, knobs, and spoon-style shelf supports.

Cherry Wardrobe
(pages 98-111)
Hardware Kit ....No. 7102-100
This kit provides the woodscrews, cherry knobs, bullet catches, and extruded brass hinges.

Tall Oak Cabinet
(pages 112-125)
Hardware Kit ....No. 778-100
Kit includes hinges, knobs, catches, strike plates, shelf supports, threaded inserts, and screws.
Cabinet Lock ....No. 778-150

KEY: TL05

MAIL ORDER SOURCES

Some of the most important "tools" you can have in your shop are mail order catalogs. The ones listed below are filled with special hardware, tools, finishes, lumber, and supplies that can't be found at a local hardware store or home center. You should be able to find many of the supplies for the projects in this book in one or more of these catalogs.

It's amazing what you can learn about woodworking by looking through these catalogs. If they're not currently in your shop, you may want to have them sent to you.

Note: The information below was current when this book was printed. August Home Publishing does not guarantee these products will be avaiable nor endorse any specific mail order company, catalog, or product.

THE WOODSMITH STORE

2625 Beaver Avenue
Des Moines, IA 50310
800–835–5084
Our own retail store filled with tools, jigs, hardware, knobs, drawer pulls, books, finishing supplies, and carving tools. Though we don't have a catalog, we do send out items mail order. Call for information.

ROCKLER WOODWORKING & HARDWARE

4365 Willow Drive
Medina, MN 55340
800–279–4441
www.rockler.com
One of the most complete all-around sources for general and specialty hardware. They carry a wide selection of knobs, drawer pulls, Shaker and mini-Shaker pegs, standard and no-mortise hinges, shelf supports, and more. Also a variety of drill bits, hand and power tools, carving tools, veneer inlays, cabinet lights, finishes, and lumber.

WOODCRAFT

560 Airport Industrial Park
P.O. Box 1686
Parkersburg, WV 26102-1686
800–225–1153
www.woodcraft.com
Has all kinds of hardware including hinges, knobs, drawer pulls, Shaker and mini-Shaker pegs, and shelf supports. They also carry a good selection of drill bits, carving tools, hand tools and accessories.

WOODWORKER'S SUPPLY

1108 North Glenn Road
Casper, WY 82601
800–645–9292
A good source for supplies including knobs, hardware, locks, power tools and accessories, point-cutting ogee bits, carving tools, finishing supplies, and more.

CONSTANTINE'S

1040 E. Oakland Park Blvd.
Ft. Lauderdale, FL 33334
954-561-1716
www.constantines.com
One of the original woodworking mail order catalogs. Find hardware, locks, hinges, drill bits, veneer inlays, Shaker and mini-Shaker pegs, and finishing supplies.

TREND-LINES

135 American Legion Highway
Revere, MA 02151
800–767–9999
www.trend-lines.com
Another complete source for hinges, drill bits, hardware, Shaker and mini-Shaker pegs, power tools and accessories.

LEE VALLEY TOOLS LTD.

P.O. Box 1780
Ogdensburg, NY 13669-9973
800–871–8158
www.leevalley.com
They offer a full range of general and specialty hardware, blind nailers, carving tools, woodworking supplies and books.

INDEX

AUGUST HOME
PUBLISHING COMPANY

President & Publisher: Donald B. Peschke
Executive Editor: Douglas L. Hicks
Art Director: Steve Lueder
Creative Director: Ted Kralicek
Senior Graphic Designers: Chris Glowacki, Cheryl Simpson
Assistant Editors: Joseph E. Irwin, Craig Ruegsegger
Graphic Designer: Vu Nguyen
Design Intern: KatieVanDalsem

Designer's Notebook Illustrator: Mike Mittermeier
Photographer: Crayola England
Electronic Production: Douglas M. Lidster
Production: Troy Clark, Minniette Johnson, Susan Rueve
Project Designers: Ken Munkel, Kent Welsh, Kevin Boyle
Project Builders: Steve Curtis, Steve Johnson
Magazine Editors: Terry Strohman, Tim Robertson
Contributing Editors: Vincent S. Ancona, Tom Begnal, Jon Garbison,
Bryan Nelson
Magazine Art Directors: Todd Lambirth, Cary Christensen
Contributing Illustrators: Mark Higdon, David Kreyling, Erich Lage,
Roger Reiland, Kurt Schultz, Cinda Shambaugh, Dirk Ver Steeg

Controller: Robin Hutchinson
Production Director: George Chmielarz
Project Supplies: Bob Baker
New Media Manager: Gordon Gaippe

For subscription information about
Woodsmith and *ShopNotes* magazines, please write:
August Home Publishing Co.
2200 Grand Ave.
Des Moines, IA 50312
800-333-5075
www.augusthome.com/customwoodworking

Woodsmith® and *ShopNotes*® are registered trademarks of August Home
Publishing Co.

Oxmoor House.

Oxmoor House, Inc.
Book Division of Southern Progress Corporation
P.O. Box 2463, Birmingham, Alabama 35201

ISBN: 0-8487-2679-0
Printed in the United States of America

To order additional publications, call 1-205-445-6560.
For more books to enrich your life, visit **oxmoorhouse.com**